CHILD COUNSELLING AND EDUCATION

CHILD COUNSELLING AND EDUCATION

(In 2 Volumes)

Child Counselling

(Volume-2)

V.C. Pandey

ISHA BOOKS

DELHI-110 033

Child Counselling and Education

Rs. 1800 (Set)
Rs. 900 (each volume)

ISBN: 81-8205-101-0 (Set)
ISBN: 81-8205-103-7 (Vol. 2)

Reprinted in 2018 in India by

Isha Books, D-43, Prithviraj Road,
Adarsh Nagar, Delhi-110 033

First Published in 2004 in India by

Contents

Preface

Making of a good society depends on the sound development of children. For a civilised, culture society we have to educate and train children properly. To lead a successful life the child should get proper guidance and counselling in each phase of his life.

Child counselling is the help given to children to develop in a balanced and wholesome manner. Growth and adaptation are key concepts of child counselling. Effective child counselling requires special knowledge, skills and insight. It is important for counsellors to recognise the dignity and worth of every child in terms of understanding their personal lives. Commitment for applying knowledge and techniques for the welfare of child underlies the philosophy of child counselling.

This book is a modest attempt to present the issues and concerns of child counselling. This is a valuable source book for students and teachers of psychology, education, social work and other mental-health professionals.

Editor

1

Child and Sexual Counselling

The term 'counselling' refers to a relationship between a counsellor and a person looking for help with a problem. The counsellor helps you to understand yourself and your problems better. Then you can use this understanding to make better choices in your life. We all go to friends or relatives for advice or support sometimes, but if the problem is complicated, we might need special help—the help of a counsellor. We shouldn't see this as a weakness, but as an intelligent way to solve a problem. People go to counselors for a number of reasons. They might be grieving the loss of a close family member, or trying to deal with a marriage that has failed. In either case they need a counsellor with a solid background of knowledge in that particular subect area.

Children and Sexual Abuse

Sexual abuse is an activity that is perpetrated in secret. The offender is often in a position of trust, and always in a position of power, in relation to his or her victim. The victim acquiesces to the authority of the offender because he or she is threatened or seduced into compliance. Often a victim's cognitive and affective immaturity renders him or her unable to appropriately judge the potential risk of the behaviours which constitute the abuse. In many ways the therapeutic process is isomorphic to that of abuse. Therapy occurs under a mantle of confidentiality. Clients enter therapy in good faith, with the expectation that a therapist will have their best interests at heart. Therapists are invested with the authority to determine the kinds of interventions that they believe will best assist their clients' recovery. As in situations of abuse, clients generally have no immediate way to judge the long-term effects of their therapy or the skills of their therapist. The difference between therapy and abuse, however, lies in the fact that ideally therapy is driven by the clients' needs, whereas abuse ignores the victims' needs. If therapy is to be effective in restoring clients' autonomy and well-being, therapists must manage treatment in ways that do not suggest or replicate the dynamics of the original abuse.

The term "sexual abuse" will be used to describe overt or covert sexual behaviour between two individuals when the following conditions exist:

1. the nature of the sexual act(s) is developmentally inappropriate for at least one of the participants;
2. the balance of power and authority between the two individuals is unequal; and
3. the two individuals have an established emotional connection.

Any definition of sexual abuse necessarily carries culturally determined values and beliefs about sexuality, self-determination and social roles. In the broadest sense, sexual abuse can be defined as: "Sexual activities that a child does not understand, to which a child cannot give informed consent or which violate the social taboos of society. The nature of the sexual acts which constitute sexual abuse vary along a continuum of intrusiveness. Activities such as voyeurism, viewing pornographic materials or age-inappropriate behaviour regarding physical health fall on one pole of the continuum. Sadistic and ritualistic abuse constitutes the other pole.

It must be noted that a client's perception of the intrusiveness of any specific sexual activity is subjective. His perceptions may change as he redefines his childhood experience through his adult understanding. It is the client's experience that needs to be addressed in therapy rather than whether the behaviour is considered objectively intrusive.

The information about the prevalence of male sexual victimization, and discusses many of the reasons why attempts to establish an accurate picture of this phenomenon are problematic. Ways in which the experience of being sexually traumatized can impact on male victims are discussed, and the primary variables that generally act as predictors regarding the severity of the resultant pathology are identified. Finally, the primary differences between male and female sexual victimization are examined using both empirical research and clinical experience to inform the discussion.

Cultural and social myths shape our ability to acknowledge many of the abusive and explosive realities that exist in culture. Sexual abuse and especially the sexual abuse of male children, has been invisible in society until very recently. Child physical abuse was not recognized or acknowledged until the 1960s and child sexual abuse in the mid 1970s. Not until the 1980s were male victims recognized and studied and their victimization found to be more frequent than previously recognized. It is difficult to accurately estimate the prevalence of male sexual victimization for a variety of reasons. In Canada, in 1984, the Badgley Report found that 33% of men are sexually victimized at some point in their lives, that 75% of these assaults occur to boys under the age of 17 and 25% of these assaults can be considered serious offenses chargeable under the Canadian Criminal Code. Estimates of prevalence vary from study to study.

A 1989 study of 592 American male college students from two different geographic regions determined that 15% of the students from the mid-western campus and 13% of the students from the southeastern campus "described al least one sexually abusive experience in childhood". A representative national sample of 2,972 American male college students found that: —7.3 % of the men reported a childhood experience that met at least one of the following three criteria for sexual abuse:

1) existence of age discrepancy between the child and perpetrator,
2) use of some form of coercion to obtain participation by the victim and/or
3) a perpetrator who was a caregiver or authority figure.

Clearly, although empirical studies have generated quantitative data identifying the problem of male sexual abuse, prevalence figures can only be estimated. The general problem of determining the extent of male sexual abuse can be summarized as follows: Many or even most sex crimes are not reported. Therefore, determining the actual number of crimes is impossible, regardless of whether the victim is male or female.

The many factors complicating the reporting process for male victims of sexual abuse will be discussed in three categories:

1) research-related factors;

2) the impact of cultural beliefs and stereotypes; and

3) clinically-related factors.

1. *Research-related factors:* Studies that attempt to determine the prevalence of male sexual abuse arrive at different estimations partly because they operationalize the definition of sexual abuse in study-specific ways. There is no standard definition of sexual abuse that comprehensively addresses sex, age, cultural and regional differences. Hence each study has a unique definition of sexual abuse and in effect, measures different kinds of experience. The samples that different studies draw upon are not standardized. Some research uses non-clinical populations such as college students, while other studies draw from clinical populations such as adolescents who are currently in treatment or adults who are imprisoned for sex-related crimes. Clearly, data describing these different populations will reflect experiences that are biased by unique variables. In addition, methodologies for data collection vary from study to study thus affecting the degree of reliability of the data.

2. *The impact of cultural beliefs and stereotypes:* The underreporting of the sexual abuse of male children is often a reflection of cultural beliefs about gender roles and socialization. Certain actions, such as male sexual victimization, remain hidden because cultural myths and values shape the ways in which they are understood.

Finklehor says "the male ethic of self-reliance ... has tended to portray youthful male sexuality in very positive, adventuresome terms... [and is] partly responsible for the serious underreporting of sexual victimization experiences involving boys." The belief that males are always powerful and able to fend for themselves has created a mythology that implies that if a boy or man admits to being victimized he is seen as less than male. Our culture has no mythology to identify the process of male victimization and boy victims are emasculated by this bias. They are either seen as being like a woman and therefore feminized, as being powerless and therefore flawed or as being interested in sex with men and therefore homosexual. None of these interpretations of victimization are useful options for a boy who has been sexually abused and is trying to make sense of this experience. Whether male children are abused by male or female perpetrators or both, the cultural interpretation of the event often minimizes its impact or puts responsibility for the abuse onto the victim.

Psychological Damage of Sexually-abused Children

Children who have been sexually abused often suffer even after the abuse has ended. Some of the psychological damage will be obvious to family members, but some of it won't. The damage may take these forms:

Guilt: Children may feel guilty, believing they are in some way responsible for the abuse.

Shame: The guilty secret may make them feel worthless.

Fear: If the offender has told them that something terrible will happen if they reveal the secret, they may be afraid.

Grief: Children may stop seeing the world as a safe and friendly place. They may mourn the loss of their sense of innocence and freedom. They may also mourn the loss of the offender if there has been a close bond between them.

Anger: They may feel intense, and often uncontrollable anger. Because they can't strike back at the offender, they may lash out at the wrong people—often the mother. Or they may hurt themselves or a pet.

Helplessness: Because they felt helpless at the time of the molestation, they may feel unable to resist sexual abuse in the future.

Depression: They may seem sad and less playful. They may lose interest in school, friends, and activities. Depending on how serious the abuse is, and on the child's nature, these feelings may show up in several ways; for example, sexual aggression, sleep disorders, irrational fears, macho or seduc-tive behavior, eating disorders, allergies, or an inability to concentrate on school work. Even if there are no symptoms it doesn't mean that the child doesn't need help—it just means that there are no obvious signs of the abuse.

Does childhood sexual abuse affect you as an adult? Yes. If you're an adult who was sexually abused as a child, you may have suffered for years from problems that never want to go away. If you're now suffering from drug or alcohol abuse, relationship breakdowns, sexual dysfunction, eating disorders, or periods when you feel out of touch with reality, unremembered childhood sexual abuse may be the cause. It's likely there was little or no counselling available when you were a child. You probably told no one or were expected to forget about it and get on with your life. Often adults who have forgotten about their own sexual abuse will have a sudden and painful memory when their own child has been molested. If this happens to you, you may have to begin counselling for both your child and yourself. This may seem hard to do. But at the same time, you may be able to see this crisis as an unexpected chance for both you and your family to become closer.

Even if you weren't sexually abused as a child, having to cope with the abuse of your own child may be the most difficult challenge of your life. If you can get counselling for yourself through this difficult period, it will also help your child to get on with his/her own counselling. How can a counsellor help? Consellor can help you or your child in several ways. Help take you and your child through the painful details of the abuse one small step at a time, so the whole experience is easier to handle and less frightening. Our natural impulse is to want to 'put the abuse behind us', where we can forget about it— or even deny that it ever happened. This is why untreated adult survivors of sexual abuse may have so many problems or symptoms they don't understand.

Counsellors are people trained to listen and respond to their clients and to help them make changes in their lives. They may have different titles such as: psychiatrists, psychologists, social workers, school counsellors, church ministers, or art therapists. But the important thing is that they are trained in counselling and should know about sexual abuse. In cities it may be easy to find a suitable sexual abuse counsellor. If you live outside a large centre, it may be harder. However, in some rural areas you may find lay counsellors. These are usually people who want to help others and have received some training from a professional counsellor. Although they may not have university backgrounds, often they can be helpful.

Counselling is especially important for sexual abuse victims because of the damage that may come from abuse that is forgotten or denied. In Thou Shalt Not be Aware, Alice Miller, a famous Swiss psychiatrist, explains that victims who bury memories of abuse run the risk of recreating the abuse; either as a victim or as an offender': Denying the abuse or pretending it doesn't matter keeps us from growing and healing ourselves.

If you're an adult, a counsellor will talk with you about specific events and feelings. For a child, the counsellor will do exactly the same things but will probably work in a different way. Children don't usually like to sit around and talk for long. In fact, they might not like to talk at all. A skilled counsellor can encourage children to express their feelings through such things as play, drawing, or letter writing. Children often believe that because they've been abused, they are different. This may make them feel isolated. In this case the counsellor may want the child to be in a group with other children who have been through similar experiences.

Group counselling allows children to help one another just as adults do when they work in a group. Because of the abuse, your child may feel 'weird' or 'not nor-mal'. The counsellor will try to help your child change those feelings by showing a genuine interest in your child's everyday activities such as sports, hobbies, computer games, and time spent with friends. The counsellor will also emphasize from time to time that the offender was the one responsible for the abuse. Most children need to be reminded of this often, because of their guilt feelings. The counsellor will probably want to spend a lot of time with you as well, especially if your child is quite young. You'll want to understand your child's feelings so you'll know the best way to talk to him/her, and to handle problems as they arise. Because your child may have a distorted idea of normal sexual development, the counsellor may use books to give accurate information about sex.

It will make things easier if you can take part in a parents' support group at the same time as your child is in counselling. In a group you can learn a lot about sexual abuse, child protection and legal systems, and what happens if the offender is prosecuted. Best of all, you'll be better able to understand your own feelings. Parents often blame themselves, and you may need help to see where the blame really belongs. Going to counselling and parents' groups takes time and energy, but there's a great payoff. You have the satisfaction of being part of your child's recovery; and you also learn about your child, yourself, and how the child protection and legal systems work.

Ideally, counselling should start as soon as possible after finding out about the abuse. Research has shown that families are most open to counselling when they are still in crisis. When families wait too long, they are much more likely to believe that they can forget about the abuse or pretend that it isn't important. All counsellors are not equal. There are good ones and poor ones, just as there are good and poor auto mechanics. Good counsellors are willing to work with social workers, police, and victims' assist workers.

There are few problems as difficult for parents, teachers, and daycare staff as deciding how to deal with children in their care who are imposing sexual activity on other children. There are many questions to consider. Should you simply ignore the behaviour and hope the child will 'grow out of it'? Or should you attempt to correct the behaviour, and run the risk of making the child feel guilty about normal sexual curiosity? How do you deal with your own discomfort in addressing the problem? Many adults in charge of young children come from homes where sex was never discussed. In today's society there is a great emphasis on sex, so we may assume that our children are sexually sophisticated. We may risk viewing children's sexual behaviour and language as a sign of the times, and do nothing about it. Or we may envy their supposed 'openness', and compare it unfavourably with our own 'repressed' childhoods.

Children today do have access to more information about sex, but it is also true that they are exposed to more misinformation. They also experience a lot of sexual pressure from the media and from society as a whole. To help children in trouble, we must base our decisions on what we know as fact, not what we imagine to be true. To know whether a child is being sexually aggressive or simply curious, we need to understand children's normal sexual development. There is a world of difference, for example, between two children in a daycare pulling their pants down to look at one another's genitals and a child forcing a pencil into another child's anus.

Unless children are interfered with, their sexual development follows a natural sequence regardless of what society may think about sex at any given time. Children are born sexual. Boys are often born with erect penises and girls with lubricated vaginas. After birth some of the following changes may take place at approximately the following ages:

— *2% Years:* Children begin to notice that boys and girls assume different postures to urinate. They may attempt to copy one another's postures. They begin to show interest in physical differences.

— *4 Years:* Children may play games of 'show'. They may use 'bathroom' talk, and call one another names like 'Poophead'. When you take them to visit friends, they may show an interest in unfamiliar bathrooms. They may role-play activities they associate with Mommy and Daddy.

— *5 Years:* Children become more modest and will demand greater privacy.

— *6 Years:* Children begin to demand practical answers about the differences in the sexes. They may want to know where babies come from and how they are made. Parents should give children short concrete explanations which don't tax their ability to listen. Children also become curious about death at this age.

— *7 Years:* There is generally less interest in sexual matters.

— *8 Years:* Renewed interest in sex takes the form of smutty jokes, sexual rhymes, provocative giggling and whispering.

— *9 Years:* Children begin to exchange sex information with friends of the same sex. They may look in books for information about their sexual organs and how they function.

— *10 Years:* Some girls and a few boys will have reached puberty by age 10. Children show greater interest in the opposite sex. There is considerable interest in smutty jokes, which will be a little more sophisticated than the jokes they told when they were 8. Don't be alarmed if children appear to skip some of these stages. All children are different and they all develop at different rates. The stages listed here are generally true, and are simply intended as guidelines to help you make an initial judgment about whether a specific child's behaviour is 'normal' or not. How is normal sexual development disrupted? It can be disrupted by the unwanted and forceful sexual attention of adults, older children or aggressive children their own age.

Forceful sexual attention may take several forms, such as:

— Continued exposure to pornographic videotapes or magazines. Pornographic material is most harmful to children if they are forced to watch it. However, it may also be harmful if it is left around the house in places where children can't miss it.

— Sexual behavior in front of children. If children are forced to watch their babysitter having sex with a visiting friend, for example, it can be a harmful experience. But parents shouldn't worry if a child inadvertently walks in on their lovemaking. The difference is that the child is not forced to watch, and the activity can be explained in a way that reassures the child.

— Disrespectful sexual attitudes and frequent use of sexual language and innuendo may encourage children to be forceful and insensitive of others.

— Caregivers failure to respect privacy or body boundaries. This can cause children to grow up unaware that others need privacy and have boundaries.

— Direct sexual abuse. When children suffer from direct sexual abuse, they are most likely to suffer from developmental disruption. This happens because sexual abuse forces children to experience sexual activity when they are not physically or psychologically ready.

When children have been sexually abused or subjected to unwanted sexual attention, they may change their behaviour in a number of ways:

— They may exhibit passive behaviours such as night fears, fear of school changing rooms, depression, school failure and withdrawal from friends and activities.

— They may exhibit aggressive behaviours such as fighting, being cruel to pets, setting fires, and acting out sexually against other children.

Although there is plenty of evidence that sexually abused children frequently act out against other children, the reason they do so isn't always clear. Common sense suggests that abused children would try to avoid repeating a frightening and distasteful activity. Unfortunately 'common sense' can easily fool us. In many cases molested children repeat the activity in which they were victims, trying to make sense of what happened. For example, a boy may have been forced to perform oral sex on an older boy. The activity may have made him feel frightened, confused and sexually excited all at the same time. Repeating the activity with a younger boy as victim takes him out of the victim role and into a new role where he is in charge. He is now less frightened and less anxious, and better understands why the older boy wanted oral sex performed on him.

When children repeat an experience in which they were victim, it is called a "repetition compulsion". We know how this compulsion works when we see the child of an alcoholic growing up either to marry an alcoholic or to become one. Boys who have been molested frequently repeat the abuse as offenders, while girls frequently repeat the abuse as victims. Boys are often ashamed to admit they have been victims, so molesting another child may be a way of calling out for help. Sometimes boys will admit that they have molested another child before they will admit to being victims themselves. Girls do not assume the role of sexual aggressor as often as boys. Research shows that those who do usually have a background of lengthy and extreme abuse.

The 'repetition compulsion' is not inevitable. It is only one of the ways in which children try to adapt to being molested. As a general rule, the more comfortable children feel about reporting a molestation, the less likely they are to act out sexually. In families where boys are expected to be stoic and self-sufficient, acting-out behaviour is much more likely. When we don't allow boys to admit to feeling powerless or helpless, we often create situations in which the only feelings allowed are anger and aggression.

Children who molest should always be viewed with compassion. If their behavior is repulsive to us, we may recoil and scapegoat them by calling them 'offenders' or 'young Jezebels'. These children need help just as much as their victims, and you should report them to social services or to the police.

Often, when they are questioned, they will admit they themselves have been abused by a teenage or adult offender. Social service workers must protect children who molest as well as their victims, because they are still vulnerable to abuse by older offenders. If children who molest are 12 years or older, they may be charged under the Young Offenders Act. The judge may take into account their youth and place them on probation with compulsory counselling if they are convicted. The judge will often rely on the experience and testimony of social workers and police to distinguish between children who have just started to offend and older teenagers who are habitually violent. The latter can be just as dangerous as adult offenders.

Children who act out sexually, and are not stopped, hurt not only other children, but may also harm themselves. Because they relate to other children in a sexual way, they may deprive themselves of a chance to have real friendships. When children have a guilty secret, it is impossible for them to be open with others. Unless someone intervenes to break the secrecy, the child who molests other children runs the risk of becoming sexually addicted.

A sense of power over others, plus sexual excitement, can be extremely rewarding, particularly since it compensates for poor self-esteem. The longer the sexual activities continue, the more addictive they become. If they continue into adolescence they are difficult to stop. Since sexual abuse of any kind thrives on secrecy, breaking secrecy is the first step towards helping everyone involved. Children who molest must be interviewed by social services or police for two reasons: to help them admit to what they have done, and to provide clues as to why they are doing it. Once they admit to molesting, they are much less likely to continue. As long as they deny what they are doing, and deny their own probable victimization, they are much more likely to continue molesting.

A teenager or adult may molest a child who then begins to molest other children. There may then be a ripple effect, with the molested children initiating still more children into sexual activity. When this happens in a school or neighbourhood, it may seem hopeless at first glance. But it isn't. Here is what you must do:

— Find the original source of the abuse. For example, locate the child who was molested by the adult and deal with the victim's trauma.

— Identify the secondary victims; that is, the victims of the first victim. Notify social services, police, and sexual abuse counsellors who will address their needs. The secondary victims may need only short-term counselling if they haven't gone through as much trauma as the original victim.

Finding out that your own child has molested another child may be one of the most difficult life experiences you'll ever have to face. Most parents go into shock initially, then through a period of denial where they try to pretend that nothing has happened. For a while they might feel as though they're on a roller-coaster ride of unfamiliar and conflicting emotions.

Every year thousands of boys and girls in this country are sexually abused. We used to think that only girls were sexually abused. Now we know that it happens to both boys and girls. Some counsellors think that just as many boys as girls are sexually abused, but that boys are more afraid to admit it's happened to them.

Men and teenage boys do most of the sexual abusing, but women and teenage girls also sexually abuse young boys. Boys and girls your own age may sexually abuse other children, but that's not as common as adults and teenagers doing it. Males sexually abuse boys more often than females do. This is because a lot of males learn to be forceful and take what they want. A lot of people think the men who sexually abuse boys do it because they are gay or homosexual. This idea is wrong. Men molest boys because they want to use their sexual power against someone smaller and weaker. They are sexual bullies. Whether they are gay or not has nothing to do with it. In fact, about 95% of the men who sexually abuse boys are not gay. If they were, they would want to spend their time with other gay men, not with young boys.

Some boys think that if a man has sexually abused them, then they must be gay themselves, or the man wouldn't find them interesting. This idea is wrong too. Men who do this do it because they are sexually attracted or 'turned on' to children. Males grow up to be either heterosexual (prefer women) or homosexual (prefer other men). We don't quite know why, but we do know it has nothing to do with having been sexually abused. Boys who are molested by men are often afraid of growing up to be homosexual. Sometimes they are afraid that other boys will find out and call them names like 'fag' or 'gay: A good counsellor can help abused boys get over these fears.

When boys are sexually abused in a painful way like Nathan was, they are often afraid of damage to their bodies. And they are often afraid of AIDS. A good counsellor will work with the doctors and nurses to help calm your fears.

The person who sexually abused you may have tricked you. He may have pretended that he was lost or that his dog was lost. He may have pretended he was going to show you how to hold a baseball bat. He may have pretended that he was going to teach you about sex.

He may have pretended that he wanted to be your friend just so he could sexually touch you. The person who sexually abused you may have started by showing you something really interesting, like a model train, or a record collection, or a fish tank, or his new truck. Then he abused you when you weren't expecting anything bad to happen.

The person who sexually abused you may have offered you money, or liquor and cigarettes, or a chance to play with some interesting toys. Sometimes boys think the abuse was their fault for accepting a gift, or letting themselves be tricked, or going to the abuser's house instead of going home on time. Sometimes kids let the abuser touch them because they really want the gift. Then they feel bad after and think it was their fault, but it's not. Adults are supposed to take care of kids, not trick them so they can sexually abuse them.

Abusers don't want to get caught, because if they do they are to go to jail. So they may tell you to keep the abuse a secret. Abusers may threaten you to make you keep the secret. They may tell you that you or your family may be hurt or killed if you tell. When this happens you feel trapped.

Abusers may offer you presents to try to get you to agree to Abusers may look for other children to abuse. Many men who abuse children do it over and over again. They really enjoy abusing children and don't want to stop. They are called paedophiles; and they are quite dangerous.

Most abusers are men and teenage boys but they can be women and teenage girls too. Sometimes boys and girls your own age are sexually intrusive with other children but that doesn't happen as often. An abuser can be someone you may live with, like a dad or a brother. Or it can be a cousin or an aunt. Abusers are sometimes people who are supposed to take care of you and protect you, like teachers, coaches, baby-sitters and doctors.

Some people think that if a man abuses a boy, or a woman abuses a girl, the abuser must be gay or lesbian. That is most often not the case. Most gays or lesbians want to be sexual with other gay or lesbian adults, not with children. Abusers are sexual bullies who like to use their power over someone younger, smaller or less powerful than they are, whether they abuse girls or boys or both. We don't really understand all the reasons why people sexually abuse children but we do know this: it's always the abuser's fault, not the child's.

The person who abuses a child is someone with more power than the child. The abuser is usually older, bigger and stronger than you are. The abuser usually knows how to scare you or make you feel guilty so you won't tell about the abuse. He knows how to trick you so you're confused and afraid to tell. Even if the abuser made you do something wrong, like lie to your parents or sexually touch a younger child, it's still not your fault. It's always the adult's fault the abuse happened because the adult is supposed to help and protect you, not abuse you.

Abusers have power over you as long as you keep the abuse a secret. You can't stop it by yourself. So the most important thing you can do to stop the abuse is tell someone. That person must then tell the police or social worker who will work to protect you. They can use the law to help make sure the abuser can't hurt you again. Think carefully about who you want to tell. Unless your mom or dad is the abuser, your parents are usually the best people to tell. But if you think they won't believe you, or that they'll blame you, or be too upset to help, then tell someone else. It's also a good idea to tell someone outside your family if the abuser has threatened to hurt someone in your family.

Myth of Sexual Initiation

Boys who are abused by a male are often seen as having engaged in homosexual acts for pleasure; this interpretation can be held by the victim himself, especially if, during the abuse, his penis responded to the sexual stimulation by becoming erect. This analysis of sexual acts between male adults and male children as consensual sexual experiences, without regard to the power and control issues which are involved, emphasizes the cultural blinders that permit continued sexual exploitation of children. Statements such as the following actively ignore the developmental differences in sexual needs and expression that exist between adults and children.

Future studies into pedophilia should not a priori categorize the adults in pedosexual contacts as offenders and the children as victims, labelling all pedosexual contact as abuse or misuse. Pedophiliac: relationships may best be viewed by the researcher initially as simply another variety of human relationships. Such statements clearly point out the difficulty some male victims of sexual abuse face when they begin to identify and examine their experience and are met with attempts to redefine this abuse as consensual sexual activity.

Our culture promotes the belief that all sexual activity is good for men, no matter what its context. Images from advertising, television and cinema often portray sexual activities in which the "emotional reactions of male victims ...are seriously distorted when compared to those of real-life victims." When sexual abuse is heterosexual and a sexually mature female victimizes a boy. he may have difficulty recognizing this as abuse, since the cultural interpretation of this event is that he "got lucky". In movies such as "The Summer of '42", sexual abuse is romanticized and represented as sexual initiation.

Myth of Female Innocence

Boys who are abused by women or girls also face social myths that can prevent their abuse from being identified. Cultural gender biases perpetuate the belief that women in general and mothers in particular, are nurturing. Mothers have cultural permission to touch their children. When this touch is sexualized, sometimes under the guise of medical or caretaking rituals, a boy may have difficulty recognizing these behaviours as abusive. Because he is also subject to the cultural myth that women's touch is nurturing rather than sexual, he may be unable to discern that the sexual behaviours; gratified his female abuser's needs rather than his own. Cultural biases skew the ways in which activities are seen and the same activities are viewed differently depending upon whether they are performed by a man or a woman. This double standard often results in inappropriate sexual interaction between an adult women and a child being ignored:

> "There is a widespread societal belief that women cannot be sexually abusive to their children and at worst their behaviour is labelled as seductive and not harmful. The same behaviour in a father is labelled child molestation."

The popular belief is that male victims of sexual abuse automatically become sexual offenders. While it is true that some sexual offenders were themselves victims of sexual abuse, committing sexual offenses is caused by complex variables which cannot be narrowed down to the single variable of previous sexual victimization. However, the cultural stereotype that victims of sexual abuse become offenders stops some victims from disclosing their abuse histories.

3. *Clinically-related factors :* Several aspects of the social service system act against the disclosure of male sexual victimization. Foremost amongst these is the fact that child protection agencies tend to deal with cases of intrafamilial sexual abuse, where they are mandated to ensure children's safety within their family systems. In his student survey, Finklehor found that, "Boys are more likely than girls to be victimized by someone outside the family." In fact approximately 83% of the persons who victimized the male students in this survey were non-family members. Thus, acts of sexual abuse perpetrated against male victims, if they are reported at all, tend to be reported to the police or the criminal justice system, not to child protection or treatment agencies. This lack of societal recognition of male victims' needs for treatment and protection perpetuates victims' silence. Male victims are unlikely to disclose their sexual abuse when they have little to gain from making their experience public. Victims of childhood sexual trauma often repress or forget their abuse-related memories. This primitive defence structure reduces the likelihood of disclosure of abuse by a victim. Even when memories are recalled, if a therapist or child protection worker is uncomfortable asking questions about the abuse or presents questions in such a way that the child does not connect the question to his abuse, the abuse may not be reported.

Awareness of the issue of male sexual victimization in the professional therapeutic community is limited by the same factors that affect the culture as a whole. Until recently, professional literature and journal articles have focused on the prevalence of male sexual victimization rather than on the impact of sexual abuse on male victims or models and methodologies of healing male survivors. An absence of information about how to work with male survivors has left many clinicians uncomfortable with or unaware of, the male survivors on their caseloads. A lack of questioning about the possible occurrence of abuse can result in an absence of disclosure on a client's part. In summary, there are many reasons why the full extent of male sexual abuse is relatively unknown and probably underreported.

Impact for Sexually Abused Males

Survivors of sexual abuse generally experience multiple and complex repercussions from this trauma All parts of the self-physical, mental, emotional and spiritual-are affected by the abuse and all of these parts can express abuse-related symptoms and effects. Abuse-related symptoms are experienced in both the short and long term. Some symptoms are crisis based and their impact is short-term; other symptoms (such as distorted cognitions or low self-esteem) are more deeply internalized by the victim and have much longer term impact. Often sexual abuse is accompanied by other forms of abuse and neglect, so that the trauma from the sexual abuse cannot be viewed in isolation. It is not always possible to determine the origin of symptoms which have multiple roots.

"From either an anecdotal self-report method or using valid, reliable instrumentation and comparative methodology, it was found that men who sought psychotherapy and had been sexually abused as children inside or outside their homes were far more psychologically disturbed than were other male therapy clients..." There are some researchers who argue that sexual interaction between adults and children or older children and younger children, is neutral or positive in its impact on a young child.

Young children are not sufficiently mentally, emotionally or physically mature to make an informed choice about whether or not to participate in sexual activities with an adult. Hence, although certain survivors of sexual abuse may identify this experience as positive or neutral in its impact on them, this is certainly not the case for the majority of victims of sexual trauma. The specific form of expression of the effects of the sexual trauma will vary from individual to individual. It is generally true that while many of the effects of sexual victimization were adaptive responses at the time of victimization, they become dysfunctional in the victims' post-abuse environment. Each person who has been sexually abused has a unique story to tell of how this event has played a part in his life. There is no single classification of impacts that can possibly recognize all the possible outcomes of sexual trauma; however, survivors share many common themes and issues. The primary focus will be on long-term impacts which become integral parts of survivor's lives, rather than on short-term acute impacts. Remember that your clients' self-reported histories are the most helpful guide to understanding the various impacts of abuse; the information given here is intended to guide you in your understanding of your clients' experience, not to replace a thorough assessment.

Researchers and clinicians have observed that the severity of the impact of sexual abuse on its victims is a function of several key variables:

— the age at which the abuse began;

— the duration and frequency of the abuse;

— the type of activities which constituted the abuse;

— the nature of the relationship between the offender and the victim;

— the number and gender of offenders involved in the abuse;

— the manner in which disclosure of the abuse occurred; and

— other attenuating circumstances in the victim's life.

Generally the younger a victim at the time the abuse begins, the greater the impact on his psychological development. Younger children call upon more primitive, less conscious defences to protect the integrity of their psyche; as the child matures, these primitive defences often lead to severe developmental impairment. Defences such as denial, repression, splitting and dissociation become problematic if the victim generalizes these coping strategies to a variety of situations in his life. The older a victim is at the time the abuse begins, the more able he is to consciously decide how he will protect himself, and fewer developmental stages in his life will be affected by his decisions.

The more often a victim is abused and the longer the duration of the abuse, the greater the likelihood that he wili be conditioned by the experience and, hence, the greater the severity of the impact of the abuse. The psychological "air" that a child breathes provides the nutrients on which his psyche grows; if this "air" which surrounds him is contaminated, his psyche will be forced to accommodate to this polluted atmosphere. In the same way that lead in inner city environments poisons children's neurological systems, so does repeated sexual abuse distort their relationships with self and others.

The use of force tends to exacerbate the impact of the sexual abuse. Threats of violence or acts of violence, threaten not only the psychological health of a child, but also his physical existence. A child's powerlessness, helplessness and rage are greater when an offender overpowers him with physical force. In some cases of ritual abuse, a victim has been forced to be an active participant in abhorrent rituals (such as when he is forced to hold the knife that performs a ritual sacrifice). Often the victim will forget that adults forced or coerced him to comply with their plans and he is overcome with self-blame and self-loathing or represses his cognitive memories of the event. Generally, "In most cases the more deviant the sexual act, the greater the negative impact."

Offenders can be complete strangers or the most intimate of family members. Because of the greater intensity of interaction when the offender is a family member or a close friend, the victim's betrayal is also greater. A victim's loyalties to his family members are generally more complex than they are to strangers, so when he is abused by a family member the breach of trust is more highly charged. Family members often continue to be significant in the victim's life and they are not easily avoided or forgotten; hence if the abuse is intrafamilial the victim's sense of loss, grief and betrayal is more severe. A victim who was seduced by a family member who was gentle and kind during the abuse often reports greater difficulty processing his residual feelings than does a victim who was forcefully raped by a stranger.

Seductive abuse strategies utilized by someone with whom the victim had an ongoing relationship create confusion and ambivalence about the nature of the abuse for the victim. Intrafamilial abuse victims generally have mixed loyalties to their abuser(s); their ambivalent feelings of caring for the abuser(s) at the same time as being fearful or rageful about his or her abusive actions can create ongoing patterns of unstable relationships.

'The greater the number of adults who take part in the actual abuse the more likely the child is to form a view of the world as inhabited only by dangerous peoples. If, as in ritual abuse, large parts of the child's world revolve around the abuse and its secretive nature, the child comes to believe that there is no other reality. Similarly, if both men and women offend against a child, he feels less safe than if only one gender abused him. Men who have had multiple perpetrators generally have greater difficulty healing; the dynamics of the abuse are more complex and the process of recovery is slower.

In general, when a victim is able to voluntarily disclose his abuse or regains his memories of the abuse in a gradual manner, it is less stressful than if the disclosure is involuntary or abrupt. If disclosure occurs when a victim is still living at home, the reactions of family members will be very important. If family members deny or refute the occurrence of the abuse, the victim's sense of helplessness and hopelessness may be augmented. If on the other hand a victim is believed and supported, his recovery from the sexual trauma is assisted. A victim's developmental stage influences the manner in which he discloses his abuse and his abilities to process others' reactions to his disclosure. Younger children often disclose by re-enacting abusive behaviours; adolescents may disclose indirectly by telling a good friend, who in turn tells a trusted authority figure. Adults tend to be more direct in their disclosure, once they acknowledge their abuse to themselves. In general, the sooner a victim discloses his abuse and receives treatment for its negative impacts, the easier his recovery. It is not uncommon for child victims to retract their abuse disclosures because the family pressures evoked by the disclosure process are so horrendous. Children are motivated to disclose by desires to have the abusive behaviour stop or in order to protect the safety of another child; they are rarely prepared for the investigation process that police and child protection agencies are required to conduct or for the upheaval in the family structure that often results.

Sexual abuse is not the only event that occurs in a child's life. If it is only a minor occurrence in the midst of other relatively benign experiences, it will have less impact than if it is one part of a potpourri of physical and emotional abuse and neglect. Three factors that affect a child's abilities to recover from sexual abuse are:

1) the basic constitutional characteristics of the child;
2) a supportive family environment; and
3) a supportive individual or agency that provides a primary support system to assist the child in coping and in developing a positive model for identification.

Sexual abuse is a multi-layered assault that is often accompanied by other forms of abuse and neglect. Therefore to isolate single symptoms or to overlook the interrelated nature of the symptoms that result from sexual abuse, is to present an inaccurate picture of most survivors' experience. This text examines the impacts of sexual abuse on male victims from a clinical view point. General post-abuse symptoms are examined before more complex abuse-specific symptoms, such as dissociation, are reviewed. The typical effects of sexual abuse on males under the following headings:

— physical impacts;

— mental impacts;

— emotional impacts;

— Posttraumatic Stress Disorder (PTSD) and dissociation;

— difficulties with male gender identity;

— sexual orientation confusion and homophobia;

— abuse-reactive perpetration and aggression;

— sexual compulsions and addictions; and

— interpersonal difficulties.

Physical impacts: Children generally lack a vocabulary to tell others of their abuse experiences or of the impact of those experiences on them. They will tend to "show" others their experience, by reenacting it or by other behavioral indicators. It is quite common for boys who have been abused to have nightmares and sleep disturbances, to be encopretic or enuretic or to display other physical symptoms of distress. Chronic somatic complaints for which there are no apparent organic cause can be indicators of abuse. Some victims develop disgust and self-hatred for their physical selves. Boys often feel betrayed by their bodies which have responded to the perpetrator's sexual overtures; their internal feelings of confusion or fear or anger were in conflict with their physical arousal. This contempt for the physical self manifests in a variety of ways, such as neglecting one's physical needs or self-abuse.

Self-abusive behaviours can take a variety of forms—a readiness to take unsafe physical risks, alcohol or drug addictions or active self-mutilation are some of the more common ones. Self-mutilation is often "an attempt to block or interrupt negative cognitions or feelings...and thus may be an attempt to survive incapacitating symptoms.... ". It is not uncommon for survivors to display their self-hatred and despair in suicidal ideation or in actual suicide attempts. Self-harming behaviours can indicate a variety of different dynamics and you must examine each client's personal beliefs in order to understand the metaphoric significance of his behaviour. For example, with clients who have Multiple Personality Disorder (MPD), self-harming behaviour may be the domain of a particular personality; unless you work with that specific personality, the client may not be able to access the emotions that fuel the self-harming actions.

When sexuality has been the way to meet a variety of non-sexual needs, a survivor may view his body and his sexuality as commodities to trade for money or lodging. Such behaviour may become part of a survivor's lifestyle. Male prostitutes and male runaways who learned as child victims of sexual abuse that their sexuality can be a means of gaining power and resources resort to using their bodies as a means of obtaining a livelihood. To be a male victim is a counter-cultural experience since men are not generally seen as vulnerable and powerless. Some male victims fear that their vulnerability is transparent and that even perfect strangers can see they have been victimized and are therefore flawed. Sometimes they become involved in counter-phobic activities such as body building and athletic activities, not for a love of sport, but as a way of becoming more powerful and hiding their "weaknesses".

Mental impacts: One of the most common cognitive distortions displayed by survivors is that they hold themselves responsible for having been abused. Children have a limited understanding of the interpersonal dynamics in which they participate. When they are abused or neglected, they understand this as being the result of inadequacies in themselves, rather than as the result of inadequacies in the adults who are abusing or neglecting them. This tendency to self-blame is often exacerbated by the abuser, who may say "You made me do this..." or "I'm doing this because I love you..." or "If you weren't so sexy, I wouldn't have to do this...". Many survivors, as adults, need assistance in understanding that a child is not responsible for the behaviour of an adult, under any circumstances. Survivors often look back on their abuse history and project adult values and judgements onto their own involvement in the experience; they forget that as children they were not sufficiently mentally or emotionally mature to make decisions about the ethics of their sexual behaviour. Helping a survivor to see himself as the child that he was at the time of the abuse can often reduce his sense of having been responsible for it.

Survivors commonly repress abuse-related memories or deny the impact of having been abused. Usually they developed these mental defences at the time of the abuse in an attempt to cope with the dissonant events in their lives. For instance, in cases of intrafamilial abuse, many child victims were placed in the dilemma of being abused by people who also expressed love and caring towards them. Trying to understand this discordant behaviour, the child may have found that by denying or unconsciously repressing his abuse memories, he could tolerate his life situation. Survivors often exhibit patterns of learned helplessness and passivity.

Although the victim mentality begins as a useful childhood coping mechanism, when it continues into adulthood, it becomes obsolete. The victimized person has become an adult, with the choices and power of a man, but he continues to think of himself as little, helpless and at fault for all the mistreatment he receives. He goes through his adult life training others to treat him poorly by being passive and not standing up for himself.... The abuse was a normal part of his childhood and nobody did anything to stop it, so he thinks that abuse is a normal, acceptable part of life. Survivors who believe they're responsible for their abuse and unable to do anything to change their life experience, often have very low self-esteem. They believe that the treatment they received from adults was what they deserved and the world has nothing better to offer them. This hopelessness and helplessness can become a self-fulfilling prophecy if the survivor does not find a way to change these inner beliefs.

Emotional impacts: Men in our culture have, until recently, received little support for the outward expression of their feelings. Survivors have often been encouraged by their socialization to suppress or repress their affect. Many male survivors are unable to identify, acknowledge or disclose their feelings; they experience affective numbness. Some homophobic men believe that only homosexual men express emotion and they develop a stoic persona to confirm their "masculinity". Some men are unaware of their emotions and they develop addictive behaviours to ensure that these emotions are suppressed. Addictions are unconscious secondary emotional processes that temporarily block out primary affect. The compulsive nature of addictive behaviour is so engrossing and temporarily satisfying that it masks the deeper emotional reality that underlies it.

Many survivors exhibit substance addictions and their relationship to alcohol, drugs or food can consume much of their mental and emotional energy. Other survivors develop process addictions and their relationships with work, sports, sex or other endeavours exhibit obsessive and addictive patterns. In this way, their work or their interest in sports, becomes all consuming because it takes on the secondary function of acting as a barrier to emotional processing. Process addictions are often socially well received and may earn a survivor the respect of his boss or his teammates. It is not usually apparent to the people who benefit from the survivor's process addictions that his activity is in fact driven by a need to block emotional awareness. When a survivor is in touch with his emotions, he is likely to experience feelings of anxiety and fear, depression, guilt, anger, rage and shame.

Initially anger is the emotion that survivors often feel most comfortable expressing. Men's rage is often connected to the homosexuality of the abuse, rather than to its expletive aspects. Anger is powerful and energy-filled and it is an affective state that is egosyntonic with masculine cultural roles. Anger and rage can become a "catch all" emotion for male victims. Because it is an active emotion, expressing anger feels more acceptable than displaying more vulnerable emotions.. Not all male survivors experience anger at having been abused. Many have difficulty accessing and expressing their rage. For many men, anger is associated with violence. Many survivors are afraid that if they contact their angry feelings, they will express them violently. Other survivors adopt a "victim" stance in their lives and respond to having been exploited with passivity and withdrawal.

People working in the rape-crisis movement, the Vietnam War veterans movement and the child sexual abuse movement have pooled their knowledge to create an understanding of the effects of severe trauma on its victims. This combined knowledge has become known as the study of posttraumatic stress. It has provided very helpful conceptualizations for those who work with survivors of natural disasters, wars, hostage-takings, rape and, most recently, sexual abuse. Victims of sexual abuse share many issues in common with victims of other disasters. These include:

— they didn't choose the frequency or duration of the traumatic event;

— their personal resources were overwhelmed by powerful, negative forces;

— their physical and psychological safety was threatened;

— they didn't know when their environment was safe and when it wasn't;

— their efforts to talk about the trauma with others are often met with incredulity and insufficient understanding, which results in emotional isolation, confusion and shame; and

— they're unable to process the trauma emotionally until they feel physically and psychologically safe.

The etiological features of Post Traumatic Stress Disorder (PTSD) provoke a variety of coping strategies by which a victim attempts to preserve his integrity. The most common PTSD symptoms include flashbacks and reexperiencing the trauma, a general numbing of mental and affective responsiveness, hypervigilance and a variety of dissociative responses. Flashbacks can involve any or all of a survivor's five senses which have either consciously or unconsciously encoded memory of the abuse. Often survivors report vague recurrent body sensations for which they have no conscious cognitive memory. These sensations or memories occur when the survivor is triggered by either internal or external stimuli which evoke the original trauma. For instance, a survivor whose abuse included posing for pornographic pictures may experience a flashback that's triggered by the appearance of a camera; or a survivor who was left alone for long periods of time after being abused may flashback to the abuse experience when he feels isolated or lonely.

The more often a trauma has been repeated and the more intrusive its nature, the deeper and stronger the survivor's neurological memory of the event. If a trigger event occurs in the survivor's current life that recalls previous abusive events, a chain of associations occurs, usually unconsciously and the client begins to re-experience the abuse incident. This re-experience will often involve a blurring between past and present; the survivor unconsciously withdraws from the present and projects past memories and feelings onto here-and-now stimuli. This trance-like event is accompanied by decreased sensory awareness and the survivor generally needs to reconnect with his present reality in order to move through the flashback. Repressed memories can return as flashbacks; they can also emerge in the form of dreams and nightmares. Survivors commonly have dreams that explicitly recall their abuse or recurrent nightmares of being pursued that symbolically evoke themes of abuse.

Briere defines the common PTSD symptom of emotional numbing as "... a loss of reactivity, detachment from others and/or constricted emotionality. Male survivors often report explicit details of their abuse without any emotionality, as if they were talking about events that had happened to someone else. Although emotional distancing has a short-term value as a means of coping with shock and crisis, if it's sustained over a long period of time, it separates and isolates the survivor from his full range of feelings. It is quite common for survivors to be afraid of identifying or expressing their feelings because they fear that their affective responses will be so intense that they won't be able to manage them.

Often survivors of trauma and sexual abuse become hypervigilant, keeping themselves prepared for the next potential assault on their personhood. PTSD is typified by hypertension and the overactivity of the sympathetic nervous system. Chronic muscle tension, an inability to sleep, restless, disturbed sleeping patterns and exaggerated startle responses are typical symptoms displayed by survivors of sexual trauma. A common reaction to trauma and sexual abuse in particular, is that the victim dissociates from the experience. A child's body may remain present during the abuse activities, but his mind and spirit separate themselves as a means of psychological self-protection. Some of the symptoms of dissociation that Briere notes are cognitive disengagement into seemingly neutral space (better known as "spacing out"), derealization (the feeling that things around you are false or unreal), depersonalization (feeling that you are different from your usual self), out-of-body experiences (the sensation of floating outside your body and travelling elsewhere) and circumscribed blanks in otherwise continuous memory.

Dissociative behaviours fall on a continuum from daydreaming to Multiple Personality Disorder (MPD). Mild forms of dissociation are common everyday experiences. However, when more extreme dissociative defences, such as splitting and repression, are used to cope with stressors, they interfere with a sense of personal integrity. Many survivors have dissociated their affect from their cognitive memory. Others have a vague, uneasy feeling that they were abused, but they cannot recollect specific abusive events. In either case, the survivor often feels crazy and partialized. Therapy has the task of helping him to reintegrate the full spectrum of his experience. When a victim is abused at a young age and the abuse is severe and prolonged and has involved several different offenders, it is not uncommon for a victim to develop highly dissociative defences, such as MPD. MPD is a sophisticated unconscious defence in which the psyche paradoxically attempts to protect its coherence by partializing its various components. Subpersonalities serve the MPD system by taking on the tasks of protectors, aggressors or victims. Generally, the subpersonalities are very distinct from one another, with very different traits and characteristics. Memories held by each subpersonality are not shared with the other parts of the system; hence, survivors with MPD often have apparent memory loss or have been told by others about actions they did, but don't remember doing.

Our culture has created a social mythology which expects men to be in control, self-sufficient and powerful. Men are not supposed to need assistance in coping with their feelings. Expressions such as "big boys don't cry" encourage males to hide their vulnerability. Successful men in our culture are portrayed as heterosexual, as sexual initiators and as protectors of themselves and others. For male survivors, the social prescription for successful manhood directly conflicts with their experience. Often survivors rewrite their abuse history, forgetting that they were powerless children at the time. They project their mature identities onto their memories of the abuse and hold themselves responsible for not having stopped their offender from abusing them.

In the course of therapy, male survivors need to examine how their ability to claim their own authentic masculinity is limited by cultural factors. Some says therapists can help clients develop a positive masculine gender identity by recognizing that rigid ideas about gender roles and stereotypes based on inadequate information are responsible for some of a survivor's personal suffering in the aftermath of abuse. Therapists can help victims to be aware that today there are new and emerging definitions of masculinity that affirm emotional expression and incorporate vulnerability.

Sexual Orientation and Homosexuality

Many male survivors have been abused by a male offender and this inevitably raises questions for the survivor about his sexual orientation and masculinity. He may be confused about whether his natural sexual orientation is heterosexual, homosexual or bisexual. Questions and concerns about sexual orientation are often a core issue for male survivors. They may express confusion about their natural sexual inclination: Dimock says that many survivors engage in sexual activity with a partner of the sex opposite to their stated sexual orientation or are unable to state their sexual preference. Generally, victims have been physiologically aroused by the offender's stimulation of their genitals. Often the sexual abuse is a victim's first orgasmic experience with another person. In attempting to understand their experience, many victims will use external cues (i.e. physical arousal and orgasm) rather than internal cues (i.e. emotional discomfort and confusion) in their attempts to identify sexual preference and orientation.

Children are not aware that many men who engage in same-sex behaviours are not homosexual. They do not analyze their experience in relation to power and control issues. Often a child will have understood his experience of being abused as a homosexual experience rather than as an abusive experience. Our society is very homophobic. Both heterosexual and homosexual men who have grown up in this culture have internalized homophobic beliefs. For gay men, the "coming out" process can be more difficult if they are survivors of sexual abuse because of their own uncertainty about the impact of the abuse on their sexual orientation. Their families and friends may discount their sexual orientation and dismiss it by saying "He's gay because he was sexually abused". Their own internalized homophobia may encourage them to see their abuse as having determined their sexual orientation, because they can then believe that recovery from the abuse will include a "cure" for being gay.

At the present time, there is no predictable relationship between sexual orientation and childhood sexual abuse. Some researchers have shown "a statistically strong...relationship between childhood sexual abuse and homosexual activity in adulthood', but whether this demonstrates cause, effect or correlation is unknown. There is some evidence that boys who are marginalized are more vulnerable to being abused. To the extent that boys who depart from traditional masculine identifies (i.e. boys who don't like sports, who are feeling-oriented, etc.) are more marginalized, they may be more likely to be abused. Research into this aspect of abuse is fraught with political and ethical concerns and the researcher runs the risk of being seen as anti-gay and homophobic.

Clearly therapists (be they male, female, homosexual or heterosexual) have an obligation to become aware of their own biases regarding sexism, racism, classism and sexual orientation. While we are aware that sexual orientation ranges from heterosexuality, through bisexuality, to homosexuality, our knowledge and understanding about it focuses on the poles of heterosexuality and homosexuality. How the continuum between these two poles is affected by innate, situational or transitional variables is not well understood. Clinicians need to pursue further research into the interface between sexual abuse and subsequent sexual identity. Therapists must ensure that their clients' interests, not their own, are served by the balance between therapeutic and political concerns that occurs in therapy sessions. To optimize the usefulness of the therapeutic process for clients, therapists need to become consciously aware of their own cultural and political biases and how these affect their interventions with clients. Victims appear to have three typical unconscious responses to the experience of sexual victimization.

1. The child knows what it feels like to be a victim and unconsciously decides "This is who I am." He accepts his victimization experience as a reflection of his self-worth, never defines his boundaries and limits and is repeatedly revictimized.

2. The child knows what it feels like to be a victim, and unconsciously decides "I'll protect others from ever becoming victims." He pursues this belief by giving

others the help and protection he never received himself.

3. The child knows what it feels like to be a victim and unconsciously decides "I'll never be a victim again." His way of regaining power is to identify with the aggressor and use abusive strategies to meet his needs.

Although male survivors can adopt more than one of these responses, identification with one position usually predominates. Many survivors, even if their primary identification is as a victim or protector, worry that they will also become a perpetrator. Obviously, not all victims become sexual offenders and not all sexual offenders were victims of sexual abuse. Certain factors lessen the likelihood that a victim will become a victimizer. Having a strong sense of self prior to the abuse experience, having a relationship with positive male role models, having supportive interpersonal relationships and developing an awareness of healthy sexual expression are some of the factors that reduce the likelihood of a victim becoming an offender.

Some victims of abuse unconsciously internalize the behaviour of their offender. Social learning theory suggests that modelling and vicarious learning play a large part in how social behaviours are shaped and expressed. For some victims, acting abusively becomes a defence against being a victim, since they believe that it is better to be powerful than weak and that you need to control others to be powerful. Identification with the aggressor may lead some survivors to acts of abuse against others as a maladaptive means of meeting their needs to be powerful. It may represent a misguided counter-phobic attempt to understand and gain mastery over their victimization experience.

Male socialization encourages action and tolerates aggression in ensuring need gratification. For some survivors, their limited repertoire of skills to meet their needs results in using controlling and manipulative behaviours with others. Bruckner and Johnson note that members of male survivor groups often admit to sexual aggression with adult partners, to physical assault of partners and to general manipulation of relationships. When survivors have themselves perpetrated against others a thorough assessment is needed to ascertain whether this behaviour is a patterned, predatory, deliberate grooming process or whether it is an isolated abuse-reactive experience resulting from behaviourial experimentation or behaviour replication. It is not within the scope of this text to address the assessment and treatment for repeat sexual offenders. However, given that some survivors will have engaged in abuse-reactive perpetration.

Often survivors who have engaged in abuse-reactive sexual activity as adolescents feel greatly ashamed of this behaviour. This double-layered shame, about being both a victim and a victimizer, must be addressed. Survivors often need to have their offending behaviour contextualized vis-a-vis their own victimization. This is not an attempt to excuse this behaviour, but rather a strategy to reduce the client's shame about it. Reducing the level of shame empowers the client to move into feeling appropriately guilty and taking responsibility for having offended, thus becoming accountable for his behaviour. Survivors need to know that a child who has been prematurely sexually awakened has his sexual energy operating without adequate judgement and maturity. As he matures, a survivor will have to examine his early sexual experience and possibly correct some unconscious dysfunctional patterns. The survivor's need to be powerful and to express his rage at having been victimized will have to be channelled into non-abusive behaviours.

Survivors who are both victims and victimizers present a challenge to many mental health professionals. Therapists are often confronted with the limitations of their fondly held theories about victims and offenders. When the boundary between victims and offenders becomes blurred, models of treatment which focus exclusively on victimization or offending processes as discrete events are no longer as useful. Many agencies separate services to victims and offenders; clients who fit both categories create a service delivery dilemma.

Sexual behaviour has a strong inherent reinforcer—namely sexual arousal and orgasm. Victims' sexual arousal patterns are conditioned by sexual abuse; by definition, sexual abuse creates dysfunctional conditioning. Since young children do not have the emotional, cognitive or social orientation with which to make meaning of adult sexual experience their abusive sexual initiation can establish patterns of arousal and sexualized coping behaviours that can be dysfunctional in later developmental stages. Friedrich, Beilke and Urquiza compared the behaviour of two groups of young boys aged three to eight years of age. One group was conduct disordered and the other was sexually abused. They found that they could discriminate who was in which group with a relatively high degree of accuracy. The variable that contributed most to this discrimination was sex problems. The sexually abused boys were significantly more sexualized as a group. The sexual behaviour of these young boys included excessive masturbation, a preoccupation with sex and re-enacting their abuse with siblings. Unless victims such as these young boys receive abuse-focused counselling at the time of disclosure, their sexuality will develop in ways that reflects their initial abusive sexual experience.

For males in culture, the first orgasm is a rite of passage and signifies entry into manhood. When this orgasm occurs in the context of an abusive interaction, it is imbued with problematic associations such as power, non-mutual exchange and sometimes violence. Some survivors have built masturbatory fantasies and rituals around the experience of their abuse and are aroused by aggressive, violent or exploitative sexual activities. The pairing of secrecy and sexual arousal often leave a victim feeling very ashamed of his sexuality, especially if he senses that his sexual expression is deviant. Some survivors are unaware that their sexual behaviour has been shaped by abuse processes and they believe that they are misfits or weird or crazy because of the nature of their sexual desires and expression. There is often an analogous pattern between a victim's abuse experience and his subsequent sexual expression. For instance, if the abuse experience involved acts of violence and sadism, the victim's subsequent sexual expression may well replicate aspects of this violence. Because of the shame surrounding this behaviour, a survivor will generally be very reluctant to let others know about his sexuality.

Many survivors report compulsive sexual behaviours such as frequent non-relational sexual activities with others or compulsive masturbation. "Compulsive sexual behaviour may be simply defined as a lack of control over one or more specific sexual activities. Such activities are most often ego-alien and the individual feels shame and remorse after engaging in such behaviours. In spite of a desire to stop, he is unable to, even when it's clear that he may be causing himself or others harm. Like other addictions, sexual addictions are usually a misguided attempt on the part of the survivor to self-medicate. Compulsive sexual behaviours are used to block states of mind (e.g. anxiety) that are intolerable to the survivor. For some survivors, sexual addictions are used to replace sexual intimacy. Masturbating with pornographic material is less threatening than having to relate sexually with a partner, especially since interactive sexual situations will often bring back memories of the abuse, either consciously or unconsciously. In some cases, survivors attempt to manage their sexual discomfort by completely avoiding sexual contact with others. In order for the client to be able to change his addictive behaviour, he needs to become aware of his addictive cycle. Becoming familiar with the sequencing of his compulsive behaviour and the states of mind that precede his addictive behaviours, helps a survivor to decode his compulsive actions and to develop functional behavioral substitutes.

Interpersonal Difficulties

Sexual abuse is a human-induced trauma and it has long-lasting repercussions on subsequent human relationships. In young children, abuse-related reactions include aggression towards others, delinquency and non-compliance. Often Victims of abuse have mixed loyalties to the abuser; although they may have disliked the one-sided aspect of the sexual relationship, they may have liked the perpetrator's attention and interest. These mixed loyalties can later manifest as an inability to distinguish between sexuality and affection, trust and exploitation and safe or abusive relationships. Victims of abuse can experience difficulty in initiating, developing and maintaining close interpersonal intimate relationships. Often the betrayal of trust that is inherent in sexual abuse leads the victim to withdraw from interpersonal relationships. This social isolation exaggerates the victim's stigmatization and leaves him less able to successfully integrate the psychosocial crisis of abuse.

Researchers and clinicians have noted that survivors of sexual abuse are more likely to be revictimized in subsequent relationships. The dynamics of this revictimization process are complex. Some victims are not well attuned to the danger signals that indicate potentially abusive situations: either they dissociate in the face of them, entering a passive ego state in which their abilities to protect themselves are absent or these signals are so much part of their normal experience that they can't imagine non-abusive interpersonal interactions. Other victims have difficulty discerning their personal boundaries and limits and are unable to identify the times when their needs for safety are not being met. One reaction to childhood victimization is that victims become hypervigilant to the moods and behaviours of other significant people in their environment. As a child, attempting to predict when an abusive event was likely to occur gave the child a marginal sense of control. Learning to read the abuser's state of mind and moods was an integral part of developing this false sense of control. This initially safety-based behaviour becomes dysfunctional in later adult relationships when a survivor cannot identify his own internal experience and is focused on the internal state of the significant others in his life. His sense of self worth becomes distorted and his own behaviour is shaped in reaction to others rather than in response to his own needs.

Survivors' interactive sexual behaviour is often very problematic. A variety of sexual dysfunctions, such as a lack of desire, problems with erection or dissociation during sexual activities can haunt a survivor. Sexual abuse generally accelerates, retards or convolutes a child's sexual development. As an abuse victim matures, his psychosexual development will reflect his abuse-related experience. In adult relationships, sexual partners will sometimes carry the survivor's unconscious projections from his abuse experience and this can be confusing and distressing for both people until such time as these projections can be identified and addressed. For example, if an offender rewarded a victim with post-abuse gifts, as an adult the victim may react negatively to any gifts he receives from his lovers. This may be confusing for his lover who expects gifts to produce enjoyment, and also confusing for the survivor who cannot understand his own response to his lover's behaviour.

Differences between Male and Female Survivors

Current research indicates that there are some significant differences between the sexual victimization of boys and girls. These differences exist both in the nature of the abuse experience itself and in how this experience is understood and integrated. Determining the prevalence rates of the sexual victimization of boys and girls is fraught with complexities. Current research studies indicate that in absolute numbers, more girls than boys are sexually abused. It remains to be seen whether these findings will change as social conditions permit men to acknowledge their victimization experiences. Research findings consistently note that boys and girls experience sexual abuse differently. Males often frame sexual abuse as a sexual initiation, rather than as a violation of their personhood.

The difference in victims' perceptions of their sexual abuse is shaped by many factors, including gender socialization, the different physiological responses of the sexes and culturally determined expressions of sexuality. Although male victims may not perceive their abuse as negative, this does not mean that they weren't negatively affected. As Finklehor discovered in his investigation of male survivors, boys were more likely than girls to cite interest and pleasure as their immediate reaction to being sexually abused. However, when he looked at the long-term effects of abuse as measured by its impact on sexual self-esteem, Finklehor noted that the boys were affected as much, if not more, than the girls. Male victims are more often homosexually abused than female victims. The reality of victimization is that boys, like girls, are most commonly victimized by men.

Researchers have found that female victims are more often abused by family members, while boys are more frequently the victims of extrafamilial abusers. Statistically, boys are at greater risk of being abused by teachers, coaches, babysitters and other adult authority figures than by members of their own family. However empirical research shows that the absolute number of boys who are sexually abused within the family is still very high. Male victims live in single parent, mother-headed households more frequently than do female victims. Many male victims lack an active male parent or nurturing, protective male model. It is more common for boys to be abused in conjunction with other children; girls are more likely to be sexually abused in isolation. In cases where the abuse is intrafamilial, the chances of a boy being one of several victims are greater.

"If a girl is abused by a parent, in 65% of the reports she will be the only reported victim. If a boy is abused, 60% of the time there will be another victim." Boys who are sexually abused are also more likely to be physically abused than girls. Not only are male sexual abuse victims at greater risk of being physically abused, it is also more likely that their sexual abuse will be violent. The types of activities that constitute abuse differ between male and female victims. Male victims are much more frequently the victims of sodomy and are more frequently participants in mutual masturbation. In addition, male victims experience orgasm more frequently during the abuse experience. Male victims are less likely to talk about their victimization experiences with family members than are female victims. Upon disclosure of the abuse, if the male victim is still a juvenile, his abuse is more likely to be reported to the police than to a child protection agency; if R is reported to protective services, the male victim is less likely to be placed in protective custody. After disclosure, male victims are less likely to receive counselling than female victims and when they do, the average length of treatment is shorter.

The clinicians interviewed for this matter were quick to point out that the clinical differences between male and female victims of sexual abuse are few compared to the similarities. Both male and female victims of sexual trauma feel isolated and marginalized. Both struggle with low self-esteem and a damaged sense of self. Ultimately, healing and recovery for both male and female victims involves embracing all aspects of one's humanity, a process which goes beyond gender. A difference between the genders that contributors frequently commented upon is the reluctance that male victims display about acknowledging their victimization. Men have greater shame attached to their victimization than women do; being a victim is a counter-cultural experience for a man. Admitting to having been victimized, to having been a powerless child, is more difficult for men. Some men completely refuse to open the door to their memories and feelings, saying "My childhood experience is in the past". This difficulty in breaking silence and disclosing abuse-related history to others results in fewer men than women seeking professional assistance to help them heal from their traumatic experiences. When men do come into therapy, fewer of them identify their history of having been abused as a presenting problem. Many victims of abuse seek counselling for relationship problems or sexual problems and have not made a cognitive connection between their present problems and their victimization history.

Contributors have observed that male survivors tend to identify sexual concerns (i.e. sexual dysfunctions, sexual orientation issues or gender identity issues) as presenting issues more frequently than female survivors. Women survivors also have sexuality issues, but these are infrequently their dominant presenting concerns; when these issues surface during the course of therapy, they have a different focus than male victim's sexual concerns. It is suggested that our culture encourages men to use sexuality, particularly their genitally-focused sexuality, as a primary component of self identify; hence, when this aspect of a man's life is not functioning well, he struggles with an impaired sense of self. Women are encouraged to identify with their relationships; for women, sexuality is only one part of other intimate behaviour. Hence, women are focused less on their sexuality and more on the quality of their intimate relationships.

The cultural script that supports women to know themselves through their relationships with others and encourages men to be more self-sufficient has other implications for abuse survivors. Bruckner and Johnson, whose experience includes providing group treatment to both male and female survivors, note that the men tend not to associate with each other outside the group, whereas the female participants frequently form relationships. Since isolation is a key issue for male survivors, encouraging them to risk creating relationships with others, including fellow group members, can be a critical step in their healing process. The now common catch-phrase "men act out; women act in" applies to sexual abuse survivors. Contributors remarked that women survivors show a greater tendency to be depressed and to engage in self-harming behaviours, whereas male survivors tend to express their anger at the abuser and exhibit aggressive tendencies toward others. Many male survivors sublimate their anger at having been abused into generalized anti-social behaviour.

In therapy, male survivors tend to be able to contact their anger and rage at having been abused long before they can feel their grief. They often display active and violent revenge fantasies. Women survivors, on the other hand, are initially more in touch with their sadness and depression and their rage at having been victimized usually surfaces later in the therapeutic process. The male clients are more dissociated from the affective components of their abuse, while their female clients are more dissociated from the cognitive components of their abuse. Male survivors often tell the story of their abuse quite matter-of-factly, describing the behaviours involved in the abuse in detail. They talk about these events as if they happened to someone else, expressing little affect or compassion.

Female survivors generally have more difficulty recalling the specific events that comprised the abuse and more difficulty telling others about it. However, they experience intense feelings related tc these events, whether or not they can accurately recall them. Therapists who have offered abuse-focused group treatment to both genders note that the men were more action-oriented than the women. Because of this readiness to take action, therapists need to ensure that their male sexual abuse clients are emotionally prepared for any behaviours which they are planning to undertake. Premature confrontation of an abuser, or ill-conceived acts of angry revenge, can be counter-therapeutic.

Treatment Models

This matter presents information about the basic tenets of therapy with male survivors. It develops a treatment model which is based on principles of partnership between the client and therapist and which supports the clients' innate abilities to recover from sexual abuse. The model describes four phases of healing, namely Breaking Silence, The victim Phase, The Survivor Phase and The Thriver Phase.

Abuse processes occur over time, in a relationship in which the offender's needs are given priority over the victim's needs. The abuse-related activities are kept a secret because of the shame that surrounds them. The therapeutic process has the potential to replicate these elements of abuse and to itself become an abusive process. If the therapy is designed to meet the therapist's needs and not the client's and if the confidentiality of the process is used to protect the therapist rather than the client, it can become a counter-productive experience for the client. The client's belief that people will attempt to use him for their own ends and that safe, intimate relationships are not possible, at least for him, will be reinforced.

However, in a manner that echoes the principles of homeopathic medicine, therapy, because of its structural similarities to the abuse process, can also heal the wounds caused by abuse. When a client can proceed through his therapeutic journey with support to reclaim his own power, therapy can be a powerful tool for recovery. Successful therapy will allow clients to experience respectful and non-exploitative power dynamics which support them in reclaiming the parts of themselves that were lost or damaged because of the abuse. The treatment model that is presented outlines a therapeutic healing process for male victims of sexual abuse.

Describing a general process of recovery or healing is a difficult task. Every recovered abuse victim has his own story to tell of this journey. However, in order to work effectively with abuse survivors, each therapist must develop a generic "map of recovery" that he or she will use to guide the therapeutic process. Although this "map" will no doubt be conceptualized in different ways at different stages of the therapist's career, at any given time, each therapist needs to be able to articulate the changes that his interventions are designed to facilitate in his clients.

As the survivor makes his unconscious coping strategies conscious, his personal autonomy increases. Flashbacks of the abuse become reclaimed memories; inexplicable fears and anxieties become associations to present environmental triggers that echo abuse-related experiences; and some chronic somatic complaints become the signals for recognizing unmet physical or emotional needs. As the survivor decodes his behaviours, thoughts and feelings he begins to recognize how his belief system was shaped by his victimization, and his reactions to this experience. This recognition opens the door for him to develop new life choices and options. The experience of learning, practising and integrating new attitudes and behaviour is a spiralling process, not a linear one. Often old patterns have to be revisited many times before they are replaced with new ones. The effects of sexual abuse are complicated by other forms of neglect and abuse that were present in the victim's childhood and compounded by the damage resulting from the development of initially adaptive but ultimately self-destructive coping behaviours. Trauma of a sexual nature shames and degrades the victim at the level of his existential core.

Survivors of abuse can never change the facts of the abuse. They cannot eradicate the abuse from their personal histories. However they can change their relationship to this history and they can change the effects these events have on their lives. For personal change to be authentic and integrated into a survivor's life, ample time to test and explore new alternative behaviours must be present. Contributors generally worked with their survivor clients for a minimum of a year and often for much longer, in order to bring about lasting and substantive change. Not all of a survivor's problems are related to his experience of childhood sexual abuse. Other life traumas play their part. Therapists must be discerning in their diagnostic skills; they must take care not to simplistically attribute their clients' issues solely to their sexual trauma if this is not an accurate assignation. Therapy for sexual abuse survivors has many facets. Reducing a survivor's sense of isolation, facilitating his emotional discharge, challenging his cognitive distortions, normalizing his experience and educating him about abuse processes are all part of the journey. Nurturing his spirituality (using this word in its most general sense) and rekindling his hope are also important.

Principles of Male Survivor Treatment

The contributors to this study are experienced therapists who have a broad range of both experience and theory to call upon in their work with male survivors. They utilize a wide range of theoretical orientations, including family systems models, feminist therapy models, cognitive-behavioral restructuring processes, hypnosis and psychodynamic approaches. All of the contributors are eclectic in their theoretical approach to working with male survivors. Although some favour one particular theoretical model over others, none of the contributors uses one theory base exclusively. They agree that using a theoretical model that is suitable to the client and his presenting issues is more important than being loyal to a theory irrespective of the client's issues. If a client is very cognitive in his presentation, they suggest initially using a theoretical orientation, such as cognitive restructuring, that will join with the client's process. More affectively focused methods of therapy, such as gestalt therapy or psychodrama, are not used until such time as the client can experience his affect with some comfort. Despite the wide range in the contributor's theoretical orientations, they agree that the following key concepts underlie successful therapy with male survivors.

Empowerment: All the contributors agree that assisting their clients to regain their personal power is an essential component of successful sexual abuse treatment. Acknowledging a client's strengths and validating the survival skills he has developed, however functional or dysfunctional they may be in his present life context, is crucial. A survivor's very presence in a therapist's office is living proof that he had what it took to survive the impact of sexual abuse. However great his need to transform his survival skills into more adaptive processes, he needs to recognize that his present level of skill has ensured his survival thus far.

The therapist and client must work in partnership while addressing the client's abuse-related concerns. If a therapist acts as an authority figure in the therapeutic relationship, he or she invites the transference that was initially formed in the abuse experience when the offender had power over the victim. Although such transference may eventually be constructively resolved, it threatens the formulation of the therapeutic relationship in the short-run. It imposes stresses on both the client and therapist that are generally unduly taxing and counterproductive. This does not mean to say that clinicians do not bring skills and awareness that can help their clients' recovery. They do. However the frame in which the therapeutic process occurs is one in which the therapist can act as a "consultant" to his client and the client is an informed "consumer" who determines the services he wishes to "purchase". Not only is the survivor the expert on his abuse-related experience, he is also responsible for his own healing process. A therapist can facilitate a client's recovery, but he cannot take responsibility for it. Both the client and the therapist need to be very clear about who is responsible for making changes in the client's life. If this is not clear, the client can remain in a victim position in which he doesn't claim responsibility for his life and the therapist runs the risk of becoming either a rescuer or a persecutor as he tries to motivate his client to change.

Many survivors are not aware of a connection between their experience of being sexually abused as a child and the problematic issues they face in their adult lives. Because they have either repressed their abuse memories or disowned their abuse experience and claim that it has had no impact on them, they don't have a context for understanding their current behaviour. Often this leaves them feeling crazy or ashamed. When symptoms are seen as "a creative adaptation to highly negative circumstances rather than an expression of psychopathology" survivors are able to start their journey of healing and recovery. As survivors reclaim their memories and discharge their repressed affect, they can begin to understand and change dysfunctional patterns in their lives. When they develop an understanding that all their behaviour makes sense, they begin to decode their experience rather than disowning or judging it. For some survivors, so-called "psychotic" episodes are PTSD flashbacks or expressions of MPD. Seeing himself as an abuse survivor who is exhibiting common abuse-related symptoms, rather than as a mental patient whose only hope is medication, can support a client in making positive change. This does not mean that some survivors will not require psychotropic drugs or hospitalization. However, in general, the sense of normalcy that survivors regain when their present behaviour is connected to past events supports the healing process.

Growth and learning model

The contributors agree that survivors need to be invited into the therapeutic process with the understanding that

"We all do the best we can at all times." Skill deficits, overwhelming emotions or confused internal states result in inappropriate or dysfunctional responses to events in a survivor's present life. Changing these maladaptive responses depends on learning and integrating new skills, increasing awareness and understanding of internal processes and acknowledging emotional states. Replacing maladaptive patterns and beliefs with functional ones and assimilating these changes in a supportive environment are essential ingredients of the recovery process. Most of the challenges that clients face in their lives do not occur in therapy sessions. Clients need support to transfer the learning that occurs during the therapeutic process into their daily lives. Therapists need to assist clients to develop structures that allow them to anchor their psycho-social growth so that it becomes habitual behaviour.

Integration

Healing from sexual abuse is, in part, a process of reclaiming lost or "stuck" parts of the self. Survivors need to be told: "Bad things happened to you. You were not bad." Often, at the time of the abuse, given his cognitive, affective and physical immaturity, the victim decided that he was being abused because he deserved to be abused. He concluded that he himself was responsible for being abused. He believed that shameful or dangerous parts of himself had caused his victimization. He then, unconsciously, repressed or dissociated those shameful or dangerous parts in a misguided attempt to make himself normal. These undervalued parts of self were put out of conscious awareness, only to intrude later in unconscious form. Most survivors need to reclaim and integrate devalued parts of themselves. Men who deny or repress their victimization experience, yet display abuse-related symptoms such as drug or alcohol abuse need to become aware that they have complex and sometimes conflicting, internal needs. They need to recognize that as well as having an adult persona, they also incorporate a damaged internal child who may continue to act problematically regardless of the survivor's chronological age. When the various parts of the self are in communication with one another and no part is devalued or ignored, the survivor will experience greater health and balance.

Survivors need to acknowledge the losses that occurred in their lives as a result of childhood sexual abuse. They lost their childhood innocence when the abuse began. Their inherent sexual clock was prematurely started. Often close family relationships are lost to them. Many must cope with the aftermath of abuse without family support. Part of the recovery process for survivors is to grieve their losses. The stages of denial, bargaining, anger, sadness and acceptance form part of a survivor's healing journey.

The earliest stage of psycho-social development in Erickson's theory of development is basic trust. This stage underlies all others and forms the bedrock for further psycho-social growth. By definition, a survivor's trust in others has been breached. Either by seductive or aggressive means, he has been violated by another human being. When a survivor enters therapy, he brings his lack of trust in others with him. At the beginning of the therapeutic process, trust in the therapist has to be earned. The therapist will have to address the client's lack of trust by ensuring that the therapeutic process is safe. This means that clients will not be expected to trust either the therapist or the therapeutic process until such time as this happens naturally. However, each client will be expected to identify his needs regarding safety in the therapeutic process. The therapist helps the client by gently but persistently soliciting these needs. In addition, clearly discussing the therapeutic groundrules and the therapeutic contract increases safety in the therapeutic process.

Although sexual abuse is a personal experience, it is intrinsicly linked to larger cultural forces. An analysis of the cultural and political forces that create sexual abuse is not generally part of therapy. However, it is impossible to address a client's post-abuse responses without acknowledging that both client and therapist are members of a culture that permits sexual violence and exploitation. The necessity of addressing cultural and social issues is even stronger when victimization due to sexual abuse is compounded by other kinds of victimization such as racial discrimination, homophobic prejudice or poverty. In such cases, the victim's issues are likely to be a complex outcome of concurrent victimization processes and they must be therapeutically addressed as such.

One part of therapy with male survivors involves debunking various social myths regarding sexual abuse. Many such myths relate to a survivor's sense of his masculinity or questions about his sexual orientation; the necessary "debunking" cannot occur without examining cultural values and social expectations. Learning how social forces have been internalized and incorporated into the survivor's sense of self thus becomes a part of successful therapy. Often, as either a direct or indirect outgrowth of therapy, survivors reexamine social and cultural values. As a result, they gain greater freedom to fully accept the realities of their own lives, including their victimization.

Male survivors of sexual abuse, like other therapy clients, tend to interpret and shape their therapeutic experience in ways that conform to their world view. If a client believes that all men are sexually inappropriate or that no one will ever be able to help him, he will bring these beliefs into the therapeutic process. He will unconsciously attempt to replicate his childhood beliefs with the therapist. Therapists need to be aware of transference and counter-transference dynamics in order to intervene skilfully. Therapists often have unresolved or partially resolved personal issues that coincide with their clients' dynamics. Under these circumstances, it is easy for a therapist to take a client's issues or "transference bait" personally. This is not helpful. Instead the therapist must work with the client to see how his patterns of understanding the world and interacting with others were established. It cannot be emphasized strongly enough how essential good supervision is in helping therapists navigate transference/ counter- transference dynamics successfully.

Survivors don't need their therapists to be models of perfection. As a consequence of their painful childhoods, survivors have often constructed fantasies of "perfect relationships" in which they imagine themselves finally having all their unmet needs recognized and addressed. These images of perfection are as dysfunctional a map for real relationships as the abusive relationships they experienced in childhood. Being authentic is an important quality that therapists can model for clients. Therapists need to respect their own human limitations—"...therapists are human beings who inevitably make mistakes and who may not always be able to maintain the empathic bond that guides accurate helping behaviours." When therapists honestly own their mistakes and take the new information gained from making these mistakes into account in their subsequent work with clients, they model a process of trial-and-error learning that helps clients acknowledge their own human limits.

Therapists who have been trained to respond to clients like a "blank screen" need to adjust this style when working with male survivors. A neutral stance can be perceived by a client as a lack of responsiveness to his pain or as a judgment about his experience; it may leave him feeling confused, frightened and isolated. Survivors require a responsive, psycho-educational therapeutic alliance which validates their experience and helps them to move beyond its negative effects. Therapists who work with male survivors need to be overtly empathic, accepting and supportive.

Therapeutic Process

From the therapist's perspective, therapy with male survivors has four distinct phases. This four-phase model of therapy is helpful both as an analogous description of the recovery process for male survivors and also as an analytical tool to assist in case management and treatment planning. The four phases are:

1. Breaking Silence
2. The Victim Stage
3. The Survivor Phase
4. The Thriver Stage

Individual clients will spend more or less time in any given phase of healing and some phases will overlap with one another. Some clients will stay in one phase for a long time, reaching a plateau in their growth; it may be advisable to take a planned break from therapy during these times. However, in general, each phase is associated with distinct issues and demands different skills from the therapist. At all times, the therapeutic process for male survivors needs to be relevant to individual needs. Identifying a client's phase of healing can help a therapist to skilfully and strategically focus the therapy to meet this client's unique requirements. Before beginning abuse-focused therapy, clients need information about the therapeutic process. Knowing ahead of time that recovery tends to be long-term rather than short-term and that the healing journey is not a linear one, helps clients to make decisions about their involvement with the therapeutic process. Each client will have to decide how to allocate his resources (e.g. time, money, etc.) to support his recovery. Relatively accurate and candid predictions about the therapeutic process, including the length of the journey, will help clients make these decisions.

Giving clients a cognitive map with which to understand the healing process can be a supportive intervention. Although the concept of a four-phase model of healing is somewhat abstract, being able to identify which phase he is currently in helps a client know where he is headed and what kind of process he can anticipate en route. Whether or not clients want such a map, it is essential that each therapist uses one to guide his interventions. The different phases of the four-phase model are described below:

Breaking silence : Acknowledging to himself that he was sexually abused as a child is the first step a survivor must take to heal from this experience. Reaching out to others for support and validation of this experience and breaking the silence that has surrounded the secret of the abuse, is an important step. Survivors come to the realization that they were abused in different ways. For some men, their memories surface during therapy for non-abuse related issues, when they begin to realize that their patterns of behaviour are the result of childhood sexual trauma. Other men have never forgotten being abused, but have discounted the impact of these events on their lives or have never labelled them as abuse. Yet others have a sudden realization while watching a TV show about sexual abuse, or reading a book which refers to sexual abuse, that they have themselves been victimized. However it happens, acknowledging his sexual victimization is the beginning of a survivor's healing process. Some men will seek support and help to cope with this realization by immediately going to see a counsellor or by attending a self-help group.

Many others wait a long time before they share this information with others. When a therapist is treating a man for other issues, but suspects a history of abuse because of the symptoms his client is experiencing, he is ethically bound to explore the possibility of childhood trauma with his client. Even if the client denies a history of abuse, the clinician must raise the possibility of childhood trauma and its associated symptoms. Clearly, if the client has no associations with having been sexually abused, the therapist should not insist on following this line of inquiry. But as long as the symptoms suggest childhood trauma, the clinician must continue to leave the possibility open. Bringing the client to awareness and acknowledgement of childhood trauma may take some time and requires rapport and trust in the therapist/client relationship. The client may also need to develop life skills (e.g. communication, assertiveness, anxiety management, etc.) before he has sufficient ego strength to manage his emotional responses to acknowledging his sexual abuse.

Some therapists are reluctant to pursue questions about abuse if their client has no memory of having been abused. "False Memory Syndrome", in which therapists are thought to create their clients' memories of abuse by planting hypnotic suggestions, is currently a topic of much debate in therapeutic circles. Until such time as this possibility can be clearly eradicated, it bears examination.

The victim stage: The main focus of this phase of therapy is to validate the client's abuse history, to build a safe therapeutic process with the client and to provide educational information about the effects of sexual abuse on its victims. Unless a client has intense flashbacks or other effectively demanding concerns, much of the work in this phase will be cognitively focused. Men often need support in acknowledging their victimization. Even if they can recall the sexually intrusive events that have happened to them, many men don't call them "abusive". Educating clients about power differences, coercion, misrepresenting adult reality, the use of threats and lies to gain compliance and so on, can assist male victims to fully claim their experience. The therapist needs to find a balance between staying focused on abuse-related material and not pushing a client beyond his own comfort zone. If the process becomes too intense or if the client perceives the therapist as trying to control the therapy process, it is quite likely that the client will shut down in the face of this replication of an abusive dynamic. To the extent that the client's memories permit, he will be asked to develop a "sexual abuse autobiography" during this phase of therapy. Remembering how he was groomed for the abuse, who offended against him, how often the abuse oecurred, what explicitly happened, what his reactions were at the time, whether or not he told anyone and what, if anything, he liked about the experience are areas to investigate at this stage. Talking openly about the abuse and continuing to challenge any denial of the experience are primary tasks for this therapeutic phase.

Clients who have defended against their abuse memories by developing substance or process addictions find themselves in somewhat of a "Catch-22" situation—if they maintain their addiction, they are unable to process their abuse history effectively; if they give up their addiction, they are often flooded by uncontrollable memories and feelings, which may lead to a relapse. Therapists have to carefully monitor addictive behaviour at this phase of therapy. If a client is not yet ready to surrender an addiction, he can be supported by the recommendation that he develop other means of addressing his anxiety before he begins to process his abuse history. Occasional relapses are predictable for addicted clients—however, when the addiction is still used as a primary coping strategy, abuse-related therapy will be counter-productive and it is generally contra-indicated.

The therapist needs to teach stress management and self-care skills during this phase, so that as the therapeutic focus becomes more affective, clients have functional ways of attending to their emotions. Ensuring that clients have active support systems in place or focusing on building these supports, are therapeutic tasks in the Victim Phase. In this phase, clients will generally feel some emotional relief at realizing that the problems they face in their lives are not the result of being crazy, but the outcome of being sexually abused as a child. As they gain information about dissociative processes and other coping strategies, they begin to feel more normal and hopeful about their futures.

The transition between the Victim and Survivor Phases of therapy is marked by the client's ability to place full responsibility for the abuse on the offender. When the client recognizes that he was a victim in an abusive relationship and that the abuse was not a reflection of his worth as a person, but of his offender's unresolved problems, he moves into the next phase of therapy.

The survivor phase: The Survivor Phase of therapy describes the often arduous work of repairing clients' emotional, cognitive and behaviourial dysfunctions. This is a push/pull stage of therapy. Client's maladaptive life patterns are slowly replaced by functional sequences as the client takes the risk of developing new coping strategies. Walking a fine line between containment and expression, and finding a workable balance of both, are the keys to success during this phase of therapy. Often clients become discouraged in this phase. Because they are reclaiming their previously blocked affective processes, they are more aware of feelings of fear, pain, rage or sadness. They feel unstable as they discard old methods of coping and substitute new ones, which are still relatively untested and awkward to use. They feel as if therapy has made them worse rather than better. Many cases of premature termination occur in this phase as clients lose their faith in ever being able to make significant changes.

At this point in therapy, clinicians must be steady and focused. They need to remind their clients that discouragement is to be expected in the Survivor Phase. The original momentum of addressing the abuse has worn off and some weariness has set in. The therapist must nonetheless continue to help the client identify his feelings and challenge his thinking errors and distorted beliefs. Throughout this phase, the therapist must affirm the client's strength and courage. By validating the painfulness and difficulty of this stage of the therapeutic work and by acknowledging the positive changes made to date, the therapist maps out the therapeutic journey, thus supporting the client's recovery. The Survivor Phase of therapy is identified by particular therapeutic tasks. Affective responses are identified and worked with during this stage. Becoming acquainted with a wide range of emotions and exploring ways in which these feeling states can be expressed, can be a slow and fear-filled process. However, as survivors become more familiar with their previously dissociated feelings, they begin to experience a greater sense of wholeness and well-being. Habitual dysfunctional cognitive and behavioral patterns are also worked with during this therapeutic stage. Thinking errors and self-defeating behaviourial sequences are identified and replaced by healthier substitutes.

During the survivor phase, new skills need to be practised outside of therapy sessions. Throughout this therapeutic stage sessions may involve both spontaneous and planned abreactive processes. At times, clients may need to take a planned break from therapy and integrate their learning before continuing the process. The transition between the survivor phase and the thriver phase is marked by the client's readiness to take back his own power; this will frequently be manifested by the client's readiness to confront his offender, either in reality or, more often, symbolically. This is not a reactive stand taken in defiance against the offender; instead it represents an integrated change in which the client no longer feels that the offender has power over his life.

The thriver phase: When the client reaches the thriver phase, he begins to feel hopeful once again. From an empowered perspective of having changed previously dysfunctional coping patterns he can articulate the ways in which he was affected by having been abused. He realizes that the outcome of successful therapy is not "living happily ever after", but having the skills and resources that he needs to address the difficulties that occur in his life. Thrivers feel responsible for their lives and they believe that they have many options to choose from in addressing their life problems, both past and present. The abuse is no longer seen as a central issue in the client's self-identification; his image of himself has shifted into the present and he trusts his adult self. During the thriver phase, the client and therapist must begin the process of termination. Termination needs to be managed so that the client can leave the therapeutic process at his own pace. In addition, clients should be given plenty of permission to return to therapy should they experience a resurgence of symptoms or should new abuse memories surface.

The therapist must be very careful not to compromise therapist/client boundaries by permitting double relationships to develop. Clients need their therapists to remain available to them for potential future consultation; any double relationship, such as when a therapist becomes a friend, lover, landlord or business partner to a client, jeopardizes the safety of the therapeutic relationship. Risk of such double relationships might arise when the therapist is himself a survivor with needs for social support from relatively "recovered" fellow survivors or when a recovering client is seen as a professional ally who can assist in furthering desperately needed services for survivors.

Group Therapy

Individual therapy provides male survivors with a safe and supportive forum where they can identify and examine their abuse-related history. An individual therapist is often the first person whom a survivor has entrusted with information about his childhood sexual abuse and how he subsequently handled this experience. Although individual therapy has a central place to play in the recovery process, it is enhanced and complimented by group treatment. Abuse-focused group therapy provides survivors with opportunities to normalize their experiences and reduce their isolation. Many adult survivors are empowered by the realization that they were not alone in having been abused by a trusted adult. Survivor groups provide clients with an opportunity to experience a social milieu where respect for personal boundaries is paramount and they can practice new skills for relating to the self and others. Group members model healing for one another and catalyze each others' growth.

Male survivor groups assist their members by providing a safe, structured and nurturing environment in which to learn new skills and resolve the trauma of sexual abuse. For many survivors this is the first opportunity they have ever had to talk with other men about hawing been vulnerable and hurt. A survivor who joins a survivors' group is openly declaring that he was abused. Joining a group is a tangible sign that his denial is over and he is willing to work with his abuse issues more directly. The support survivors receive from their fellow group members takes a number of forms. Being listened to and believed is a powerful validation of each survivors' victimization experience. Hearing other members' abuse-related stories often evokes previously repressed feelings of compassion or anger within survivors. Initially these feelings are projected onto other group members; eventually, they are reclaimed and integrated into the self. Sharing emotionally with other men without this intimacy being fraught with sexual undertones opens new possibilities of male friendship for many survivors.

Group membership gives survivors opportunities to become aware of maladaptive interactive processes and to practice new inter-personal skills. Either by direct interactions with other group members or through role-playing in the group, members learn how to resolve conflict nonviolently, how to get their needs met and how to give and receive nonsexual affection. Giving as well as receiving help enhances clients' self-esteem and counteracts their sense of powerlessness. Group members model both effective and ineffective coping strategies for one another. They give each other direct and indirect feedback on many levels. Frequently, group interventions occur indirectly. Group members experience vicarious learning as they witness their peers grow and change. "Each time someone takes more charge of his life, it underscores the reality of recovery for everyone." However, group treatment is not a panacea for all survivors. For some clients, a group experience can be overwhelming. If a client's internal resources are not strong enough to counter the weight of the group process, a group experience can be counter-therapeutic. Each individual client has much less control of his experience in a group than he does in individual therapy. The fact that clients spark one anothers' memories and catalyze one anothers' growth can be either positive or negative, depending on the client's readiness.

The assessment process for potential group clients sets a tone for subsequent group experiences. Time spent on a thorough and comprehensive assessment is time well invested. In order to obtain useful information, assessment questions need to be direct, concrete and behaviourial. Group screening serves a function for both client and therapist. Clients can use the assessment interview as an opportunity to find out about group treatment and to gather the information they need to make a decision about whether or not to engage in this process. Clinicians use screening interviews to solicit data about potential clients' abuse histories and their recovery process to date in order to assess their potential readiness for a group experience.

During the screening interview, a client is expected to tell the group therapists about his abuse history in sufficient detail for the therapists to have enough information to be able to skilfully facilitate the client's growth in the group. Clients should also receive information about the group's treatment goals, philosophy and process. It's helpful to give clients handouts about the group, such as a list of acceptable and unacceptable behaviours; in the group, or information about the group's purpose and structure. The contributors assess the following specific issues to determine a client's readiness to participate in an abuse-related therapy group:

The client's ability to talk about his abuse: Survivors must be able to talk about their abuse with some degree of comfort before joining an abuse-related group. They should have at least one clear memory of having been abused. If they talk about their abuse as "it", or are unable to say or hear words that refer specifically to abusive processes, they are not ready to join a group.

Support: Clients who have no supports outside of the therapy group are not good candidates for group treatment. A group member should have access to at least one close friend or a 12-step support network to supply social support outside of the group. Ideally a client engaged in group treatment should also be engaged in concurrent individual therapy, at least on an as-needed basis. Group therapists should obtain a release of information from clients during the assessment process, so that they have permission to contact the client's individual therapist if necessary. In some situations, a shortage of suitable individual therapists or a client's lack of financial resources may rule out the possibility of concurrent individual therapy. In such cases, before admitting a client to their group, the leaders need to be very sure that the client's self-care skills and social supports are sufficient to meet the demands of group membership.

Motivation: Group clients should be able to discuss how their sexual victimization is currently a problem in their lives. They should also be able to articulate desired goals they intend to work toward during the group process. If clients are referred to group treatment by their individual therapist, it is important to ensure that the interest in group therapy belongs to the client and not his therapist. Clients who attend a group because someone else thinks they should are not good candidates for group treatment.

Interpersonal skills: Group members need to have adequate interpersonal skills to be able to participate in a group. A client who is scapegoated by other group members because of poor social skills is only revictimized or patronized by group treatment. Until such time as a client has sufficient social skills to fully participate in a group, he is better served by other treatment modalities.

Self-care: Potential group members should be able to describe self-care strategies to deal with both their own pain and the pain of listening to others. They must demonstrate that they not only are aware of such strategies, but that they actually put them into practice.

Homophobia: Actively homophobic clients are not well-suited to abuse-related group treatment. Abused men need to have space to explore their sexual orientation and masculine identity during group treatment and adamantly heterosexist attitudes curtail this exploration. Both gay and straight men are treated in the same abuse-focused groups. Some contributors said that they used to separate groups into gay and straight, but noted that they no longer observe this practice. The focus in male survivor group treatment is on the common human experience of having been abused, not on the issue of sexual orientation.

Contributors discussed a paradox—although many male survivors are very concerned about the implications of having been abused by a man (if their perpetrator was male) and many of them are quite homophobic, they have a strong desire to establish closer relationships with men. They noted that having both gay and straight men in a group initially causes consternation. At first, the men are very sensitive to each other's sexual orientation, as they establish their own comfort in the group. However, when clients come to know one another, and to understand the differences between pedophiles and homosexuals, this tension eases. By the end of the group sexual orientation has become an irrelevant issue as the group members open up to one another and share their humanity.

Present life functioning: Clients who are actively addicted or very recently recovered addicts are not suitable candidates for group treatment. Suicidal or homicidal clients are too emotionally unstable to join a group. Clients currently in physically or sexually abusive relationships need to address these issues directly before they enter a survivors' group. A client who is actively psychotic or currently processing a major life crisis is not a candidate for group treatment.

Abuse-reactive perpetration: Therapists must ask clients if they have engaged in abuse-reactive perpetration. You will have to determine how to evaluate acts of abuse that happened when a client was an adolescent. A general rule-of-thumb is that a client who has committed any patterned, repetitive acts of perpetration, or who has committed acts of perpetration in the last five years, is disqualified from participating in a survivors's group.

MPD: Clients who have MPD can be suitable group members, provided they have sufficient control of their various alter personalities. Clients who can develop therapeutic contracts about how they manage their dissociation and who can ensure that their persecutor alters will not be brought into the group, can be group members. The group therapists need to educate the other group members about MPD and the process of splitting into after personalities, in order to normalize this process.

A variety of group models to work with sexually abused males: single-leader groups, dual-leader groups, structured and unstructured groups, open and closed groups are all offered by different therapists in different locations. Some of these models are based on theoretical principles, others are based on practical necessities. However, whether or not they facilitated a group themselves, all the contributors agreed on the usefulness of group treatment.

The first stage is a closed, structured eight to 10 week psycho-educational group, which suits clients who are in the victim phase of therapy. Clients who wish to pursue group treatment further, are well served by a second stage, open-ended, unstructured group which focuses on resolving abuse-related trauma and developing functional life skills. The level of processing and the intensity of this second-stage group are suited to clients in the survivor phase of therapy. There are many reasons why this model is suitable for survivors of sexual abuse. As with individual therapy, safety is the guiding principle in offering group treatment to survivors. Initially, when survivors begin to attend an abuse-focused group, they are nervous and hesitant. They feel anxious about discussing their victimization with others. A structured psycho-educational group, in which the focus of the group is known in advance, is a safe entry into an unfamiliar group process.

Each week the psycho-educational group focuses on a selected theme, such as sexuality, coping strategies, self-care, abuse dynamics and so on. Clients are given written materials before each group or exercises which they are asked to complete prior to the group session. The group structure is flexible and the leader tells clients to ask for time in the group to address their personal concerns on an "as-needed" basis. No one expects any group member to self-disclose unless he chooses to do so. All the clients in the psycho-educational group begin the group and end the group at the same time. This structure provides newcomers to group therapy with an equal opportunity to develop safe and predictable relationships in a group context. It also means that the group members move through the various stages of group development on the same schedule. The initial session focuses on group rules and procedures, the middle sessions focus on abuse-related material and developing group process and the final session acts as a celebration of growth and sharing. This gentle entry into abuse-focused material supports and empowers clients. It also provides the therapists with an opportunity to fully assess the group members' capacity to handle group process within a contained structure.

The psycho-educational group permits clients who are not yet ready to move into a more intense process-focused group to successfully complete a group experience. They can then concentrate on enhancing their skills until they're fully prepared to continue in a process group. The second-stage group is more demanding of both clients and therapists. This group is unstructured, in the sense that it relies on the clients to generate the material that is addressed each week. It is less predictable for both clients and therapists since the agenda cannot be known in advance. It is also more fluid and more interactive than the psycho-educational group. Clients may be asked to participate in each other's work and they are expected to be active participants in the group process.

The second-stage group is open-ended. This means that clients determine how long they stay in the group based on its usefulness to them. Contributors who run groups for male survivors estimate the average length of time a client stays in a group is generally between one and two years. Because group members have different entry times into the group, the established group members take on the role of enculturating and supporting new members. Abuse-focused groups are a hybrid of self-help and therapist-led processes. The sharing and support clients offer one another are essential components of recovery. However, at certain times, the therapists' skills in handling abreactive situations or helping clients decode their transference reactions, are crucial to clients' healing. Therapists must develop discernment about when to facilitate the group process and when to sit back and let the group members carry the ball. The groups that contributors work with have from six to 10 members. A group with eight members is ideal; however, one or two members more or less will not interfere with the delivery of quality service.

The contributors run their group sessions for differing lengths of time; 1 - 1½ hours was the shortest group session and three hours the longest. Group sessions should be held weekly, although the second-stage process may take several scheduled breaks throughout the year.

This two-stage model recommends that group membership be reserved for male survivors only. Most survivors, both male and female, initially benefit from working with group members of the same sex with whom they can more easily let shame and embarrassment surface. However, some contributors work with mixed-gender groups and report success with this model. Mixed-gender groups are best reserved for clients who wish to pursue further group therapy after they have completed an all-male second-stage group. A mixed-gender group is best able to help a client who's in the thriver phase of therapy.

Group Groundrules

Both first and second-stage groups need to develop a set of groundrules to provide safety and structure to the group process. Although many groundrules are common among different groups, each group needs to ensure that it's groundrules fit its unique identity. Spending time during the first session of a psycho-educational group to develop a set of groundrules is an essential task. In a second-stage group, the groundrules need to be reviewed each time a new member joins the group. Although certain groundrules remain consistent throughout a group's life, others change with the group's developmental stage. Many survivors will at first be unable to articulate their needs in regards to making the group a safe environment. They are unused to thinking of their needs and unused to having an opportunity to voice them. Negotiating conflicting needs can also be a foreign experience for many survivors. Because of these factors, the groundrules need to be revisited from time to time to ensure that they're still appropriate and timely.

Here are some of the key groundrules that contributors use to make their groups safe environments for their members. It is very important that group leaders use the groundrules to hold the group members accountable to the group process. Violations of the groundrules must be addressed. Many survivors come from families which were chaotic. Having predictable and consistent limits set within the group is an essential step in preparing the ground for the client to take risks and begin to heal.

Groups Process

Each individual session should have a predictable opening, middle and ending stage. Establishing some predictability is a way of making the group into a safe and healing environment. Most groups begin with a check-in, where every group member takes some time to speak to the rest of the group. The focus of this time can be to let the group know how he has been doing since the last session or to identify issues he wants to address in the current session. However the check-in is conducted, it needs to be predictable. It also needs to have clear time and content boundaries so that members do not use the check-in to start to do therapy-focused work. Runaway check-ins that become the focus of an entire session reinforce dysfunctional crisis-focused behaviour. Even when a client is in crisis, he needs to be supported and contained through the check-in so that everyone has the opportunity to address the group before any one member takes the floor. The middle section of the session will vary depending on whether it is a first or second-stage group. In a first-stage group, unless a client has requested time to process an issue, the group will focus on psycho-educational material. Although some affective work may occur, this is not the primary purpose of the group process. A listing of topics that contributors have used with their first-stage groups includes:

— legal and criminal aspects of sexual abuse
— typical roles in sexually abusive families
— types of offenders
— sex education and information about normal sexual development
— sexual and non-sexual intimacy
— assertiveness
— relationship styles—codependency vs. interdependency
— conflict resolution
— domestic violence—physical, sexual and emotional abuse
— child development
— parenting skills—consequences vs. punishments
— building self esteem
— self-care and stress-reduction techniques
— self-defeating behaviours

In an eight to ten week group, it would be impossible to address all aspects of abuse-related behaviour. The members of the first-stage group should be asked to select the topics that are the most salient to them and these should be the focus of the sessions. In a second-stage group, the middle stage of the session is unpredictable. This time is used to work with issues that clients identify during the check-in. The exact format this takes will depend upon the style and skills of the group leaders. Whether the focus remains on the individual who raised an issue, or whether an issue is worked on by the group as a whole, tends to be a function of the group leadership style, the nature of the issue, the level of safety and trust within the group and the respective ego-strengths of individual group members.

For instance, if a client identifies feelings of shame during check-in, it might be suggested that he work on this individually. This would mean that he would discuss the times when he feels ashamed and he would be offered interventions that would assist him to move through his shame. These interventions may or may not involve the other group members directly. For instance, group members could be asked to act as a mirror for the client and to feed him back both his views of himself and the group members' respective views of him. Alternatively, all the group members could be enlisted in a shame-focused exercise. They could be asked to write down five of their most shameful experiences on separate pieces of paper. These pieces of paper are placed in an envelope, which is circulated through the group. Each member is asked to pull out one sheet of paper and to read it out aloud. The men's reactions to these anonymous disclosures are then processed. In this case attention is not put on one individual group member; rather an issue is dealt with by the group as a whole.

Whichever style occurs in the group, after any intense processing it is important that everyone has a chance to debrief his experience. Acknowledging the importance of all group members, be they quiet or vocal, close to the end of their healing journey or just starting it, is very important. In a second-stage group, although the process must be safe, it may not be comfortable. The group leaders will challenge these transferential patterns that clients bring into the group. Clients may be distressed as their habitual ways of interacting with others are challenged and brought into consciousness. Group leaders need to monitor the types of issues that clients bring into the group and to ensure that there is a reasonable balance of intense process-focused work and enjoyable social interaction. Clients' successes need to be celebrated and shared in equal measure with their pain. The group must not only concentrate its energies on resolving old traumas, but also on building functional new behaviours, such as acknowledging positive events and effective outcomes.

At the close of every session, it is recommended that clients participate in a ritual closing. Survivors need time to pull themselves together before they leave the group and return to their regular lives. If the group (or some of its members) has been involved in intense processing, the members need time to debrief this work. Bringing closure to the group process is important. After intensive processing, some groups give a group howl or another appropriate vocalization, before closing the session. Some contributors offer a weekend retreat for their second-stage groups. The group spends a weekend together and stays in a relaxed, comfortable setting. Having a longer time together allows the group members to enter a deeper and more sustained emotional process. Often, as the members speak of their abuse-related histories, new content and feelings emerge. The longer timeframe permits the group to engage in powerful expressive and symbolic work. When the time comes for clients to terminate the group process, whether the group is a first or second-stage group, their departure must be conducted in a thoughtful and appropriate way. Clients need to be well prepared for termination. They need plenty of time to replace the support they have received within the group with other non-group resources. They need to have permission to return to group or other therapeutic processes, should the need arise. Most importantly, however, they need to be aware of the changes they have made by having participated in the group and they need to celebrate their successes. Many clients are reluctant to fully embrace their triumphs because they fear that this will somehow tempt fate. Unintentionally, they discount their own hard-won achievements. The group leaders must address this subtle discounting and support clients in honouring their accomplishments.

Group Leadership

In abuse-focused group therapy, it is important to have two group leaders, especially in a second-stage group. Survivors trigger one another's responses in a group and often more work occurs than one therapist can handle alone. With two therapists in each session, one can take the role of being the primary leader and the other can monitor the less active group members. Quiet clients may in fact be quite dissociated and may need support and assistance to return to the here-and-now process of the group. The two group leaders need to be well matched in their knowledge and skills. Both need to be able to nurture, challenge and confront clients as the need arises. They need to work together as a team, because group members will often unconsciously try to split them into good therapist and bad therapist, replicating old family patterns. Both therapists should expect transference reactions from clients from time to time; this may run the gamut from being hated to being adored. Group leaders must ensure that they have adequate time between group sessions to examine these reactions and process their own counter-transferential responses. Good supervision is essential to assist the group leaders to separate here-and-now processes from there-and-then transference.

Some contributors argue that the two group leaders should be male, whereas others believe that a male/female co-leadership team is a more appropriate model of group leadership. Both points of view have merit. A male/female team gives the group members opportunities to practice self-disclosure with both sexes and to observe mutually respectful. male/female interactions. Indeed, role-modelling a healthy male/female working relationship is often cited as one of the most important benefits of male/female co-leadership. A male/male team challenges group members' beliefs about men. Seeing two male leaders working cooperatively and being either nurturing or confronting as the situation demands, challenges clients' preconceived ideas about masculine behaviour. Most contributors agree that the skilfullness of the therapists in working with abuse-related issues is the most important factor. The fact that they work well as a team and are knowledgeable and experienced outweighs considerations of gender. Prior to joining a group, potential members should meet both leaders. If a client is unprepared to work with a male/male team or a mixed gender team, he can be helped to find other treatment resources.

2

Childcare Counselling

Care consists of the actions necessary to promote survival, growth and development. Caring for a child means responding to basic needs. The basic needs of development go beyond protection, food, and health care to include the need for affection, interaction and stimulation, security provided through consistency and predictability, and play allowing exploration and discovery. These needs appear together.A supportive environment will respond to all of a child's needs which will, however, be defined somewhat differently and be given different priorities by different cultures. At a minimum, the following child care activities can be specified:

— providing security,
— sheltering,
— clothing,
— feeding,
— bathing,
— supervising a child's toilet,

— preventing and attending to sickness,
— nurturing and showing affection,
— interacting with and stimulating a child,
— playing and socializing the child to its culture.

Defining child care in this way implies that programmes of child care and of integrated child development should be the same. Child care is used in the broad sense described above, including health and other elements of custodial care, but looking beyond them to include care directed to the psychological, social, and emotional welfare of children. But child care is commonly used in a much narrower way. Moreover, the meaning attached to "care" is different for different groups attending to young children. In the health community, for instance, care is fundamentally health care defined in terms of preventing or attending to infection and disease. Appropriately, child care is linked to care for the mother in maternal and child health (MCH) programmes. When associated with programmes designed to improve the "productive " role of women, child care refers to the arrangements made to look after a child while the mother works. Often, that arrangement is "custodial, " assigning to another person or institution the temporary responsibility for assuring that a child has shelter, clothing, food, and attention to health needs. This association with custodial care means that child care programmes are usually put in a different category from child development programmes.

In fact, child care programmes have not, for the most part, placed much emphasis on stimulation and education components intended to foster the mental and social development of children. If child care is approached from a social welfare perspective, it is usually associated with institutionalized care, and often with programmes for indigent, abused, abandoned children. These programmes also have a strong custodial tradition. However, when discussing programmes of child care, it is well to look beyond centre-based or institutional care and to include also direct care by a mother, and delegation of responsibility for care to extended family members or to others in a personal social network. The foregoing discussion of terms may seem to have been a bit laboured to some readers while others will perhaps find it oversimplified. However, existing misconceptions and the general lack of clarity that marks many discussions seems to demand both the attempt to clarify and to present these central concepts in straightforward language, and we trust, to show how the concepts of child survival, growth, development, and care are used in this document.

Survival, growth, and development: relating health and nutrition to social and psychological development The way in which people think about survival, growth and development is mirrored in the way they conceive the relationships among health, nutrition, and psycho-social well-being. Most of the world thinks about health in a holistic way. Physical, social and spiritual well-being are not separated.

In the view most commonly found among trained physicians, a two-way relationship between health and nutrition is recognized. Sickness increases the possibility of malnutrition and vice versa. However, the relationship between either nutrition or health and psychosocial well-being is seen as a one-way relationship, runing from N to PS or from H to PS. The debilitating effects of physical health on social and emotional development are recognized, but a reverse effect, of psycho-social development (or debility) on physical health is given much less attention. Similarly, the effect of nutritional status on psycho-social development is accepted, and thought to occur primarily as malnutrition affects growth and development of the brain, or, the energy level of a child. Nutritional interventions are (appropriately) thought to affect a child's social and psychological, as well as physical development. But psycho-social development interventions are not recognized as having an affect on nutritional status or on growth.

Although this formulation may seem a caricature to some readers, particularly those who see all of these components as of one piece, the relationships depicted are frequently reflected in major lines of action and in the implementation of programmes. Slowly, however, a new view of the relationships between health, nutrition, and psycho-social well-being is emerging. In this view, two-way effects are pictured between psychosocial well-being and both health and nutrition, as well as between health and nutrition. If this newer formulation is accepted, then actions to strengthen social and psychological well-being must be included in health or nutrition programmes focussing on "survival." This viewpoint affirms that improvements in the social and psychological condition of caregiver and child can affect survival and physical development. The evidence to support this position is strong and growing.

Somewhere between the obvious and the uncertain, we know more than we think we know about early childhood development and about programming to facilitate and foster that development. The field has grown rapidly in the last two decades, bringing new knowledge and some changes in orientation. At the same time, experience has been accumulating at a rapid rate. Undoubtedly, the field will continue to develop and we will continue to improve our knowledge on the basis of concrete experiences. However, a more than reasonable base of knowledge and experience already exists that is sufficient to guide programming, even while we are filling in gaps in our knowledge.

Consider the following affirmations, derived from the literature on child development, each with an important implication for programming. The statements illustrate scientifically derived knowledge that is useful for programming. Some of the statements are obvious, but bear repeating because of their programme implications. The less obvious statements could be the subject of some debate, but even these would be accepted as reasonable working hypotheses by most experts in the field of early childhood development.

1. A child can see and hear at birth and is also born with predispositions that prepare it to perceive, learn from, and make demands upon the external world. An infant can communicate from birth by crying and through its facial expressions and movements. The implications are important. From birth, an infant can interact with and learn from its environment. Therefore, programmes designed to enhance development can include the newborn, helping parents to be responsive to and promote communication through their interaction with the newborn.

2. Infants differ from birth in their disposition to activity, irritability, and fearfulness, among other characteristics, and therefore differ in what they require from their environment and in their reaction to what caregivers do. The implication is that the same actions by caregivers can produce different

effects in different children. Therefore, parents need to be alert to how each particular child responds to the conditions around them. They need to be aware and flexible, and to possess a range of skills and expectations to match the temperament of a given child.

3. Cognitive and social development are related to the growth of brain cells and the development of neural connections. Thus, health and nutrition conditions that damage the brain, even prenatally, when the most growth is occurring, will influence development. In addition, stimulation that provides the brain with exercise will help to improve the connections made and set a stronger base for later development.

4. Children are amazingly resilient, particularly in the earliest years when they seem to have a series of built-in mechanisms to help them develop. A child's development may be delayed, or damage may occur, as a result of problems at birth or because the environment after birth is cruel. However, unless early, prolonged, and severe difficulties (e.g., an extended period of severe malnutrition) occur, a child has the potential to recover and develop normally. Caregivers therefore should be aware that the fact that a child has suffered from poor health or has been moderately malnourished does not automatically mean its development will be delayed. Recuperation is possible, but as always, prevention is better than cure: preventive programmes beginning with pre-natal care of the mother are preferable.

5. In addition to needs for food, shelter, health care and protection, young children have basic psychological

and social developmental needs. These include: a need for love and affection; a need for interaction (including both stimulating and reacting to the child); a need for consistency and predictability in their caregiving environment; and a need to explore and discover. Evidently, programmes of integrated attention to the child should respond to these basic needs as well as to the needs for food, shelter, health care and protection.

6. Although all children have certain basic needs, each child will have a set of individual needs, determined by its own genetic makeup, by the immediate conditions in the family that satisfy (or do not satisfy) some of the basic needs, and by conditions in the community and larger society, both of which set goals and impose limits on the child affecting its development. Programming must take into account these differences in individual needs and in the conditions at the level of family, community, and society that affect development. A programme formula, to be applied to all children and circumstances, is therefore inappropriate.

7. There is a two-way relationship between psycho-social development and the health and nutritional well-being of a child. A child that is alert and/or a child that cries is more likely to obtain a response and to be fed than a child that is listless. Thus, activities that help a child to develop socially and psychologically will make the child more alert and will, therefore, also help to improve the nutritional status and health of a child and its chances for survival.

8. There is a synergistic relationship among the various facets of development; the physical, social, intellectual and emotional facets are part of a whole so that modifications in one area bring change to the others as well. In infants as well as in adults, cognitive processes are related to emotional states because they are related to the onset, control, and reduction of anxiety. In consequence, multi-faceted approaches to programming are needed.

9. The cognitive development of infants living in environments with little variety is generally lower than that of infants living in environments that contain variety. The implication is that attention should be given to determining the degree of variety present in different environments and to either reinforcing or adding to that variety, according to the needs of the particular child.

10. The social experience of a child will usually have a much stronger influence on future achievement, IQ score, and socially deviant behaviour than condition at birth. In short, a benevolent environment is critical. It is possible for recuperation to occur in such an environment, even in relatively high "at risk" circumstances related to conditions at birth.

11. All children develop, but some children develop faster than others and their development is qualitatively different. Although developmental norms may be useful for judging a large population of children, they should be applied with caution to individuals.

The eleven statements above are given as examples of the knowledge base that can be drawn upon in the design and implementation of programmes for early childhood care and development. But there is another source of knowledge that needs to be taken into account, namely, "traditional wisdom, " or "experience". Unfortunately, failure to recognize and draw upon traditional wisdom with respect to significant childrearing practices is common. Until recently, a similar failure to recognize the value of traditional health practices was evident, though traditional medicine has begun, in the last ten to twenty years, to be regarded with greater respect. Several examples of practices affecting survival, growth, and development will help to make the point. In many cultures, norms are set for the pregnant or lactating woman that include attention to her psychological state. The importance of avoiding stress is recognized and these customs should be honored, both from the standpoint of physical health for the woman and from the standpoint of helping the survival, growth and development of the fetus or the infant.

Many cultures have nutritional taboos that are designed to keep the weight of babies low. Although low birth weight is taken as a characteristic of "risk" by academic health standards, high birth weight appears to be a characteristic of risk by experiential standards. When one considers the average stature of women in the rural highlands of Guatemala or in Bangladesh, the product of centuries of under-nutrition, or, if one considers circumstances in which rickets has traditionally affected pelvic growth, then the traditional wisdom makes sense and imposing so-called scientifically derived standards would be a mistake.

Again, massage of newborns and infants is widely practiced in traditional cultures. Though in decline, this is a practice that benefits both growth and development of young children. Breastfeeding on demand is another traditional practice that is also declining. That practice has been incorporated into the package of survival strategies but its importance to social and emotional development is seldom discussed.

Though sleeping with babies seems to be frowned upon in modern health circles, it is a common practice in many cultures. It provides warmth, security and tactile stimulation to a child while allowing breastfeeding on demand during the night. As traditional wisdom is given its proper place, and when the currently applicable wisdom is separated from that which no longer applies, the conclusion is reinforced that we know more than we think we know.

Childcare Arrangements

Interest in childcare intensified as more women entered the labour force and sought to balance both family and work. The need for child care may increase further as welfare reform encourages recipients, who often have young children, to seek work. This section describes the number and characteristics of children in different child care arrangements and the characteristics of their families. The data come from the fall 1995 Survey of Income and Programme Participation (SIPP) and continue a series that dates back to 1985. Child care arrangements for preschool- and grade-school-age children is briefly discussed. These two age groups differ in their needs and activities in that the primary focus of child care for infants and preschoolers is on meeting their basic needs. For older children, more attention is on structured activities, educational programs, and socialization.

Caring Children under 5 Years Old

The multiple arrangements families use for childcare, this section turns to more detail on the patterns of use and then turns to how the arrangements vary with other characteristics of the family. The section concludes by summarizing some historical trends and by giving detailed information about the role of HeadStart.

In 1995, 14.4 million (75 percent) of the 19.3 million children under 5 years of age were in some form of regular child care arrangement during a typical week. About 8.5 million children (44 percent) were cared for in multiple arrangements (two or more per week). Overall, children using a regular arrangement averaged 2.0 arrangements. About one-quarter (4.9 million children) of preschoolers had no regular child care arrangement. The vast majority of them (96 percent) had a designated parent who was neither employed nor in school and presumably available during the day to care for the children. Virtually any preschool-age child whose parent was either employed or in school was in some type of regular child care arrangement during their parent's work or school hours (98 percent), compared with fewer than half of preschoolers with a parent who was neither employed nor in school (43 percent).

The high prevalence of child care use among preschoolers with a parent who was neither employed nor in school may be due to these parents using child care arrangements for enrichment purposes or educational development. Use of multiple child care arrangements is also more common among children whose parents were employed or in school than among other children. Preschoolers of employed parents who were in child care arrangements had an average of 2.2

arrangements per week: 73 percent of these 22.5 million arrangements were used during the parent's work hours. Preschoolers of parents who were in school also averaged 2.2 arrangements per week, suggesting that parents who have structured schedules that take them out of the house for set periods of time face similar complexities in arranging for child care providers.

Preschoolers of parents who were not employed nor in school, on the other hand, used an average of only 1.4 arrangements per week. Parents use child care similarly during their non work/school hours, regardless of their employment or enrollment status. More than half of both groups of children did not have a regular non parental arrangement during non work/school hours, and presumably were being cared for by their parents. Fewer than 35 percent were in one regular arrangement, roughly 10 percent were in two arrangements, and only around 2 percent were in three or more arrangements during their parent's non work/school hours.

Types of child care arrangements

Since many children are in more than one type of arrangement, these percentages total more than 100 percent. Of the 19.3 million preschoolers, 50 percent were regularly cared for by a relative. Grandparents were the single most frequently mentioned care provider, with 5.8 million preschoolers, or 30 percent, in this type of arrangement. Parents relied on the child's other parent (18 percent, usually the father) more than other relatives (15 percent). Some preschoolers were cared for by the designated parent while working (5 percent) or by siblings (2 percent). Non relatives also played a prominent role in the care of preschoolers. In 1995, 49 percent of children under were cared for by a nonrelative on a regular basis. Similar proportions of preschoolers were cared for in either an organized facility (30 percent) or by some other nonrelative either in the child's home or in the provider's home (29 percent). In addition, comparable proportions of preschoolers were in a day care center or in a nursery or preschool (15 percent and 14 percent, respectively). Children under 5 years old were also cared for by family day care providers (13 percent), and similar proportions were cared for by other non relatives in the child's home or the provider's home (9 percent each). This last category probably consisted of friends or neighbors of the family who were not officially licensed as family day care providers.

Arrangements used during the parent's work and non work hours Of the 19.3 million preschool-age children in 1995, 11.2 million had a designated parent who was either employed or in school. Similar proportions were cared for by either relatives or non relatives as childcare providers (about 61 percent of children) while the parent was at work or in school (these percentages exceed 100 percent because some children were in both types of arrangements). Use of regular child care arrangements tends to be less common during the parent's non work/school hours. For example, only 26 percent of children under 5 were cared for by relatives as regular care providers during their parent's non work/school hours, compared with 62 percent of children under 5 during their parent's work/school hours. This relationship holds true for most of the arrangement types.

Some similar patterns of child care emerge regardless of the time period examined. In particular, care by grandparents was prevalent regardless of when the arrangement was used. The proportion of children cared for by a particular provider shows only one dimension of child care. Examining the number of hours spent in the arrangement can shed light on how and with whom children may be spending significant periods of the day. Time spent with either a parent or sibling was not collected during the non work/school hours as we attempted to separate "family time" from child care arrangements used by the family during the designated parent's work hours. On average, children under 5 spent 28 hours per week in child care. If cared for by non relatives, preschoolers spent an average of 39 hours per week in nonrelative care, but those cared for by relatives spent only 23 hours per week in relative care.

Preschoolers spent the most time in day care centers and with family day care providers both an average of 33 hours per week), and they spent the least amount of time in sibling care (11 hours per week). Preschoolers received care from a grand parent and their other parent for similar amounts of time each week (18 hours per week and 17 hours per week, respectively) among children who were in these arrangements. Preschoolers spent more time in various child care arrangements during their parent's work/school hours (35 hours per week) than during their parent's non work/school hours (8 hours per week). This difference is to be expected as employed parents are likely to need child care for reasonably longer stretches of time. In addition, preschoolers spent more time in the care of a non relative than in the care of a relative during their parent's work/ school hours (33 hours and 24 hours per week, respectively) and also during their parent's non work/ school hours (20 hours and 12 hours per week, respectively). The fact that relatives provided fewer hours of care than non relatives suggests that parents use relatives as supplemental care providers.

Primary Arrangements

Primary and supplemental arrangements used by parents, the amount of time children spend in these arrangements per week, and some of the most common child care combinations. Primary, secondary, and tertiary arrangements are defined in terms of hours per week. During the parent's work/school hours, non relatives were more likely than relatives to be the primary providers of child care for preschoolers. In 1995, 55 percent of preschoolers were cared for by non relatives as the primary provider during the parent's work/school hours, while 48 percent were cared for by relatives. A large proportion (28 percent) were primarily cared for in an organized facility. An interesting pattern emerges when looking at the secondary and tertiary arrangements used to care for preschoolers during the parent's work/school hours. More than half (56 percent) of preschoolers using a secondary care arrangement were cared for by a relative and only 31 percent were cared for by an on relative.

A similar pattern exists for the tertiary care arrangement during the parent's work/school hours and also when the designated parent was not at work or in school. In particular, large proportions of children are cared for by their grand parents while parents are not working or in school, a time when parents presumably could care for their children. Parents may welcome or even encourage involvement of their own parents in the everyday lives of their children on a regular basis.

Regular contact with other family members may also provide another type of social interaction for children. This greater reliance on relatives for supplementary care arrangements is understandable as families seeking additional care provision will attempt to secure providers at little or no financial cost, and relatives often meet this criterion. Hours spent in primary and supplemental arrangements

Among preschoolers who had multiple child care arrangements, an average of 10 hours per week was spent in their secondary arrangement, and 6 hours per week was spent in their tertiary arrangement. Children under 5 spent nearly twice as much time in their primary arrangement during their parent's work/school hours as in their parent's non work/school hours. In secondary arrangements, children also spent more time in care during their parent's work/school hours than outside such hours. While relatives may be more likely to pitch in and help out as asupplemental arrangement, they generally are used for fewer hours per week than non relatives regardless of whether the care is during the parent's work/school hours or during the parent's non work/school hours. Preschoolers secondarily using a relative during the parent's work/school hours spent only 9 hours per week in that arrangement compared with 12 hours per week for preschoolers secondarily cared for by a nonrelative.

Common Childcare Combinations

When parents require a combination of child care arrangements to cover their work schedule, they must choose among professional providers, relatives, neighbors, and friends. The most frequently used combination was an organized facility (such as a day care center) and a nonrelative, which would include friends and family day care providers (28 percent). About one quarter were cared for by the child's other parent and a non relative. The child's other parent and grandparents are key child care providers. In 1995, 20 percent of preschoolers were cared for by the other parent and the grandparent combination during the parent's work/ school hours. Similar proportions of preschoolers were cared for either by the other parent and by an organized facility or a grandparent and an organized facility (18 percent and 16 percent, respectively). Smaller proportions of preschoolers combined other relatives with either the other parent or a grandparent. Examining the multiple arrangements of preschoolers shows that relatives, especially grandparents, pitch in as supplemental care providers.

Family Characteristics

Child care use by family characteristics such as marital status, race and ethnicity, educational level, family income, and child's age.

Marital status: Interesting relationships emerge when the marital status of the parent is considered. Preschoolers of never-married parents were more likely to be cared for by a relative (55 percent) than by an on relative (40 percent), with grandparents playing a large role in the care of these children. While 40 percent of children of never-married parents were usually cared for by a grand parent during the week, this arrangement applied to 29 percent of children of previously-married or married parents. Children living with both married parents were much more likely to be cared for by their other parent (21 percent), usually the father, than children living with a single parent (12 percent), demonstrating the importance of living arrangements in determining the father's involvement in the care of their children. However, the sex of the single parent seems to make a difference with regard to whether the child is cared for by the nonresident parent on a regular basis.

Preschoolers living with a single father were about three times as likely (32 percent) to be cared for by their nonresident parent as preschoolers living with a single mother (11 percent). This difference suggests that mothers are more regularly involved in the care of their children even when they do not live with them. How are children in different living arrangements cared for during their parent's work/school hours? Children living with married parents were cared for by similar proportions of relatives and non relatives during the work/school hours (62 percent and 61 percent, respectively). However, children of previously-married parents relied more heavily on non relatives (74 percent) than on relatives (50 percent) during the parent's work/school hours. Half of children under 5 living with a previously-married parent were cared for by organized care facilities.

Race and his panic origin: About 32 percent were cared for by a grand parent, and similar proportions were cared for by other non relatives. While similar proportions of pre schoolers of non-Hispanic Black parents were in relative and nonrelative care, these children were often cared for in an organized facility (35 percent). However, preschoolers of Hispanic parents were more likely to be cared for by a relative (43 percent) than a nonrelative (34 percent). Common to all groups is the heavy reliance on grandparents as care providers among relatives providing childcare. Hispanics have lower levels of multiple child care use than the other racial and ethnic groups (28 percent). All three of the other racial and ethnic groups have similar levels of multiple care arrangements (about 47 percent).

Educational level: Parental educational level appears to be a factor in the decisions parents make regarding care for their preschoolers. Parents with at most a high school diploma relied more often on relatives than non relatives. Conversely, parents with a higher educational level—at least some college—relied more often on non relatives than relatives. Similar patterns exist during the parent's work/school hours, except the variation in use of multiple arrangements disappears. Use of a nonrelative's care during the parent's non work/school hours is also related to the parent's educational level. Children under 5 of parents with at least some college were more likely to use care by an on relative during the parent's non work/school hours (26 percent), than children of parents with less than a high school education (20 percent). However, the use of organized child care facilities shows little difference by the parent's educational level, regardless of their work or school status.

Family income: Families in poverty rely more on relatives than non relatives to provide child care. About 41 percent of preschoolers in families below the poverty level were cared for by relatives and 32 percent were cared for by non relatives. In families not in poverty, children were about equally likely to be cared for by relatives as by non relatives—about 53 percent in each. About 23 percent of poor preschoolers and 32 percent of nonpoor preschoolers were in an organized facility. This difference derives from whether a child has a parent who is employed or in school. For children with a parent at work or in school, about 35 percent of both poor and nonpoor preschoolers were in an organized facility while their parent was at work or at school. In addition, about 68 percent of poor preschoolers received care by relatives, compared with 61 percent of nonpoor children, while the parent was working or in school. Outside of a parent's hours at work or at school, the poor and nonpoor were about equally likely to rely on relatives for care—about 26 percent of both groups of preschoolers.

Child's age: Use of non relatives as child care providers varies widely by age. For example, use of organized facility care increases dramatically by age: only 19 percent of children less than one year old during their parent's work/school hours but 50 percent of children 3 to 4 years old did so. Care by two other arrangement types—other non relatives and grandparents appears to work in reverse of organized facilities, as the proportion decreases with age of the child. The percent of children who were cared for by an "other nonrelative" falls from 44 percent of children under 1 year old to 36 percent for children 3 to 4 years old. Children cared for by a grandparent falls from 33 percent for children under 1 year old to 27 percent for children ages 3 and 4. Care by the other parent does not differ by the age of the child. Taken all together, the SIPP data suggest that parents of preschool children face different constraints securing child care during their work/school hours depending on the child's age. Parents may have difficulty securing infant care at organized facilities because infant care is not provided, or they may prefer their very young children to be cared for in a home environment. As children age, however, school readiness may weigh in as an important factor in the choice of child care, thus explaining the high proportion of children 3 to 4 years old in organized facilities. Multiple child care arrangements also appears to be more common when a child is 3 or more years old than among younger children.

Child care data were first collected in the SIPP in 1985, which now provides the opportunity to examine 10 years of child care trends for preschoolers with employed mothers. In 1995, 10 million preschoolers lived with employed mothers, up from 8.2 million in 1985. Fewer than half (43 percent) were cared for by either a parent (including the mother herself) or by some other relative in 1995, lower than in 1985 (48 percent). Organized child care facilities and other types of nonrelative care made up at least one-half of all primary arrangements in 1995, a pattern similar for every survey year since 1985, except for in 1991. In 1991 fathers reached an all-time high as a primary care provider for preschoolers of employed mothers. The use of non relatives has had an erratic trend over the period from 1985 to 1995, with parents' reliance on non relatives waxing and waning in response to economic and other situations.

In 1985 and 1995, the proportion of preschoolers who were in nonrelative care was 28 percent. In 1993, only 22 percent were cared for in a home-based arrangement by a nonrelative of the child. Care by non relatives in the child's home remained steady at roughly 5 percent throughout the entire 10-year period; thus, the significant changes in care by non relatives in informal settings can be attributed to changes in the care of preschoolers by non relatives in the provider's home. During the same 10-year period, the use of organized facilities for preschoolers fluctuated. From 1985 to 1990, the proportion of preschoolers being cared for in organized facilities rose from 23 percent to 28 percent, and it has wavered since then. Rates of family and relative care also have varied during this 10-year period. Care by fathers, while remaining around 15 percent between 1985 and 1988, increased sharply to 20 percent by 1991.

However, by 1995, this proportion had dropped back down to around 17 percent. Interestingly, the overall declining trend in care by mothers while working was interrupted in 1991 as well, when it reached a level similar to the 1985 level, and then it decreased to 5 percent by 1995. Care by grandparents did not change much across the late 1980s and early 1990s. The lower levels of child care by mothers and fathers in 1995 relative to 1991 supports prior research suggesting that the relatively higher use of father and mother care in 1991 was in response to the economic recession at the time. Apparently parental care of preschoolers is more responsive to changes in the economy than care by grandparents, who seem to be a stable component of child care arrangements.

Head Start Programme

For many parents, reliable childcare is an integral component of their ability to find a job and remain employed. Federal programs such as Head Start aim to improve school readiness among children from low-income families by integrating child care with high quality early education. In addition, HeadStart programs provide the participants and their families with links to social and health services, job training, and schooling, while encouraging parental involvement. Head Start eligibility is determined prior to enrollment based on income level and other special needs, such as disability of the child. Because the SIPP asks questions on current socioeconomic and demographic characteristics and not when the child first enrolled in Head Start, characteristics may have changed since the child's enrollment. Furthermore, Head Start programs may enable parents to further their education or gain employment which would increase their income level over time. For these reasons, some children currently in Head Start may have characteristics which would normally not have qualified them for enrollment; however, they are still enrolled because they initially qualified. These caveats should be kept in mind when considering current characteristics of children enrolled in Head Start.

The fall 1995 SIPP estimates show that 710,000 children under were enrolled in a federally funded Head Start program. According to the SIPP, the majority (74 percent) of children enrolled in Head Start were either 3 or 4 years old; smaller proportions were 5 years old (18 percent) or under 3 (8 percent).

Because many poor families with children are headed by single parents, it is not surprising that HeadStart serves more single-parent households than married-parent households. For example in 1995, 62 percent of HeadStart enrollees lived with a single parent, including 25 percent who lived with a previously-married parent and 37 percent who lived with a never-married parent. Among children in Head Start, equal proportions were non-Hispanic White or Black, comparatively fewer were Hispanic. For children in Head Start, 42 percent had a parent who was a high school graduate, but only 24 percent had some college education, and very few had completed four or more years of college (5 percent). In 1995, 55 percent of parents of HeadStart enrollees were not employed in the fall of 1995, 28 percent were employed full-time, and 17 percent were employed part-time.

About two thirds of the Head Start enrollees lived in families that received some government assistance (62 percent): 52 percent received food stamps and 31 percent received Women, Infants, and Children (WIC) benefits. Participation in other government programs may reflect the degree to which the family is integrated into networks that assist low-income populations. Enrollment in Head Start differs by region of residence and metro politan status. Children enrolled in Head Start were more likely to live in the South (45 percent) or the West (27 percent), than in the Northeast or the Midwest (both about 15 percent). More enrollees lived in central cities (47 percent) than in other areas. These variations may reflect differences in levels of poverty, knowledge of programs, and availability of programs.

With changes in welfare reform, federal agencies and programs, including Head Start, are looking forways to facilitate transitions from welfare to work. Because childcare problems can hinder low income parents looking for employment, Head Start is contemplating ways to expand its program to reach more members of the low-income community. The following comparison of Head Start participation among a group of children who are potential candidates for enrollment promotes a better understanding of the variations among those who participate in Head Start and those who do not. Official Head Start guidelines or eligibility criteria are not used here to define potential candidates, since each Head Start program determines eligibility based on a set of programmatic, community, and family considerations, which include but are not limited to poverty and the child's need based on disabilities. Rather, potential candidates are defined simply as those children ages 3 and 4 living in families at 185 percent of the poverty level or lower in 1995, a group that encompasses low income families who are eligible for many government assistance programs. In this analysis, the family income level of the potential candidates is higher than the poverty line because poverty is episodic—a transitory condition for many—and low-income families are at risk of experiencing multiple short-term spells of living in poverty.

Only 401,000 (11 percent) of these 3.8 million potential candidates were enrolled in Head Start in the fall of 1995. Head Start enrollees were more likely than nonenrollees to be living with a single parent who had never married -54 percent compared with 24 percent and less likely than nonenrollees to be living in a married couple family (30 percent and 14 percent, respectively). Fathers and other relatives play an important child care role among poor families. Children of unmarried parents may not receive care from both parents and these families may seek free day care services from Head Start. Head Start enrollees were more likely to be non-Hispanic Black than were nonenrollees. Head Start programs may be more accessible to Black families because of their history of serving this minority group since the onset of the Head Start program in the 1960s and because of the trust the program has earned in Black communities.

The two groups were quite similar when comparing the educational and employment characteristics. About one-quarter of the designated parents in both groups had attended 1 to 3 years of college, and more than half were not employed. This similarity is expected as these children were selected into this "potential pool" because they were living in families with low incomes. Across the board, higher proportions of Head Start enrollees than nonenrollees lived in families that received government assistance. Head Start participant families were much more likely to receive AFDC (50 percent) than nonenrollee families (29 percent). They were also more likely to receive food stamps. This finding suggests that families with children enrolled in Head Start programs may be better connected into networks of assistance and are more aware of the variety of government assistance programs available to low-income families. Some families may not know that they are eligible for Head Start even though they may qualify for the program because of their low income levels. Lack of access to a Head Start program may also be an impediment to enrollment. A larger proportion of the Head Start enrollees lived in the South (44 percent) compared with nonenrollees (30 percent), and many fewer enrollees lived in the Midwest (11 percent) compared with nonenrollees (24 percent). This difference may reflect variations in the number of and accessibility to programs in different regions.

Head Start programs, although used by a small fraction of the overall population, were an important source of child care or school readiness for many poor families. Overall, children in Head Start spent about 68 hours per week in the program. Head Start was the primary care provider for 79 percent of Head Start children; for 31 percent, it was their only arrangement. Even though the HeadStart program was used by families for a large portion of their child's daytime hours, many families still found it necessary to seek out other care providers to cover all their child care needs. Child care provided by relatives plays a more important role than that provided by non relatives among Head Start participants (46 percent and 32 percent, respectively), with grand parents playing the most prominent role. This pattern is to be expected because Head Start families typically have low incomes and tend to rely on less expensive supplemental care arrangements, such as family members or relatives, rather than nonrelative care arrangements.

Among potential Head Start candidates, actual Head Start enrollees tend to use more child care arrangements than nonenrollees (an average of 2.3 arrangements compared with 1.3 arrangements per child, respectively). They also spent twice as much time in child care - 41 hours per week in all of their child care arrangements combined compared with only 23 hours. Although enrollees and nonenrollees were cared for by relatives to a similar extent, nonenrollees were more likely to be cared for by non relatives (excluding Head Start and school). Among the potential pool, 19 percent of nonenrollees were in a nursery or preschool compared with 3 percent of HeadStart enrollees. This difference suggests that low-income families may seek educational and school readiness programs for their children through enrollment in childcare arrangements, such as a nursery or preschool, if Head Start slots or programs are not available.

Children 5 to 14 Years Old

Multiple child care arrangements families use for grade-school-age children, this section examines different patterns of use by characteristics of the family. More and more parents and policymakers are asking what grade-school-age children are doing when not in school? In 1995, virtually all of the 38.2 million children 5 to 14 years old (98 percent) were in a regular child care arrangement, including school, during a typical week. Three quarters of grade-school-age children (28.7 million) were cared for in multiple arrangements. Overall, grade-school-age children were regularly in an average of 2.8 arrangements per week.

Multiple arrangements are more common among children who separents are employed/in school than among those whose parents are not—children of employed parents were cared for in 3.4 arrangements per week compared with 1.6 arrangements for children whose parents were neither employed nor in school. Most of the 79.0 million arrangements of children of employed parents were used during their parent's workhours (68 percent). Among children whose parent was in school, the majority of arrangements occurred during the parent's school hours (60 percent).

Older children experience a wider array of daily activities than do preschoolers. They may have extended peer groups of friends at school and participate in various after school or enrichment programs that are not available to younger children. To capture these activities, the child care arrangements shown in the tables for grade-school-age children differ from those shown for younger children. Relatives are important contributors to the overall care of grade school-age children - 43 percent regularly received care from a relative. A slightly higher proportion of children received care by a grandparent (17 percent) than by the other parent (16 percent). Care by a sibling is not common for grade-school-age children (9 percent), but is more common than among preschoolers.

Grade-school-age children are less likely to be cared for by non relatives (such as organized care facilities or other nonrelative care in the child's home or the provider's home) than by relatives. Only 17 percent of children 5 to 14 years old were cared for by these types of non relatives on a regular basis. This relatively low use of non relatives may be due to the high rate of school enrollment for these children as well as their involvement in other structured activities. Nearly all grade-school-age children (93 percent) were in school and a large proportion (39 percent) participated in enrichment activities such as sports, lessons, clubs, and before- or after school programs. In addition, 18 percent (6.9 million) grade school-age children cared for themselves on a regular basis without any adult supervision.

In general, parents are more likely to use arrangements during their work or school hours than during their non work/school hours, primarily because many parents care for their children themselves during this time. In 1995, there were 24.7 million grade-school-age 'children whose designated parent was either employed or in school. Fifty-two percent were in relative care during their parent's work/school hours and 25 percent were cared for by the child's other parent. Only 18 percent of children 5 to 14 years old were cared for by a relative during the parent's non work/school hours. Care by non relatives was less common than care by relatives during the parent's work/school hours -18 percent compared with 52 percent. Nonrelative care during the parent's non work/school hours was also low (7 percent). Comparing the use of school, enrichment activities, and self care across the two different activity schedules of the parent reveals some important findings. Among children whose parent was employed or in school, 88 percent were in school during their parent's work/school hours. Many parents'work/school schedules overlap substantially or coincide with their children's school hours, thus reducing the overall need for child care arrangements.

Thirty-five percent of children of employed/in-school parents regularly participated in at least one enrichment activity during the parent's work/school hours. Although fewer participated in enrichment activities during their parent's non work/school hours, enrichment activities were the most frequently used arrangement, aside from school, during this time (27 percent). These findings suggest that enrichment activities play a large role in what children are doing when outside school, regardless of their parent's employment or enrollment status. Some parents may use enrichment programs as a type of child care provider, especially if they occur after school and before the parent returns home from work. However, many activities, for example Saturday morning soccer leagues, are scheduled outside of parents' work or school hours. Among children whose parent was either employed or in school, 20 percent regularly spent time inself care during the parent's work/school hours. This figure is more than twice the proportion for grade-school-age children who regularly spent time in self care during their parent's non work/school hours (9 percent).

The amount of time a child spends in a particular arrangement can have a lasting effect on development. Overall, grade-school-age children spent 43 hours in child care per week—the greatest number of hours were in school (35 hours per week). They were regularly cared for by relatives and non relatives for approximately 15 hours per week each. Children 5 to 14 years old spent about 8 hours in enrichment activities per week and about 6 hours per week in self-care situations.

Of the 24.3 million grade-school-age children with a primary arrangement during the parent's work/school hours, 80 percent were in school at this time. Comparatively small proportions of grade school-age children had relatives (14 percent) and non relatives (5 percent) as their primary arrangement. Only 2 percent of grade-school-age children were either in enrichment activities or in self care as their primary arrangement. The role of enrichment activities becomes more apparent when one looks at the secondary and tertiary arrangements. In 1995, 24 percent of grade-school-age children participated in enrichment activities as their secondary arrangement, and 30 percent participated as their tertiary arrangement when their parent was at work or in school. In addition, greater proportions of grade-school-age children cared for themselves as their secondary or tertiary arrangements than as their primary arrangement (13 percent and 17 percent compared with 2 percent).

Enrichment activities are also important supplemental arrangements when their parents are not working or attending school. Grade-school-age children were nearly two times as likely to participate in enrichment activities as their secondary arrangement during the parents non work/school hours (44 percent) than during the work/school hours (24 percent).

On average, grade-school-age children spent 28 hours per week in their primary arrangement during the parent's work/school hours compared with 22 hours per week during the parent's non work/school hours. About 25 hours per week was spent in relative and nonrelative care during the parent's work/school hours. The number of weekly hours spent in enrichment activities is twice as high during the parent's work/school hours than during their non work/school hours (14 hours compared with 7 hours per week, respectively). The longer hours noted during the parent's work/school hours suggests that they use enrichment activities to meet both their child care needs and to promote child well-being.

The variations in child care use regarding family characteristics such as marital status, race and ethnicity, educational level, and family income.

Grade-school-age children of married parents were more likely to receive care by the other parent 20 percent) than were children of single parents, while children of unmarried parents were most likely to have grandparents as their principal source of relative care. Children of married parents were also more likely to participate in enrichment activities 42 percent) compared with those of previously- or never-married parents (38 percent and 22 percent, respectively). Higher proportions of grade-school-age children of previously-married parents took care of themselves (22 percent) compared with children of married parents (18 percent) or children of never-married parents (8 percent). Overall, 64 percent of grade school-age children of never married parents were in multiple arrangements, a lower proportion than children of previously or currently married parents (about 76 percent). However, children of all three marital status groups experience multiple care arrangements about the same extent (all approximately 78 percent) when parents are at work or at school.

Similar proportions of grade-school age children of non-Hispanic Black and non-Hispanic White parents use relative care (both 44 percent), but Hispanics tend to use relative careless frequently (38 percent). Use of nonrelative care (organized facility or other non relatives) was also similar among non-Hispanic White and Black parents. In addition, children of non-Hispanic White parents were more likely than the other three racial/ ethnic groups to participate in enrichment activities (45 percent), while Hispanic children were least likely to participate in enrichment activities (27 percent).

White children were also more likely to be in a self care situation at some time during the day (21 percent) than either non-Hispanic Black children or Hispanic children (both 12 percent). The cumulative result is that children of non-Hispanic White parents are most likely to use multiple child care arrangements (80 percent), while children of Hispanic parents are least likely to use multiple arrangements (63 percent). Higher participation in enrichment activities and self care among grade-school-age children of non-Hispanic White parents seen above repeats itself regardless of the parent's activity schedule.

Parents with one or more years of college education are more likely than parents with less education to use nonrelative care and have their children participate in enrichment activities. This pattern prevails during and outside the parent's work or study hours. Greater use of care by non relatives probably reflects higher income and the ability to purchase such care by parents with higher levels of education.

Children living in households above the poverty line experienced a wider variety of child care arrangements.

Eighty-two percent of grade-school-age children living in nonpoor families were cared for in multiple arrangements, compared with 54 percent of those living in poverty. Compared with grade school-age children living in poor families, higher proportions of children living in nonpoor families use nonrelative care, enrichment activities, and self care. During the parent's work/school hours, grade-school-age children were cared for by relatives and non relatives similarly regardless of the families' poverty status; however, participation in enrichment activities remains higher among children living in nonpoor families (36 percent) than in poor families (27 percent). A similar pattern is seen during the parent's non work/school hours.

During the parent's work/school hours, grade-school-age children in nonpoor families are more likely to care for themselves (21 percent) than are children in poor families (15 percent). This difference may arise if a larger proportion of parents of children in nonpoor families work full-time and therefore need child care for longer amounts of time during the day. However, a slightly higher proportion of grade school-age children living in nonpoor families compared with poor families were in self care during their parent's non work/school hours (9 percent and 8 percent, respectively).

Because there is interest in a comprehensive view of the regular weekly experiences of children, greater detail is provided on enrichment activities. For some parents, enrichment activities may be a form of child care. In 1995, 15 million children between the ages of 5 and (39 percent) participated in at least one enrichment activity during the week. The most frequently mentioned enrichment activity for grade-school-age children was sports (22 percent). Similar proportions of grade-school-age children participated in lessons and clubs (16 percent and 15 percent, respectively). A smaller proportion of grade-school-age children participated in before- or after-school programs (6 percent). Overall, 24 percent participated in one activity per week while 15 percent participated in two or more activities.

On average, grade-school-age children spent 8 hours per week in enrichment activities among those who participated in enrichment activities. Although the lowest proportion of children participated in before- or after-school programs, these children spent 10 hours per week doing so, the greatest average number of hours per week in an enrichment activity. Grade-school-age children spents even hours per week in sports; they spent fewer hours per week in lessons or clubs (four hours and three hours per week, respectively). Participation in sports activities is almost three times as likely among 12- to 14-year olds (34 percent) than among 5- to 8-year olds (13 percent). However, children 5 to 8 years old participated in before and after-school programs similarly compared with children 9 to 36 years old (both 6 percent). Children 12 to 14 years old were less likely to be enrolled in before- or after-school programs (4 percent). Girls and boys were about equally likely to participate in at least one enrichment activity, but the type of activity differs. While boys were more likely than girls to participate in sports, girls were more likely than boys to participate in lessons or clubs. Similar proportions of both girls and boys were enrolled in before- or after-school programs.

Participation in specific enrichment activities differs by the child's living arrangements. A higher proportion of children living in a married-couple family participated in lessons (18 percent) than children living with a single mother (12 percent). Similarly, participation in clubs is higher among children living in married-couple families than among children living in single mother families (16 percent and 10 percent, respectively). Enrichment activities, which may involve expenses to families, may be least affordable by single mothers. Participation in before- or after-school programs, which are more likely to be of low cost or free as part of the school curricula, did not differ significantly by the child's living arrangements. Enrichment activities may be costly in terms of money and time to transport children to and from the site. The differences by income persist regardless of the type of activity. In addition, the number of enrichment activities in which a child participates differs by the income level of the family. Half of the children living in families at or above 200 percent of the poverty line participated in at least one enrichment activity, while one quarter of the children living below the poverty line did so. In sum, children from economically advantaged families are more likely to be exposed to activities that would assist their development and transition to adulthood than children in families with fewer economic resources.

Self Care

Self care can be an important part of the natural process of independence, allowing children structured opportunities for successful transitions to adulthood. While some children may encounter self care in a safe environment, with neighbors and parents checking in periodically, other children may experience self care in a less structured and unsafe environment. Parents base their decisions to allow their children to care for themselves on a number of factors including the age and maturity level of the child, the environment in which the child will be in self care, the financial resources and parental time available to provide alternative care arrangements, and the perceived risks associated with self care.

In 1995, 6.9 million (18 percent) of the 38.2 million children 5 to 14 years old were reported to be inself care on a regular basis. The majority of these children were of middle-school age, 12 to 14 years old (65 percent). An upward trend exists in the use of self care by the age of the child, from 2 percent among 5 year olds to 48 percent among 14 year old. Grade-school-age children are separated into two groups depending on the generally accepted age cut-offs for elementary and middle school.

Because being in school is considered a child care arrangement, self care is not a prevalent primary care arrangement for grade-school-age children - 1 percent of children 5 to 11 and 7 percent of children 12 to 14 years old. However, use of self care as a secondary or tertiary arrangement is more prevalent, especially among older children. Among children 12 to 14 years old who have two or more arrangements, 24 percent were in self care as their secondary arrangement. Among children with three or more arrangements, 23 percent were in self care as their tertiary arrangement. Self care is a less prominent supplemental arrangement for children 5 to 11, with 4 percent in self care as a secondary arrangement and 6 percent as a tertiary arrangement. On average, children 5 to 14 years old in self care spent six hours per week doing so. Fifty percent spent less than five hours per week in self care, while only 13 percent spent more than 10 hours per week in self care. Children 12 to 14 years old spent an average of 2.4 hours more per week in self care than children 5 to 11 years old and were more than twice as likely to spend more than 10 hours per week in self care than those aged 5 to 11 (16 percent and 6 percent, respectively).

Research indicates that the amount of time a child will be in self care is associated with the amount of parental time available to care for children, which in turn, depends on family structure and labour force participation. In 1995, grade school-age children living in a single-parent household were not significantly more likely to be inself care than children living in a two-parent family (18 percent each). However, when the sex of the single parent is considered, large differences emerge. It is important to simultaneously consider the marital and employment statuses of the parents when examining the prevalence of self care. Use of self care was greatly reduced among children living in a married couple family where one or neither of the parents worked, and in single-parent families where the parent did not work. This suggests that families with less time (married couples who are both employed or single parents who work) are more likely to have children who are in self care.

Due to the strong and significant correlation between parent's employment status and self care, changes in mothers' labour force participation (due to welfare reform for example) may be associated with changes in the proportion of children in self care, especially if affordable child care is not concurrently available.

Children in self care were more likely to live in families with higher average monthly family incomes than the overall population of children. For example, the average monthly income of families with children 5 to 11 years old in self care was $4,512, whereas the average monthly family income of children not in self care was $3,664. The same pattern exists for children 12 to 14 years old. In 1995,11 percent of children living in poverty, 16 percent of children living just above the poverty line (between 100 and 199 percent of poverty), and 22 percent of children living at or above 200 percent of the poverty line were in self care. Since families with higher incomes are likely to have both parents working, some of the income correlation with self care is likely to be related to employment rather than the income. In addition, families with higher incomes tend to live in safer neighborhoods and parents may be more comfortable with self care.

Children who participated in enrichment activities were more likely to be in self care than those who did not. While 49 percent of children 12 to 14 years old who participated in enrichment activities spent some part of their day in self care, a much smaller proportion (33 percent) of children 12 to 14 years old who did not participate in enrichment activities were in self care. A similar relationship also exists for children 5 to 11 years old. This pattern may occur because parents see these activities as building more confidence and responsibility in their children or because the time that would be spent in self care is significantly shorter.

Expenditures for Caring Children under 15

Of the 19.9 million employed women with children under 14 years of age in the fall of 1995, 41 percent (8.1 million) reported they made a cash payment for child care for at least one of their children, the highest percentage recorded since 1985, with the possible exception of 1988. In 1995, a family paid an average of $85 per week for child care. In constant 1995 dollars, child care costs increased from $59 in the winter of 1985 to $85 in the fall of 1995, an increase of 44 percent. In addition, families are spending a greater portion of their family in come on child care per month. The proportion of family income spent on child care increased from 6 percent in 1986 to 7 percent in 1995. In 1995, relatively fewer poor than nonpoor families paid for child care (33 percent compared with 41 percent). Poor families paid about the same amount per week for childcare as nonpoor families ($75 compared with $86). However, larger variations in the cost of child care exist when one considers the broader income distribution. For example, those with monthly family incomes under $1,500 (approximately $18,000 annually) paid an average of $71 per week, while those with monthly family incomes of $4,500 or more (approximately $54,000 or more annually) paid $101 per week. In 1995, poor families who paid for care spent five times more of their budget than nonpoor families on child care (35 percent compared with 7 percent). This large gap in the proportion of income paid for child care by poverty status has persisted over the period 1987 to 1995.

Special Care for Girl Child

Education for girls helps them and their future children. Girls and women are enabled to fulfil their potential. Fewer women will die in pregnancy and childbirth unnecessarily. Fewer infants will die. More children will be better nourished and healthier all around. Families will have additional income. More women will marry later and more will have fewer children. More women will serve in leadership roles. More women will be involved in financial decision-making. More women will contribute to social policy. More girls and more women will enjoy the full range of their rights.

- Get all girls into school
- Help all girls stay in school
- Ensure that all girls learn what they need to succeed.
- Thirty per cent fewer girls will be out of school
- The quality of schools will improve in at least 50 countries Progress in learning outcomes and gender parity.

Ensuring a child the best start in life depends on an integrated approach to early childhood care and development. Such a start lays the foundation for ensuring all other rights. This integrated approach requires inputs from health, including women's health, nutrition, water and environmental sanitation, psycho-social care and early learning and child protection. Immediate benefits: child survival, healthy growth, healthy development, less disease, fewer illnesses. Mid-term benefits: a child's thinking and language skills, emotional and social skills, school readiness and self-esteem. Subsequent benefits: success in school and later in life as an active member of society.

- Focus most intensely on children under three years old
- Strengthen the capacities of families to care for children, especially those most vulnerable
- Increase the access of families and communities to good-quality basic services and adequate livelihoods

— Promote gender equality and ensure the rights and status of women

— Strengthen and integrate national policies for the young child.

— Reduction in infant and child mortality rates

— Healthier infants and children under five

— In 80-100 countries with the greatest needs and/or greatest disparities, implementation of integrated approaches to service delivery that fulfil all the rights of the young child.

— More effective birth registration systems for both boys and girls

— Improved care practices of families and communities in every country

— More children under three in good-quality community or group childcare.

Immunizations and micronutrient supplementation save millions lives every year. Almost every child can be reached with vaccines and supplements, even under the most difficult conditions. Immunization and micronutrient supplementation have a high impact on the health of entire populations. They are affordable and cost-effective. They help families and communities improve childcare practices. They strengthen primary health care systems and can control disease outbreaks.

— Save all infants and all children under five from preventable deaths and disabilities

— Prevent the spread of childhood diseases

— Get all childhood vaccines to all children

— Use immunization 'plus' as an entry point for other

health interventions.

— 80 per cent immunization coverage in every district in 80 per cent of countries
— No polio, anywhere
— Deaths from measles cut by half
— Elimination of maternal and neonatal tetanus
— Twice as many countries with adequate vitamin A coverage.

HIV/AIDS is among the most significant threats to fulfilling the rights of children and women. No region is safe from its spread. HIV/AIDS exacerbates poverty, malnutrition, armed conflict, gender inequities and sexual exploitation. HIV/AIDS exhausts the resources of families, communities and government services. HIV infections can be prevented. The ways and means exist to provide care, support and protection for those who are affected by HIV/AIDS.

— Prevent HIV infections among young people
— Prevent parent-to-child transmission of HIV
— Expand care for children and parents living with HIV and AIDS
— Expand protection, care and support for orphans and children affected by HIV/AIDS.
— Complete impact analyses of HIV/AIDS, disaggregated by gender and age, for every country
— National policies, strategies and action plans implemented in all countries affected by HIV/AIDS
  — to reduce risks for young people
  — to prevent parent-to-child transmission of HIV
  — to ensure protection and care for children orphaned by or vulnerable to HIV/AIDS.

Protection is a universal imperative and the right of every child. Violence, abuse, neglect and exploitation threaten children throughout their life. Children, including those born healthy, and young people are more vulnerable than adults to being hurt, neglected, abused and exploited. Their survival is at risk and their full development compromised. Millions of abused and exploited children suffer out of sight as violence against children occurs within families, in schools and communities and in institutions. Build a 'protective environment' for children that fortifies them against abuse and exploitation in the way that good nutrition and good health care fortifies them against disease.

— Get the facts for each country

— Implement laws, policies and programmes that protect children

— Prevent violence and abuse by supporting families and communities

— Mitigate the impact of violence through recovery and reintegration programmes.

— A strong and protective environment for children that will

— Reduce violence against children

— Eliminate the worst forms of child labour

— Increase protection for children in armed conflict

— End discrimination in all its forms.

— Set the mechanisms in place for family- and community based care for all children without primary caregivers.

3

Counselling Adolescents

Adolescent victims of sexual abuse are no different from adult survivors in the ways they are affected. Both feel betrayal, stigmatization, shame and anger. Both have questions about masculinity and sexual identity. Developmentally, however, adolescent victims are different from adults, and their therapy must reflect these differences. Adolescents are still forming their physical, psychological and sexual identities. They have more changeable personas than adults, and are more willing to experiment with a variety of different, and often contrary, psycho-social styles. Adolescents are very influenced by their peers. For most teenagers, being accepted by their peer culture is paramount; the parts of self that they most consciously identify with generally reflect the values of their current peer group. Adolescent males who have been sexually abused are reluctant to incorporate experiences they consider deviant (such as their sexual abuse) into their sexual personas. Adolescent boys tend to accept the myth that says they are expected to know all about sexual matters, no matter what the limits of their personal knowledge. Admitting they have concerns about sexuality is considered "uncool". For many adolescent victims, the power of culturally approved mythologies about sexuality and masculinity overwhelms their own experience. Because of this, many of them deny their victimization. They either repress their memories of having been abused, or rewrite their histories and describe the abuse as consensual.

Since many offenders are skilful at giving responsibility for their actions to their victims, this misconstruction of reality is generally also supported by the perpetrator. Other victims clearly see their abuse as exploitive, but deny its having had any impact on them. Ironically, it is often easier for adolescent victims to discuss their sexual offences against others than it is to discuss their own victimization because offending behaviours conform better to cultural expectations about masculine power and control. Many adolescent victims who participate in counselling first enter treatment facilities as adolescent sexual offenders.

Adolescent victims who do not act out their abuse-reactive behaviours in ways that cause concern to others are frequently never treated, especially if their discomfort with their victimization keeps them silent. Adolescents tend to think of themselves as invincible. They are not usually aware of the circumstances and/or needs of their childhood that left them vulnerable to being abused. They blame themselves for their victimization. Still forming their identities, they don't see their relationship difficulties or dysfunctional behaviours as being related to sexually victimization. They don't have an extensive history of intimacy problems to motivate them to examine the origin of these difficulties. Instead, they tend to see themselves as secretly flawed or they accept their difficulties as inevitable, characterological traits.

Counselling Adolescent Male Victims

Therapy is a counter-cultural experience for adolescent males. Male self-reliance, independence and action-based behaviours are challenged by the therapeutic process. For many adolescent victims, participating in therapy has connotations of "being crazy" or "sick". It's a challenge for clinicians to package therapy so that it can be a helpful and non-stigmatizing experience for adolescent victims. Whether his sexual abuse was intrafamilial or extrafamilial will have an impact on an adolescent victim's therapeutic experience. In either circumstance, the adolescent victim's family needs to be involved in treatment if he is living at home. If the abuse was intrafamilial, other family members will also need to be involved in extensive counselling processes. It the family members want to remain together, their treatment will involve intensive individual, group and family therapy. Even when families have responded appropriately to the disclosure of abuse, the adolescent male victim's recovery will be enhanced by family therapy.

For adolescent clients who live independently from their families, family therapy may be impossible. Adolescents in foster or residential care, or those living on their own, need support within their immediate community if they are going to address their victimization. If this support does not exist or if there are other more pressing issues that are preoccupying the adolescent, focusing on abuse-related events is counter-therapeutic. Waiting until an adolescent is ready to address his victimization is a very important aspect of the therapeutic process. An adolescent needs the support and caring of his family and community to fully integrate and resolve his victimization. The victim's family (or community) also needs assistance. If inadequate parental supervision contributed to the boy's victimization, the clinician must address this, especially if there are young children in the family. Some families overprotect children who have been victimized; they excuse all aberrant behaviours, no matter what its origin, because of the abuse.

Counselling adolescent male survivors of sexual abuse takes a different focus from that taken with adults. Counselling is the operative word, rather than therapy, since the process concentrates on skill building rather than trauma resolution. This does not mean that trauma resolution does not occur. It does. However, with adolescent clients, abreactive-type processes are not invoked in the same way that they are with adult survivors. Very few adolescent victims have a sufficiently mature personality, or sufficiently well-developed ego strengths to undertake voluntary abreactive processing. However, in their favour, adolescent victims have rarely built up the same entrenched dissociative processes which cause abreactions and hence they can often process their abuse-related experiences more directly.

Adolescent clients need to deal with the impacts of having been abused which are currently affecting their lives. Often this means that treatment focuses on issues such as sexual expression and sexual identity. They need to be helped to see that sexuality is, in itself, a positive force in their lives, but that non-consensual sex is damaging. They need to be helped to distinguish between peer contacts and power contacts in regards to sex. Their understanding of sexuality needs to be expanded to include more than genital sexual arousal. Clinicians also need to prepare adolescents for the possibility that they may need to re-visit their sexual abuse and its impact on their lives as they pass through different developmental stages. This possibility must be handled with a light touch to ensure that it doesn't become a self-fulfilling prophecy. However, it is common for sexual abuse victims to examine their abuse-related experiences as they mature. For instance, when an abuse victim becomes a father and fully understands the vulnerability of children in the face of adult power, his grief for his own lost childhood may be reactivated. Hence, counselling needs to be a positive experience for adolescent clients to keep the door open for future therapy, should the need arise.

Assessing adolescent clients requires a skilful and light touch on the part of the assessing clinician. If assessments are to provide useful diagnostic information, clients must co-operate by giving truthful and detailed answers to the questions asked. In order for this to happen, the client must be confident that the assessment process will help him. Some adolescents respond to an invitation to "lift the burden of secrecy" that has surrounded their abuse. If they see talking about their abuse as a means of relieving their feelings of stigmatization and low self-esteem, they will co-operate more easily with the assessment process.

Most adolescent males are not used to talking explicitly with adults about their sexuality. In fact, if this has happened at all, it has generally occurred within the context of being sexually abused. Hence, an assessing clinician must make his or her role and intent very clear to abused clients, so that they don't think that the assessment is an elaborate new grooming procedure. Explaining the assessment procedure and the assessor's role to adolescent clients is an essential first step in establishing a trusting relationship. This is especially important if the assessor will not be the client's ongoing therapist. Clients need to know in advance if they will be assessed by one clinician, but treated by another.

Using a medical analogy can help adolescent victims understand why they have to reveal intimate information about their abuse. The assessing clinician can tell the client that if someone experiencing severe stomach cramps were taken to an emergency ward, the doctor who examined him would need to know why he was having so much pain before treating him, otherwise the patient might be subjected to surgery when in reality he only needed to get rid of some stomach gas. In the same way an assessment enables the clinician to be skilful in his interventions. The information that he receives from the client assists him to formulate an effective treatment plan. During a good assessment the clinician will educate the client about both abuse and treatment processes.

Since adolescent male victims often feel a great deal of shame about having repeatedly been involved in abuse, they need to be reassured about the normalcy of their behaviour. If an assessing clinician tells the client that abuse victims usually have very good reasons for not telling anyone about the abuse, and asks the client if he had reasons for not telling, this eases the clients shame for not having told when the abuse began. Adolescent clients also carry shame about their physical arousal during the abuse. Sharing basic physiological information can assist the assessment process. When an adolescent client understands that if his penis is stimulated, it will become erect, no matter who is stimulating it or why, he feels less ashamed discussing his arousal. In a humorous way, the assessing clinician can remind an adolescent client that his penis doesn't have eyes or a brain or any other way to determine who is stimulating it.

The clinician needs to show adolescents that when an event happens, it can be understood in many different ways. They may have interpreted their physiological response to the abuse by thinking "I'm very sexy" or "I'm gay" or "I'm a pervert"; these interpretations may have limited their understanding of the abuse. Helping clients to see how they made sense of being victimized can give them permission to become less self-blaming in their interpretation of these events. This can increase their ease in discussing abuse-related matters. Often a simple analogy can help clients see how interpretation changes our understanding of an event. For example, if you have been expecting a telephone call from a friend who doesn't call, you'll react differently if you think your friend has had an accident from the way you'll act if you think your friend is mad at you.

Adolescent clients need to know that their strengths as well as their weaknesses are important to the assessing clinician. The assessment process should focus on gathering information in as much detail as possible. This includes information about the clients successes and positive coping skills. If a client displays cognitive errors, such as being very self-blaming, these need to be noted, but not challenged, during the assessment. The treatment stage of therapy is the time to change thinking errors, not the assessment stage. If the assessor prematurely challenges dysfunctional cognitive patterns, the client may feel unheard or misunderstood; and may subsequently withdraw from disclosing any further personal information.

Frequently everyone in an adolescent's life, except the adolescent himself, wants him to get treatment. If an adolescent is not motivated to address his abuse-related issues, treatment will only reinforce his experience of dysfunctional power dynamics. An adolescent client needs to know that he is a partner in the treatment process that he is in charge of what he will tell the clinician about himself, and when he will do so. Forcing an adolescent into treatment before he is motivated is counter-therapeutic. The only exception to this rule occurs when an adolescent is abusing younger children and must be held accountable so that he doesn't continue to endanger others.

During the assessment process, an adolescent client's ego strengths and ability to handle anxiety must be determined. If focusing on his sexual abuse will increase his destructive behaviour towards himself or others, it is not advisable to proceed. Many adolescents do not have sufficiently sophisticated coping strategies to contain the emotions that surface when they recall their abuse. If this is the case, their treatment must focus on building self care skills, rather than on abuse-related material per se. An adolescent client's dissociative tendencies need to be assessed prior to treatment. Dissociative adolescents are often self-destructive, experience drastic mood swings, and act out behaviourally in ways that are inconsistent with their primary personas.

Treatment Process

Adolescent victims of sexual abuse exhibit the same wide range of symptoms and strengths as their adult counterparts. However, due to their youth, adolescents have had less opportunity to internalize dysfunctional coping mechanisms. They are at a developmental stage that encourages experimentation, and are often more willing than adult to try out new behaviours provided they don't feel embarrassed or humiliated doing so.

Therapist's style: Therapists who work with adolescents must be comfortable with this age group. They need to be able to work with erratic mood swings and attitudinal challenges without becoming parental. The therapist needs to be confidant in his or her own role, but not authoritarian. The therapist must be comfortable with adolescent clients' jargon and language. Adolescent communication styles and sexual nomenclature come in and out of fashion; the therapist needs to keep abreast of these trends.

Gender of therapist: Adolescent male victims are generally more at ease discussing their sexuality with a male therapist. Knowing that the therapist has a similar psycho-physiological reality from which to discuss sexuality enhances the clients' level of comfort. However, if an adolescent client was abused by a male, discussing the abuse with a female therapist may initially feel safer. It is important that clients' preferences about the gender of their therapist be respected and honoured.

Clear boundaries and limits: Therapists must explicitly state that during the course of counselling, adolescent clients will be expected to talk about their sexuality, but that they will always be in charge of how much, or how little, they say. Therapists who work with adolescent survivors need to approach sexuality with a "no big deal" attitude and convey a direct and relaxed approach to sexual issues. Typically, adolescent clients will test their therapists' abilities to handle sexual material. The therapists' responses will determine the extent to which the client engages in the therapeutic process. Therapists can assume that a client won't disclose the full extent of his abuse until he feels confident that he is safe to do so.

Not only must the therapist be explicit regarding his or her expectations that the client's sexuality will be discussed during his counselling, but he or she must also be explicit in regards to other therapeutic boundaries and limits. Adolescent clients need to know the therapist's boundary of confidentiality. Therapists must state that they will break therapeutic confidentiality if they're concerned about the safety of the client or anyone else. For instance, if the client discloses information about other abusive incidents, the therapist is legally bound to report them. If other members of the client's family are also in treatment, the client needs to know how information will be shared between the different treatment providers. You also need to clarify whether your client will be given information from other family members' sessions, and vice versa.

Counselling Process

Treatment with adolescent victims generally proceeds best if it is short-term. It needs to clearly focus on the presenting problem or issue that is most pertinent to the client. Partializing treatment so that it deals with one piece of work at a time is a good strategy to use with adolescent survivors. Creating a succession of small successes boosts clients' self-esteem. It also ensures that the treatment process is a positive experience for the client, thus increasing the likelihood that he will use therapeutic resources in the future. For example, if an adolescent victim is acting out by being aggressive with authority figures, his therapeutic contract might focus on anger expression and developing safe and effective ways to manage his angry feelings. The therapist might make some attempt to connect his present anger with his past betrayal, but the primary focus of therapy would be on assisting the client to address his here-and-now concerns. Once he had learned and integrated these new skills the contract would end. The therapist would encourage the client to renew therapy if in future he developed new psycho-social problems or showed other symptoms related to his sexually abuse.

Adolescents often engage more quickly with the therapeutic process if they can approach abuse-specific issues with a little distance. This can occur in a variety of ways. One method is to use externalizing techniques, such as drawing or other art media. Asking an adolescent male survivor to draw what he would like to do to his perpetrator can be a door opener to discussing anger, and constructive means of channelling intense feelings. Often boys have chosen dangerous or socially unacceptable ways to express their anger, and they need to find safe ways to discharge this emotion. Some boys are so afraid of the power of their rage that they have shut down their angry responses, and their anger is sublimated into other areas of their life. For clients like these, ft is very beneficial to develop assertiveness skills and learn to separate anger and violence.

Psycho-educational materials help adolescent clients process their abuse. They not only fill in information deficits that the clients may have, they also act as door openers for more personal disclosures. For example, if a client is reluctant to share any information about the specifics of his abuse you can give him a set of flash cards that have different types of touching described on them. Ask the client to sort the cards into three piles: OK touch, not-OK touch and unclear touch. His choices, and his reasons for making these choices can then be discussed. You can ask more participatory clients to generate their own list of different types of touch.

Sometimes reading adolescents stories which were originally intended for younger children can stimulate discussion about events in their childhood. The client's developmental age is often younger than his chronological age. Provided that he doesn't experience being read to as condescending, his inner child will often be activated by more juvenile reading material. This kind of stimulation can "unfreeze" parts of the self that shut down at the time of the sexual abuse. In a similar manner, showing videos and movies that deal with abuse can be an indirect way of accessing abuse-related material. Separating the parts of self that a client accepts from those that he rejects or is uncomfortable with, can be a first step in working towards integration. It may help to refer the different parts of the clients as "sad Bob", "angry Bob" or "scared Bob" and talk about them as if they were separate. To reshape a client's sexual behaviour into more age-appropriate forms, it's often necessary to work with the clients' sexual fantasies.

Using guided imagery can be helpful in this regard. For example, after bringing your client into deep relaxation, ask him to imagine a place of safety for himself that is the most beautiful place that he knows. Tell him that he will have complete privacy in this place and ask him to think about what he'd like to do sexually that would give him the biggest possible turn-on. Ask him if it involves anyone else. It he says "yes", ask him to note the person's name. Ask your client to thank the person for joining him in his fantasy and to let the person leave the fantasy in the smoothest possible way.

Then you gradually bring the client back into the counselling session. The fantasy and the role of the person or persons the client called into his fantasy are debriefed. If the client's arousal patterns are based on deviant behaviours, he is helped to develop more orthodox associations to sexual stimulation. Adolescent clients need help to develop safety plans to reduce the possibility of being revictimized, or to put in place should they actually become revictimized. This is especially important for clients who were intrafamilially abused and who continue to live at home. In cases where the abuse was intrafamilial, all the family members need to be involved in developing "fire drills" to put into effect should any member of the family have concerns about either their own, or another family member's safety. These "fire drills" can consist of ensuring that all family members, especially the victim, has a trusted person to whom they can turn if they have safety concerns.

In some cases, they involve family contracts about how certain family members agree to interact with one another. Whatever form they take, they're essential to ensure that adolescent clients are familiar with both preventative and crisis-based self care strategies.

Group Treatment

Group treatment is a particularly effective treatment modality for adolescent victims of sexual abuse. Given that adolescents are peer-focused and many have negative associations with one-to-one contact with an adult because of their victimization, group treatment is a safe and effective form of treatment. The group process breaks the adolescent victim's isolation and helps them to destigmatize their victimization. Peer contact with other victims encourages adolescent survivors to openly acknowledge their abuse experience. A group format gives clients options about how much or how little of themselves they disclose, since they are no longer the single focus of a therapists' attention. For many adolescent victims, being able to move in and out of the spotlight makes the group process more comfortable than individual counselling sessions, where they're always the centre of attention. The control this gives adolescent clients generally increases their feelings of safety and hence they participate more freely in the treatment process.

Therapist Issues

Because therapy is an interactive process, the well-being and integrity of the therapist has a fundamental impact on the course of therapy for the client. Clients will intuitively be aware of inconsistencies between what a therapist says and what he or she does. This section of the text describes important self care strategies for therapists to incorporate into their work and lives. It suggests seven ways to recognize and manage therapists' counter-transference. Providing therapy to male survivors has many intrinsic rewards. The intimacy of the therapeutic process and the chance to participate in a client's heating and growth provides a therapist with both professional and personal satisfaction.

A therapist's confidence and effectiveness build as he or she develops specialized skills for working with survivors and as his or her intuition in applying these skills becomes more finely tuned. However, empathetic listening to survivors' experiences leaves the therapist open to vicarious experience of trauma and loss. The phenomenon of vicarious traumatization, or traumatization by proxy, is one that all therapists who work extensively with clients who have experienced childhood trauma must learn to manage. Finding the balance between being able to absorb and respond therapeutically to the events that clients disclose, and distancing themselves from this information as a means of self protection, is an ongoing issue for therapists.

Not only do therapists vicariously experience their clients' trauma, but they may be directly affected if a client's story triggers unresolved issues from the therapist's past history. Some therapists report violent and disturbing dreams after working with survivors. Clinicians who work with abuse survivors need to have ongoing supervision to help them process their responses to their clients; in some cases, personal therapy is an important component of therapist self care. Therapists who work with clients who have been sexually abused often become more vigilant about their own, or their childrens' personal safety. Several contributors commented that after working with many survivors of sexual abuse they view the world more cynically and less trustingly than before. There are certainly some personal costs for the therapist who works extensively with abuse survivors. Because therapy is an interactive process between two people, both are subject to being influenced by the other. However, given the nature of the therapeutic contract, it is essential for therapists to develop strategies to handle their own counter-transference so that they don't act it out in therapy. In addition, therapists must become aware of their own thematic life issues so that they don't unconsciously play them out with clients. Here are some common counter-transferential concerns that therapists experience and procedures to reduce their negative impact on both client and therapist.

Counter-transference with Male Survivors

Therapists, as well as clients, internalize cultural attitudes and gender scripts. To the extent that the therapists are unconsciously acting out such scripts and attitudes, they may unknowingly project them onto their client relationships. Such contamination of the therapeutic process needs to be identified, challenged and transformed. Just as therapists support their clients in challenging ways of living that are no longer useful, so they themselves need to be challenged and supported in developing and enhancing their therapeutic skills. The emotions and dysfunctional behaviours that male survivors present can elicit a range of responses in the therapist. It is not unusual for therapists to begin to develop the same kinds of defences shown by their clients during their work together. Therapist dissociation, minimization, avoidance, helplessness and other similar parallel processes can occur. Generally, a change in the therapist's affective state or behaviour indicates the presence of counter-transferential dynamics. Other therapists will redirect their client's attention to less emotionally charged material when their own anxiety levels begin to rise. If a therapist starts to dread his sessions with a particular client, or begins to feel overwhelmed and incompetent in the face of a client's issues, he or she is probably experiencing counter-transference. Learning to notice these cues and using them as signals for self-examination can reduce the negative impact of these dynamics on the therapy.

Another aspect of counter-transference occurs when a therapist begins to see a client as "special" and deserving extra attention. Extending the length of sessions at no extra cost to the client, or meeting with a client outside of scheduled sessions or in other ways changing the normal boundaries of the therapeutic relationship, indicate that the therapist is exhibiting counter-transferential dynamics that need to be addressed in the therapist's supervision. At times it is necessary to change the normal boundaries of the therapeutic relationship and hold longer sessions or meet more frequently. However, the therapist needs to ensure that these changes are the result of sound clinical judgement, not unconscious counter-transference. Whenever a therapist's interaction with a client is driven by his or her own needs, rather than by the clients' needs, he or she is opening the possibility of replicating the original abuse dynamics. Being aware of this potential hazard, and working to avoid it is an important aspect of therapy with survivors.

Managing Counter-Transference

Contributor's suggestions for managing counter-transference and providing self care:

— a partnership attitude to providing therapy;

— personal therapy for the therapist;

— identifying one's personal limits and boundaries;

— supervision;

— peer support;

— advocacy; and

— personal life satisfaction.

Therapists who work with male survivors often need to remind themselves that the power to heal from childhood trauma lies in the client, not in the therapist. Like a good gardener, a therapist can nurture and fertilize his clients' growth. They may assist in removing noxious weeds or other hindrances to full recovery. However, as with growing plants, the therapists need to trust that their clients have an inherent ability to respond favourably to appropriate interventions. Victims of abuse need to be in control of pacing their recovery process. A therapist who adopts an authoritarian stand with clients will generally elicit counter-therapeutic transference. Therapists who see themselves as facilitators who can guide their clients' recovery, rather than as experts who can prescribe cures, are more likely to help their clients. Not only is sharing power in therapy an essential component of restoring the clients' capacity to make autonomous decisions, but letting go of a need to control the process reduces therapists' work-related stress.

Several contributors commented on the importance of therapists being responsive to their clients, and the issues they present, without taking responsibility for them. Clients need to be given complete ownership of their own actions, beliefs, behaviours and cognitions. The therapist's task is to be able to respond to all aspects of the client non-judgmentally. Therapists must avoid taking a parental stance with clients since this will generally counteract the desired outcome of increasing the client's autonomy. Therapists express a partnership attitude toward their clients when they own their own shortcomings and imperfections. Inevitably, all therapists make mistakes with their clients. For instance, a therapist may misjudge the timing of an intervention, or he may interrupt a client prematurely to give well-intentioned feedback. To the extent that therapists can claim mistakes such as these, they provides their clients with a model for honest human interaction. Therapist's personal integrity and the congruence between their words and deeds influence the success of therapy as much as their professional knowledge and expertise.

Therapy for the Therapist

There are several important reasons why therapists who work with adult survivors of childhood trauma should have undergone, or be engaged in, psychotherapy. Probably foremost of these is that by coming to terms with their own psychological scripts, therapists are less likely to project their own injuries onto others—most notably their clients. It is important to understand the process of therapeutic change not just intellectually, but also experientially, in order to genuinely engage and track his or her clients. Due to the intense nature of therapy with survivors of childhood sexual trauma, it is likely that therapists will face their own psychological vulnerabilities. Each therapist will have idiosyncratic triggers that particular clients will provoke. For instance, one therapist may typically overwork on behalf of clients who are very depressed, in response to his own family script about how to handle depressed feelings. Another therapist may become angry or afraid when clients identify issues similar to his or her own childhood trauma, thereby unconsciously inhibiting the clients safety to work on these issues.

Personal therapy helps therapists to more easily separate their own processes from those of their clients. Therapists will be better able to identify their own vulnerable areas and to work more effectively with clients who provoke them. Good personal therapy should assist therapists in developing skills that make him more fully present in both their work and personal lives. It should provide them with skills to respond to their own personal process should a client unknowingly trigger a problematic association. If a therapist is conducting therapy with clients while in personal therapy, it is essential that he or she have good clinical supervision to keep personal issues distinct from client issues. Therapists need to be respectful of themselves and to structure their time in self-supporting ways. For instance, personal therapy appointments need to be scheduled at a time when you can be self-focused and do not immediately have to return to client-focused concerns. There may be times when you will have to lighten your workload if you're working intensely on personal issues.

Therapists who work with survivors of childhood trauma need to create clear and predictable boundaries in their work to support both their clients and themselves. For clients, knowing the therapist's groundrules about issues such as scheduling extra sessions or handling unpaid fees provides safety and predictability. For the therapist, setting up clear boundaries is good self care. Therapists must have clear policies about missed appointments, receiving crisis phone calls, extended sessions, fee payments and so on. When to schedule vacations and the length of a typical work day are decisions that need to be tailored to a therapist's personal taste and style.

Other boundaries are more general in nature and focus on broader issues. Managing case-load composition in ways that respect your own needs is a vital aspect of boundary setting. When determining what types of clients the therapist will work with and the size of his or her caseload, the therapist must be thoughtful and realistic about his or her circumstances. In general, it is advisable for therapists who work with sexual abuse survivors to maintain a mixed case load. Clients who are recovering from childhood sexual trauma are usually candidates for long-term therapy. Having opportunities to work with short-term cases and a variety of presenting problems, can help to keep the therapist refreshed and energized. It is important that the boundaries that a therapist makes are flexible enough to change to meet new eventualities, but rigid enough to meet the purpose for which they were intended. Ensuring that clients are aware of their therapists' work-related boundaries is a key ingredient of ensuring that therapy is a safe and predictable process.

Almost inevitably, clients will ask their therapist why they do the work they do. Therapists who choose to work with sexual abuse survivors have a multitude of reasons for doing so. These reasons need to be clear to the therapist; often they emerge during the course of the therapist's own therapy. Although a therapist must be judicious about the personal information they tell clients, you should be prepared to honestly answer your clients' inquiries about why you work with sexual abuse survivors. Sexual abuse, has involved a violation of a client's personal boundary. In the therapeutic process, therefore, the therapist must be vigilant about respecting his or her clients' boundaries while simultaneously respecting his or her own. Providing clients, and therapists, with a safe environment in which to engage in the therapeutic process is paramount and any lapse in maintaining clear boundaries which may jeopardize this safety must be avoided.

4

Negative Engagements and Ineffective Rewards

Social cognitive theory is rooted in an agentic perspective in which people function as anticipative, purposive, and selfevaluating proactive regulators of their motivation and actions. A theory embodying feed-forward selfregulation differs from control theories rooted solely in a negative feedback control system aimed at error correction. Among the mechanisms of human agency, none is more central or pervasive than beliefs of personal efficacy. Whatever other factors serve as guides and motivators, they are rooted in the core belief that one has the power to produce desired effects; otherwise one has little incentive to act or to persevere in the face of difficulties. Selfefficacy beliefs regulate human functioning through cognitive, motivational, affective, and decisional processes. They affect whether individuals think in self-enhancing or selfdebilitating ways, how well they motivate themselves and persevere in the face of difficulties, the quality of their emotional well-being and their vulnerability to stress and depression, and the choices they make at important decisional points.

Self-efficacy Beliefs and Decisional Behavior

The higher the perceived self-efficacy to fulfill educational requirements and occupational roles is, the wider are the career options people seriously consider pursuing, the greater is the interest they have in them, the better they prepare themselves educationally for different occupational careers, and the greater is their staying power in challenging career pursuits.

Efficacy beliefs predict occupational choices and level of mastery of educational requirements for those careers and predict persistence in technical or scientific pursuits when variations in actual ability, prior level of academic achievement, scholastic aptitude, and vocational interests are controlled. Self-development during formative years forecloses some types of occupational options and makes others realizable. A multifaceted longitudinal project examined, by use of the path-analytic method, how sociostructural determinants operating in concert with different facets of perceived self-efficacy at the beginning of junior high school predict the types of occupational pursuits students seriously consider toward the end of junior high. The impact of familial socioeconomic status and parents' self-efficacy and aspirations on their children's occupational preferences is entirely mediated through the children's perceived occupational self-efficacy and academic aspirations. Perceived occupational self-efficacy rather than actual academic achievement is the key determinant of the kinds of career pursuits children seriously consider for their lifework and those they disfavor.

Multivariate investigations using panel designs with path analytic and structural equation modeling are now commonly used to estimate the unique contribution of efficacy belief to subsequent performance after controlling not only for past performance but for a host of other possible determinants. The entire system of direct and mediated relations in the causal structure is tested, not just the contribution of isolated predictors. Tests are conducted on the goodness of fit between the posited conceptual model and the empirical data and on how well alternative conceptual models fit the data. The issue of past performance and the determinative function of perceived self-efficacy can, of course, be addressed experimentally rather than by partialing out variances statistically. This experimental strategy was used in an intraindividual experimental design with sequential microanalytic comparison of the relative predictiveness of prior performance and perceived efficacy.

Contrary to the view that perceived self-efficacy simply reflects past performances, the same performance attainment gave rise to widely different levels of perceived self-efficacy. Having achieved the same performance level at the midpoint of the hierarchical coping tasks, some phobics judged themselves capable of performing only 10% of the higher level tasks, others 20%, still others 35%, and some felt supremely efficacious to perform 100% of the tasks. Efficacy beliefs predicted at an 84% level of accuracy performance on the highly threatening tasks that the phobics had never done before. All that past performance could tell phobics in regard to coping tasks that they had never attempted was that they could do what they had just done, which has no predictive value.

Behavior is not a cause of behavior. Correlations between prior and subsequent behavior simply reflect the degree of commonality of their determinants. If the determinants are similar across time, the performances will be highly correlated. Performance is not an unadulterated measure of ability; it is heavily infused with many motivational and self-regulatory determinants. Past performance is thus a conglomerate index encompassing the set of unmeasured sociocognitive factors operating at the time. Perceived self-efficacy is an important part of that constellation of unmeasured determinants of performance. Thus, past performance is itself affected by beliefs of personal efficacy. Efficacy beliefs are autocorrelated and affect both prior and later performance. Using unadjusted past performance scores thus also removes some of the effects of efficacy beliefs on future performance. Therefore, control for past performance ideally should use the residual after partialing out the prior self-efficacy contribution to variance in performance.

The field has moved beyond the simple-minded view that efficacy beliefs are just reflectors of performance to analyses of the unique contribution of efficacy beliefs in multifaceted causal structures. In these structural analyses, the relation of past performance to subsequent performance is heavily, if not fully, mediated through efficacy beliefs, goals and aspirations, outcome expectations, and other sociocognitive determinants.

Diverse lines of research examining coping with different types of stressors and taxing demands have provided converging evidence for the influential impact of perceived ability to exercise control on anxiety and stress reactions. People who are arbitrarily led to believe that they can control aversive events display lower autonomic arousal and less performance impairment than do those who believe that they lack personal control, although they are subjected equally to the painful events. The same is true for stress reactions to clinical pain. Bogus physiological feedback that patients were effective relaxers raised beliefs in their efficacy to cope with their oral surgery. Self-efficacy enhancement surpassed relaxation and sedation drugs in reducing self-rated anxiety as well as anxiety reactions and behavioral agitation during surgery, as rated by the oral surgeon and dental assistant. Regardless of type of ameliorative treatment the patients received, the more their efficacy beliefs were raised by the preparatory ministrations, the lower the anxious agitation was.

Social cognitive theory posits dual control systems in selfregulation of motivation and action-a proactive discrepancy production system working in concert with a reactive discrepancy reduction system. People are aspiring and proactive organisms, not just reactive ones. Their capacity to exercise forethought enables them to wield adoptive control anticipatorily rather than being simply reactive to the effects of their efforts. They are motivated and guided by foresight of goals, not just by hindsight of shortfalls. People are not primarily motivated by discrepancy reduction. They motivate and guide themselves through proactive control by setting themselves challenging goals and performance standards that create negative discrepancies to be mastered. They then mobilize their effort and personal resources on the basis of their anticipatory estimation of what it would take to fulfill those standards. Reactive feedback control comes into play in subsequent adjustments of effort to achieve desired outcomes. After people attain the goals they have been pursuing, those individuals with high perceived self-efficacy set a higher standard for themselves. The adoption of further challenges creates new motivating discrepancies to be mastered. Thus, discrepancy reduction is only half of the story and not necessarily the more interesting half.

The greater challenge is to explain why people inflict on themselves high standards that demand hard work and beget a lot of stress, disappointments, and failures along the way rather than to explain why they should seek tranquility by matching a standard.

Creating and removing discrepancies are two sides of the same goal-directed coin. Discrepancy reduction is a concomitant of motivating self-challenge, not the prime motive of action. If it were, people would simply set their goals to match whatever they had already done, thus ensuring no discrepancy. Furthermore, the very concept of discrepancy reduction, even as part of the full goal-seeking process, is misleading. It is not discrepancies that people seek to eliminate but goals and valued outcomes that they seek to attain.

In the pursuit of difficult challenges, people have to override a lot of dissuading negative feedback if they are to realize what they seek. Resilient belief that one has what it takes to succeed provides the necessary staying power in the face of repeated failures, setbacks, and skeptical or even critical social reactions that are inherently discouraging. Those beset by self-doubts become the early quitters rather than the successful survivors. Success under rapid change requires overriding even current positive feedback. Efficacious adaptability has become a premium at the organizational level. Organizations must be proactively innovative to survive and prosper in the rapidly changing global marketplace. Innovative proaction brings future preemption in the competitive arena. Organizations face the paradox of preparing for change at the height of success. Those organizations that get locked into the technologies and products that produce their current success and that fail to change fast enough to the technologies and marketplaces of the future quickly fall victim to the inertia of success. The growing primacy of proactive or "feed-forward" agency in adaptation and change in all aspects of life in the electronic era is discussed more fully elsewhere.

In expectancy-value theory, motivation is governed by the expectation that given performances will produce particular outcomes and the value individuals place on the expected outcomes. However, people act on their beliefs about what they can do as well as their beliefs about the likely outcomes of performance. Indeed, they exclude entire classes of options rapidly on self-efficacy grounds without bothering to analyze costs and benefits. Adding perceived self-efficacy to rational models of decision making increases their explanatory and predictive power. Some expectancy-value theories include an expectancy that given performances are achievable through effort. However, many tests of expectancy-value theory do not include the effort expectancy. Most people believe that high effort is likely to enhance performance attainments; however, there is an important difference between belief in the utility of effort and belief that one can get oneself to mobilize and sustain a required level of effort in the face of impediments, failures, setbacks, and bouts of discouragement along the way.

The latter concerns perceived personal efficacy; the former concerns beliefs in the instrumental value of a particular means. Agentic efficacy beliefs are good predictors of performance, whereas means beliefs are weak differentiators and predictors. Perceived self-efficacy for effort regulation is but one aspect of self-management that contributes to level and quality of performance. Success in performances that requires ingenuity, resourcefulness, and adaptability demand more than just dint of effort. People, therefore, judge their efficacy for other essential aspects of self-management including their cognitive and social facility and resilience. Moreover, in taxing endeavors people have to judge their efficacy not only to sustain their motivation and task-oriented focus but to manage distressing emotional states and selfdebilitating thought patterns, which can impair their execution of activities.

Control Theories

Control theory of human functioning was developed by Powers as an outgrowth of the cybernetic model in engineering to show how mechanical devices are regulated through feedback based on the results of their previous motions. The core idea is the negative feedback loop in which a deviation from the desired programmed state or reference value detected by a sensor automatically triggers movements that will drive the system toward the preprogrammed state. This model takes discrepancies between the programmed state and the perceived input from the output of the system as the fundamental driving force behind motion within the system. "Action is driven by the difference, or error". If there is no disturbance, there is no adjustment. The system either maintains its present movements or remains at rest. According to this conceptual scheme, the nervous system embodies a hierarchy of interconnected feedback loops with upper-level loops providing the reference signals that serve as goal settings for subordinate loops.

An odd aspect of perceptual control theory is the claim that "people act to control perceptions, not actions". Taken literally, an organism that is focused solely on regulating perceptions would not survive for long. People act to develop their knowledge and capabilities and to exercise some measure of control over their everyday lives. They obviously do so through their construals and constructions of reality, but the aim of their purposive actions is not just to manage their perceptions but to manage their life circumstances. Despite claims to the contrary, Powers's control theory is founded on austere materialistic reductionism. In this view, the human organism is "nothing more than a connection between one set of physical quantities in the environment (input quantities) and another set of physical quantities in the environment (output quantities)". Experiments in which subjects are instructed to control a cursor by manipulating a stick are used to verify the theory. In the posited "behavioral law," action is "determined strictly and quantitatively by the inverse of the feedback function and is, therefore, a property of the environment and not of the subject". Powers also noted, "We are not modeling the interior of the subject, so we need not worry about how this effect is created". Such a view is hardly conducive to understanding human motivation and action, which are extensively cognitively regulated. Powers stated that machine language is better than "natural language" because it reduces ambiguity.

Many problems arise in a cybernetic model of human motivation and action. Machines are not conscious. They operate automatically and nonvolitionally. People are not nonconscious organisms locked in negative feedback loops driven automatically to reduce disparity between sensed feedback and inner referents. They can and do respond with a wide variety of possible reactions to performance shortfalls. They act proactively and can choose and change the standards they aim for, use multiple and even conflicting standards, make judgments about their capabilities for different options, process feedback in many different ways, use various methods of developing task strategies, use diverse combinations of conscious and nonconscious knowledge, engage in many types of problem-solving activities, and operate across many different time spans. The connections between sensing and action are not mechanical. The cybernetic model ignores the vast knowledge of cognitive self-regulation of human motivation and action.

Control theory is rather barren psychologically. It has identified little in the way of new processes aside from the ones already known. Other than stating that people act to reduce detected discrepancies, it has little additional content. Control theory does posit hierarchical goal systems, but that idea is not unique to control theory. Powers described, in stilted machine language, four ways of increasing motivation:

a) raise the goal,
b) underrate achievement,
c) increase importance of the goal, and
d) present obstacles.

The conditions under which these types of interventions may or may not increase motivation were identified and tested years ago within the framework of goal theory and social cognitive theory. In efforts to create a psychocybernetic system, control theorists have had to incorporate "add-ons" into the model. There is no single control theory with a determinate set of propositions. Rather, there is a multiplicity of control theories that take different forms depending on the particular mix of sociocognitive factors grafted on the negative feedback loop. Fifteen hypotheses were taken from goal theory, eight from expectancy theory, three from attribution theory, two from satisfaction theory, one from social cognitive theory, one or two from script theory, and others were just statements of the obvious (e.g., people have goal hierarchies). The ingredients in this theoretical conglomerate may contain valid ideas, but none of them have anything to do with control theory. The rich eclectic embellishment of the negative feedback loop is more akin to cafeteria theorizing than to integrative theorizing as claimed. These cognitive components certainly are critical to understanding human action, but again, they have little to do with the basic control theory.

Some argues that other motivation theories did not deal adequately with affect, argued that affect would be a function of the rate at which discrepancies are reduced but not of current goal-outcome discrepancies. However, goal theory had already shown that affect was, in fact, a result of both goal-outcome discrepancies and progress toward the goal. Accomplishments that surpass earlier ones bring a continued sense of self-satisfaction, but people derive little satisfaction from smaller accomplishments or even devalue them after having made larger strides. People who are prone to depression display even greater affective reactivity to their pattern of progress. They are more self-satisfied with accelerating strides, but they find even less satisfaction in modest improvements after large attainments.

All that they found, however, was that when people were assigned a goal and were given feedback regarding their performance relative to the goal, they would use the feedback to adjust their actions so as to better match the goal. This conception essentially dismantles a stable regulatory function by the feedback loop. If personal goals simply reflect past performance, then the feedback loop is stuck with a continually fluctuating internal goal setting reflecting the rises and declines in prior performance. In social cognitive theory, humans are proactive and are more apt to look forward than to look backward, locked in a negative feedback loop. They extend their aspirations distally well beyond their proximal performance level and override a lot of negative feedback along the way in pursuit. Through this proactive self-management they turn high aspirations into reality. Conditions of rapid change demand a forward-looking perspective for human success. Neither perceived self-efficacy nor goals are simply reflectors of past performance. A given performance attainment can give rise to diverse self-set goals depending on level of perceived self-efficacy. Thus, when people fail to fulfill a challenging standard, some become less sure of their efficacy and lower their goals, but others remain confident and persist in the face of failure and even raise their goals. Surpassing a taxing standard through sustained strenuous effort does not necessarily raise efficacy beliefs.

Although for most people, high accomplishment strengthens beliefs of personal efficacy, many who drive themselves to hard-won success are left with self-doubts that they can duplicate the feat and so adopt more modest goals for future pursuits. Strength of perceived efficacy and goal commitment predict whether people redouble their efforts, react apathetically, or become despondent when they fail to fulfill a valued standard. There is more to self-regulation than control by means of feedback loops. A comprehensive theory must encompass the variety of agentic factors known to influence human selfregulation. These factors include proactive adoption of aspirant standards serving valued purposes; selfappraisal of personal efficacy to fulfill various goal challenges; anticipatory regulation of the strategies, resources, and effort needed to turn cognized standards into reality;

material and social outcome expectations for fulfilling or failing to meet the standards; affective self-evaluative reactions to the quality of one's performances; and self-reflective metacognition focused on the accuracy of one's efficacy appraisals, the appropriateness of one's goals and the adequacy of one's strategies for realizing them, and the meaning of one's pursuits.

Describing agentic functions as higher level loops contributes little to our understanding of these proactive functions. These are the very interior cognitive processes that Powers dismisses as of little interest because "we are not modeling the interior of the subject". The self-regulation of learning through performance and error correction is a drawn out process. If knowledge and skills could be acquired only by negative response feedback, human development would be greatly retarded, not to mention exceedingly tedious and hazardous. Moreover, limited time, resources, and mobility impose severe constraints on what people can directly explore to gain new knowledge and competencies. However, humans have evolved an advanced cognitive capacity for observational learning that enables them to abbreviate the acquisition process by learning directly from modeled information, not just enactive experience. They extract the generic structure embodied in modeled exemplars, use the symbolic representation to construct appropriate courses of action, and then refine their skills through a conception-matching process. By drawing on symbolic modeling through the electronic media, observers transcend the bounds of their immediate environment and sole dependence on learning by means of error correction. In Powers's theory, neither self-satisfaction nor selfdissatisfaction serves as a motivator. It is solely shortfalls that drive behavior.

Social cognitive theory accords affective selfreactions motivating functions. The theory also makes an important distinction concerning the performance on which self-satisfaction is conditional-self-satisfaction with past performance versus the future level of performance with which one will be satisfied. This distinction carries important theoretical and methodological implications. The backward negative feedback theorizing focuses on self-satisfaction with past performance, whereas the feed-forward orientation of social cognitive theory emphasizes the level of future attainment required for self-satisfaction, which provides a self-motivating incentive. Selfsatisfaction made conditional on future level of performance is more predictive of performance than self-satisfaction with past performance.

Evidence disputes Powers's theory that neither selfsatisfaction nor self-dissatisfaction with discrepant attainments has any effect on performance. Cybernetic machines do not respond emotionally to their own performances; humans do. Humans react self-critically to performances that are deficient or that violate their personal standards and react with pride and self-satisfaction when they attain what they value. Studies have been conducted that experimentally vary the direction and the level of discrepancy with microanalysis of the impact of affective self-reaction. The higher the discontent with large and moderate substandard performances, the higher the subsequent effortful performance. Affective self-reactions serve as significant predictors of subsequent performance within each of these discrepancy levels. Other studies have similarly shown that affective self-reactions to one's performances contribute to variance in subsequent individual and group performance.

Not only is perceived self-efficacy an extraneous implant in perceptual control theory, but Powers did not seem to agree on how it debilitates performance. Discrepancy shrinkage and speed are by no means the same processes, because for any level of goal discrepancy, one can have speedy or slow realization of it. Furthermore, control theorists have never validated either of these propositions.

The first major problem is the theoretical disconnect between the posited perceptual control theory and the actual theory being tested. According to Vancouver et al., they tested predictions from Powers's perception control theory, in which action is driven by negative discrepancy between perceived input and a programmed standard. However, the predictions they offered are conditional on perceived selfefficacy -high perceived self-efficacy allegedly shrinks the apparent negative discrepancy, thereby lowering motivation through complacency. However, perceived self-efficacy is not part of the perceptual control theory that they claimed to be testing. The theoretical discordance involves a nonconscious feedback control system reflecting on its personal efficacy and thereby constructing its perceptions of performance incongruities. Similarly, the complacency mechanism they posit for negative motivational effects is at odds with the theory they espouse. Powers contended that mere discrepancy is the motivator and that neither selfsatisfaction nor self-dissatisfaction with discrepant attainments has any effect on performance. Cybernetic systems do not respond emotionally to their own performances.

Another theoretical problem is the failure to specify the impact of counteracting self-efficacy and goal determinants. Vancouver et al. focused heavily on demonstrating that self-efficacy is a performance debilitator but completely ignored the effect of the coacting goal partner. High perceived self-efficacy presumably slackens performers' efforts, but it also promotes high goals, which create large discrepancies that drive performers. The former is demotivating; the latter is motivating. Vancouver et al. did not specify how these counteracting influences get resolved to produce a joint impact. There are also disconnects between theorizing and experimental design in Vancouver et al.'s research. According to perceptual control theory, high self-efficacy is a debilitator only when performance is ambiguous or unknown, thus allowing leeway to decrease the perceived goal discrepancy. A serious test of their theory would, therefore, require comparing the effects of selfefficacy on performance under ambiguous versus explicit performance feedback. However, in their studies, Vancouver et al. tested their theory solely under conditions of explicit feedback in which the negative efficacy effect should not occur and then claim that the findings corroborate their theory. In dealing with the methodological mismatch, they claimed in retrospect that the feedback did not really "capture the entire feedback space" because control theory has many hierarchical loops. Unless these upper loops are clearly specified and measured, the theory is essentially nonfalsifiable.

Vancouver et al.'s studies did not work in the way they had expected-negative effects for self-efficacy but positive effects for goals. Instead, self-set goals had a negative effect on performance as well, although their theory predicted a positive effect of goals on performance. Their methodological remedy for the alleged fault with the goal measure by assigning goals also failed their theory-although assigned goal conditions differed, self-set goals still had a negative effect on performance. They dismissed the negative goal effects that contradicted their perceptual control theory as "spurious" because they could not think of a mechanism for the discordant finding. In a subsequent test of their perceptual control theory, Vancouver et al. discarded goals. It is meaningless to test control theory while stripping it of goals. Powers regarded goals to be essential. Feedback loops need goals for discrepancies that are presumed to drive behavior. Moreover, to judge perceived selfefficacy for a goalless activity makes no more sense than judging one's self-efficacy for high-jumping without specifying the height to be cleared.

Inter and Intra-individual Designs

Verification of functional relations requires converging evidence from different research strategies. This is because any given methodology has limitations as well as advantages. Moreover, the methods vary in scope of application, in ecological validity, and in the generalizability of the data they produce. Converging evidence from complementary methodologies increases confidence in the functional properties of sociocognitive factors. The same is true for positive goal effects. Intraindividual designs are informative in verifying functional relations between variables over time. Such designs have been used successfully in studying both self-efficacy and goal effects. But there is nothing inherently superior in such designs, and they may even yield misleading findings under some conditions. There is often far less variance within individuals than between individuals on critical determinants. Without variance, one cannot find causal or even correlational relations, or if one does find them, the size of the relation may be greatly attenuated with the result that the contribution of a given determinant is underrated. Thus, a factor such as goal commitment gets dismissed as insignificant in intraindividual analysis because of little change over time.

Vancouver et al. regarded interindividual experimental designs as suspect on the assumption that efficacy beliefs may reflect intergroup performance differences. This argument fails to recognize the controls for performance that have been used in such studies. The interindividual designs in which efficacy beliefs are varied directly rather than by enactive means, individuals' prior performance, competencies, abilities, and so forth, remain the same but their beliefs in their efficacy are raised or lowered merely by bogus feedback. Random assignment to experimental conditions provides a further safeguard against group differences in ability and performance level. Multiple controls are likewise applied in evaluating the unique contribution to performance of naturally developed levels of perceived self-efficacy. Experimental laboratory approaches have the advantage of providing some indication of the relative importance of factors that cannot be easily isolated in naturalistic situations by varying the factors of interest while holding constant other potential contributors. However, the scope of controlled experiments is severely limited. It is precluded for phenomena that are not reproducible in laboratory situations because such phenomena require a lengthy period of development, are the products of complex constellations of influences by different social sources operating interactively, or are prohibited ethically.

The impact of pernicious socialization practices on children's sense of efficacy and aspiration and the extraordinary resilience of some children to severe adversity are not subject to experimental studies. All too often researchers select simple activities that permit at least some change in a single sitting with the predictable caveat that the generalizability of the findings should be tested under more meaningful real-life conditions.

Controlled field studies that systematically vary psychosocial factors under real-life conditions provide greater ecological validity, but they too are limited in scope. Finite resources, limits imposed by social systems on what types of interventions they permit, hard to control fluctuations in quality of implementation, and ethical considerations place constraints on controlled field interventions.

Controlled experimentation must, therefore, be supplemented with controlled investigation of variations in psychosocial factors that are produced naturally linked to possible determinants. For reasons already given, the latter approach is indispensable in the social sciences. For example, longitudinal investigations address the complex interplay of sociostructural, familial, education, and self influences in shaping the course of lives that are socially situated in historical contexts.

Path analysis and structural equation modeling evaluate the patterns of influences as a whole and help to disentangle the unique contribution of sociocognitive factors within the posited causal structures. There are no experimental analogues for these complex, multicausal structures governing human self-development, adaptation, and change. Given the complex multicausality of human functioning and the social and ethical constraints on the opportunity to apply experimentally designed influences, no single investigatory approach can provide a full explanation of behavior.

Determinants of Intraindividual Change

Meaningful tests of the contribution of perceived self-efficacy to performance in intraindividual change over time have several requirements. The structure of the ongoing activity should permit progressive changes in perceived self-efficacy and performance rather than sequentially disjoined activities. In the disconnected activity structure there is nothing learnable that is transferable or controllable from one task to another.

A second requirement for informative research on the functional properties of efficacy beliefs is the use of a dynamic rather than a static environment. Tasks that allow meaningful progressive changes but in which the same activity is performed repeatedly in the same session under invariant conditions not only are minimally informative but can be misinformative. With nothing changing situationally, little being learned, no impediments or stressors to shake performers' self-assurance, and nothing to intrude on attentional focus or disrupt execution of the activity, performance quickly stabilizes, yielding the mundane finding that prior performance correlates highly with subsequent performance. Such static environments reveal little of interest beyond the initial trial.

Vancouver et al. selected a disjoined guessing game in which participants had to guess patterns randomly preset before each game. The disconnectedness precludes any growth of perceived self-efficacy and performance from one game to another. Guesswork also makes ratings of perceived self-efficacy basically trifling. Moreover, the guessing game includes a confound that cannot be disentangled. It is impossible to separate sheer guesses from correct discernment of the solution on a particular game. Indeed, the authors coded some performances as "missing" because participants guessed the correct arrangement on the very first try by sheer luck. When participants guessed correctly, they probably assumed they were becoming more skilled, and therefore they momentarily raised their self-assurance and goals only to have their hope dashed because the task precluded translation of self-belief and goals into improved performance.

When they guessed incorrectly, they probably assumed that they were less able and lowered their goals only to be surprised again by an uptic. This is just the result one might expect on a guessing game.

The obtained sawtooth pattern would produce a weak negative relation of both self-efficacy and goals to performance as an artifact rather than a genuine control process. This can, of course, be easily verified by having participants perform activities that permit skill acquisition and controllability of performance. The peculiarity of the guessing game that yields negative goal effects is most likely responsible for the negative self-efficacy effects as well.

Perceived self-efficacy is measured in terms of judgments of personal capabilities and the strength of that belief. Vancouver et al. had participants estimate the number of attempts it would take to find a solution. The anchors on the strength measure varied from extremely likely to extremely unlikely.

In the context of a guessing game, the anchors suggested estimates of chance rather than explicit judgments of personal capabilities. As one would expect for a guessing game, participants estimated their chances, on average, as around 50% with little variance around this 50-50 probability level.

Negative Self-efficacy Effects

No psychosocial factor, or any other factor for that matter, ever bears an invariant relation to human behavior. Social cognitive theory specifies certain conditions under which an elevated sense of efficacy can have negative effects. Vancouver et al.'s proclaimed discovery of negative efficacy effects is nothing new. The examples Vancouver et al. cited were reported and analyzed in some detail in the volume on the exercise of control through self-efficacy belief. Vancouver et al.'s conceptual and empirical claims of invariant debilitating effects of belief in one's capabilities in intraindividual change do not survive close scrutiny. Self-efficacy theory adopts a conditional view regarding negative effects of an elevated sense of personal efficacy. For example, the functional value of high perceived self-efficacy differs in preparatory and performance aspects of functioning. In preparing for challenging endeavors, some self-doubt about one's performance efficacy provides incentives to acquire the knowledge and skills needed to master the challenges. However, one must distinguish between different aspects of perceived self-efficacy. In the skills development phase, a high sense of learning self-efficacy serves a positive promotive function. Thus, informative peer modeling raises, by observational means, children's beliefs in their own efficacy for learning, which, in turn, predicts both their rate of progress during instructional sessions and their eventual level of mathematical competency.

Thus, even in the preparatory phase of functioning, one need not undermine a sense of efficacy to motivate self-investment in activities, as the control theory under discussion would prescribe. On the contrary, instilling a strong sense of learning efficacy enhances the development of competencies. In managing challenges in performance situations, people need a resilient sense of efficacy that they can achieve desired results by their efforts and try to remain unfazed by setbacks or failure. One cannot execute well-established skills while beset with self-doubt. In applying what one knows, a strong belief in one's performance efficacy is essential to mobilize and sustain the effort necessary to succeed. Control theory would have coaches send their team on the playing field in a self-doubting frame of mind; otherwise they will play complacently. A resilient sense of efficacy provides the necessary staying power in the arduous pursuit of innovation and excellence. During difficult endeavors, people have to invest a great deal of time and effort and have to be willing to take risks under uncertainty. Those of high perceived self-efficacy focus on the opportunities worth pursuing, whereas the less self-efficacious dwell on the risks to be avoided. Among patent inventors, it is those of high perceived self-efficacy who are most likely to start new business ventures.

Venturers who achieve high growth in companies they have founded or who transform those they have bought have a vision of what they wish to achieve, set challenging growth goals, and have a firm belief in their efficacy to realize their goals. Marked discontinuity in environmental circumstances and in adaptational styles are other conditional factors. The very resilient self-efficacy that brings success in tough ventures may perpetuate adherence to practices of questionable utility. Thus, for example, managers of high perceived self-efficacy are more prone than those of low self-efficacy to escalate commitment to unproductive ventures and practices. The corrective for the perils of success is not diminishment of personal efficacy. Such a disenabling remedy would undermine human aspiration, innovation, and performance accomplishments in endeavors presenting tough odds. Some of the problems stem from misreading the environment rather than misjudgment of self-efficacy. The challenge is to preserve the considerable functional value of resilient self-efficacy but at the same time to institute informative monitoring and social feedback systems that help to identify practices that decline in utility.

Social cognitive theory is founded on an agentic perspective to human self-development, adaptation, and change. This theory specifies four core features of human agency, which include intentionality, forethought, selfreactiveness, and self-reflectiveness. People form intentions that include plans and strategies for realizing them. The temporal extension of agency involves more than future plans, however. People set goals for themselves and anticipate likely outcomes of prospective actions to guide and motivate their efforts anticipatorily. Agents are not only planners and forethinkers, they are self-regulators as well. They adopt personal standards and monitor and regulate their actions by self-reactive influence. They do things that give them satisfaction and a sense of self-worth and refrain from actions that bring self-censure. People are not only agents of actions, they are self-examiners of their own functioning. They reflect on their efficacy, the soundness of their thoughts and actions, the meaning of their pursuits, and make corrective adjustments if necessary. Goal theory is similarly rooted in an agentic perspective.

The ontological foundations of control theory in its different versions have never been clearly articulated. This is no easy task given that this theory of cybernetic regulation is a discordant hybrid of agentic functions grafted on a mechanical feedback control system devoid of consciousness or any self-reflective capabilities. To further complicate matters, agentic functions have crept even into the allegedly automatic feedback system, although somewhat dissonantly, as when the cybernetic system is humanized by being equipped with complex information-processing components, endowed with a consciousness, and even granted a free will; furnished with scripts, causal attribution judgments, and calculation of utilities for alternative options; and affixed with affective self-evaluative motivators and self-efficacy beliefs from social cognitive theory.

Moral Disengagement and Inhumanities

Moral agency is manifested in both the power to refrain from behaving inhumanely and the proactive power to behave humanely. Moral agency is embedded in a broader sociocognitive self theory encompassing self-organizing, proactive, self-reflective and self-regulatory mechanisms rooted in personal standards linked to self-sanctions. The self-regulatory mechanisms governing moral conduct do not come into play unless they are activated and there are many psychosocial maneuvers by which moral self-sanctions are selectively disengaged from inhumane conduct. The moral disengagement may center on the cognitive restructuring of inhumane conduct into a benign or worthy one by moral justification, sanitizing language and advantageous comparison; disavowal of a sense of personal agency by diffusion or displacement of responsibility; disregarding or minimizing the injurious effects of ones actions; and attribution of blame to, and dehumanization of, those who are victimized.

Many inhumanities operate through a supportive network of legitimate enterprises run by otherwise considerate people who contribute to destructive activities by disconnected subdivision of functions and diffusion of responsibility. Given the many mechanisms for disengaging moral control, civilized life requires, in addition to humane personal standards, safeguards built into social systems that uphold compassionate behavior and renounce cruelty. The disengagement of moral self-sanctions from inhumane conduct is a growing human problem at both individual and collective levels. Psychological theories of morality focus heavily on moral thought to the neglect of moral conduct. People suffer from the wrongs done to them regardless of how perpetrators might justify their inhumane actions.

The regulation of humane conduct involves much more than moral reasoning. A complete theory of moral agency must link moral knowledge and reasoning to moral action. This requires an agentic theory of morality rather than one confined mainly to cognitions about morality. An agentic theory specifies the mechanisms by which people come to live in accordance with moral standards. In social cognitive theory, moral reasoning is translated into actions through self-regulatory mechanisms rooted in moral standards and self-sanctions by which moral agency is exercised. The moral self is thus embedded in a broader sociocognitive self theory encompassing self-organizing, proactive, self-reflective, and self-regulative mechanisms. These selfreferent processes provide the motivational as well as the cognitive regulators of moral conduct. In early phases of development, conduct is largely regulated by external dictates and social sanctions. In the course of socialization, people adopt moral standards that serve as guides and as major bases for self-sanctions regarding moral conduct. In this self-regulatory process, people monitor their conduct and the conditions under which it occurs, judge it in relation to their moral standards and perceived circumstances, and regulate their actions by the consequences they apply to themselves. They do things that give them satisfaction and build their sense of self-worth. They refrain from behaving in ways that violate their moral standards because such conduct will bring self-condemnation.

The constraint of negative self-sanctions for conduct that violates one's moral standards, and the support of positive self-sanctions for conduct faithful to personal moral standards operate anticipatorily. In the face of situational inducements to behave in inhumane ways, people can choose to behave otherwise by exerting self-influence. Self-sanctions keep conduct in line with personal standards. It is through the ongoing exercise of self-influence that moral conduct is motivated and regulated. This capacity for self-influence gives meaning to moral agency. Selfsanctions mark the presence of moral oughts. The exercise of moral agency has dual aspects-inhibitive and proactive. The inhibitive form is manifested in the power to refrain from behaving inhumanely. The proactive form of morality is expressed in the power to behave humanely. In the latter case, individuals invest their sense of selfworth so strongly in humane convictions and social obligations that they act against what they regard as unjust or immoral even though their actions many incur heavy personal costs. Failure to do what is right would incur self-devaluation costs. In this higher-order morality, people do good things as well as refrain from doing bad things.

Moral standards do not operate invariantly as internal regulators of conduct, however. Selfregulatory mechanisms do not come into play unless they are activated and there are many social and psychological maneuvers by which moral self-sanctions can be disengaged from inhumane conduct. Selective activation and disengagement of personal control permits different types of conduct by persons with the same moral standards under different circumstances. The disengagement may center on the reconstrual of the conduct itself so it is not viewed as immoral; the operation of the agency of action so that the perpetrators can minimize their role in causing harm; in the consequences that flow from actions; or on how the victims of maltreatment are regarded by devaluing them as human beings and blaming them for what is being done to them. The sections that follow document how each of these types of moral disengagement function in the perpetration of inhumanities.

Moral Justification

One set of disengagement practices operates on the cognitive reconstruction of the behavior itself. People do not ordinarily engage in harmful conduct until they have justified to themselves the morality of their actions. In this process of moral justification, detrimental conduct is made personally and socially acceptable by portraying it as serving socially worthy or moral purposes. People then can act on a moral imperative and preserve their view of themselves as a moral agent while inflicting harm on others. Regional variations in the social sanctioning and use of violent means are predictable from moral justifications rooted in a subcultural code of honor. Rapid radical shifts in destructive behavior through moral justification are most strikingly revealed in military conduct. The conversion of socialized people into dedicated fighters is achieved not by altering their personality structures, aggressive drives or moral standards. Rather, it is accomplished by cognitively redefining the morality of killing so that it can be done free from self-censure. Through moral justification of violent means, people see themselves as fighting ruthless oppressors, protecting their cherished values, preserving world peace, saving humanity from subjugation or honoring their country's commitments. Just war tenets were devised to specify when the use of violent force is morally justified. However, given people's dexterous facility for justifying violent means all kinds of inhumanities get clothed in moral wrappings.

Widespread ethnic wars are producing atrocities of appalling proportions. When viewed from divergent perspectives the same violent acts are different things to different people. It is often proclaimed in conflicts of power that one group's terroristic activity is another group's liberation movement fought by heroic fighters. This is why moral appeals against violence usually fall on deaf ears. Adversaries sanctify their own militant actions, but condemn those of their antagonists as barbarity masquerading under a mask of outrageous moral reasoning. Each side feels morally superior to the other.

Euphemistic Labeling

Language shapes thought patterns on which actions are based. Activities can take on very different appearances depending on what they are called. Not surprisingly, euphemistic language is widely used to make harmful conduct respectable and to reduce personal responsibility for it. Euphemizing is an injurious weapon. People behave much more cruelly when assaultive actions are verbally sanitized than when they are called aggression. In an insightful analysis of the language of nonresponsibility, identified the different varieties of euphemisms. One form relies on sanitizing language. By camouflaging pernicious activities in innocent or sanitizing parlance the activities loose much of their repugnancy. Soldiers "waste" people rather than kill them. Bombing missions are described as "servicing the target," in the likeness of a public utility. The attacks become "clean, surgical strikes," arousing imagery of curative activities. The civilians the bombs kill are linguistically converted to "collateral damage." In an effort to sanitize state executions, a United States senator proclaimed that, "Capital punishment is society's recognition of the sanctity of human life." This memorable verbal sanitization won him the uncoveted third-place award in the national Doublespeak competition. Sanitizing euphemisms are also used extensively in unpleasant activities that people do from time to time. In the language of some government agencies, people are not fired, they are given a "career alternative enhancement," as though they were receiving a promotion. Being disfellowshipped is getting one's self fired by the Baptists. In the Watergate hearings, lies became "a different version of the facts."

The television industry produces and markets some of the most brutal forms of human cruelty under the sanitised labels of "action and adventure" programming. The acid rain that is killing lakes and forests is merely, "atmospheric deposition of anthropogenically derived substances." The nuclear power industry has created its own specialized set of euphemisms for the injurious effects of nuclear mishaps. An explosion becomes an "energetic disassembly." And a reactor accident is a "normal aberration." The agentless passive style in depicting events serves as another linguistic tool for creating the appearance that reprehensible acts are the work of nameless forces rather then people. It is as though people are moved mechanically but are not really the agents of their own acts.

Advantageous Comparison

Advantageous comparison is another way of making harmful conduct look good. How behavior is viewed is colored by what it is compared against. By exploiting the contrast principle, reprehensible acts can be made righteous. Terrorists see their behavior as acts of selfless martyrdom by comparing them with widespread cruelties inflicted on the people with whom they identify. The more flagrant the contrasting inhumanities, the more likely it is that one's own destructive conduct will appear benevolent. The massive destruction in Vietnam was minimized by portraying the American military intervention as saving the populous from Communist enslavement. Expedient historical comparison also serves self-exonerating purposes. Exonerating comparison relies heavily on moral justification by utilitarian standards. The task of making violence morally acceptable from a utilitarian perspective is facilitated by two sets of judgments.

— Nonviolent options are judged to be ineffective to achieve desired changes, thus removing them from consideration.

— Utilitarian analyses using advantageous comparisons with actual or anticipated threats by one's adversaries affirm that one' injurious actions will prevent more human suffering than they cause.

The utilitarian cost-benefit calculus, however, can be quite slippery in specific applications. The future contains many uncertainties and ambiguities. Human predictive judgment is, therefore, subject to a lot of biases. As a result, calculations of long-term human costs and benefits are often suspect. There is much subjectivity in estimating the gravity of potential threats. Moreover, violence is often used as a weapon against small threats on the grounds that they will escalate and spread to where they will take a heavy toll on human suffering if left unchecked. The frequently invoked "domino effect" reflects this type of escalative projection error concerning the likely course of events. Judgment of gravity justifies choice of options. But preference for violent options often biases judgment of gravity. Assessments of conflictful realities and the best means to deal with them can be flawed by biasing social processes as well as by inferential errors from uncertain information. Cognitive restructuring of harmful conduct through moral justifications, sanitizing language, and exonerating comparisons is the most powerful set of psychological mechanisms for disengaging moral control. Investing harmful conduct with high moral purpose not only eliminates self-censure. It engages self-approval in the service of destructive exploits. Functionaries work hard to become proficient at them and take pride in their destructive accomplishments.

Displacement of Responsiblity

Moral control operates most strongly when people acknowledge that they cause harm by their detrimental actions. The second set of disengagement practices operates by obscuring, or minimizing the agentive role in the harm one causes. People will behave in ways they normally repudiate if a legitimate authority accepts responsibility for the effects of their conduct. Under displaced responsibility, they view their actions as stemming from the dictates of authorities rather than being personally responsible for them. Because they are not the actual agent of their actions, they are spared self-condemning reactions. Self-exemption from gross inhumanities by displacement of responsibility is most gruesomely revealed in socially sanctioned mass executions.

In psychological studies of disengagement of moral control by displacement of responsibility, authorities explicitly authorize injurious actions and hold themselves responsible for the harm caused by their followers. The sanctioning of harmful conduct in everyday life differs in two important ways from the direct authorizing system examined by Milgram. Responsibility is rarely assumed that openly. Only obtuse authorities would leave themselves accusable of authorizing harmful acts. They usually invite and support harmful conduct in insidious ways for personal and social reasons. Through surreptitious sanctioning practices they can shield themselves from social condemnation should the courses of action go awry. They also have to live with themselves. Sanctioning by indirection enables them to protect against loss of self-respect for authorizing human cruelty. In detrimental schemes, authorities act in ways that keep themselves intentionally uninformed.

Disengagement practices operate within sociopolitical structures that shape their expression and affect their prevalence. Cultural hatreds create low thresholds for the disengagement of moral self-sanctions. Inhumanities toward human beings cast in devalued categories and invested with vile attributes become not only permissible but righteously approvable.

Diffusion of Responsibility

The exercise of moral control is also weakened when personal agency is obscured by diffusing responsibility for detrimental behavior. There are several ways of doing it. A sense of responsibility can be diffused, and thereby diminished, by division of labor. Most enterprises require the services of many people, each performing subdivided jobs that seem harmless in themselves. After activities become routinized into detached subfunctions, people shift their attention from the morality of what they are doing to the operational details and efficiency of their specific job. Group decision making is another common practice that gets otherwise considerate people to behave inhumanely. When everyone is responsible, no one really feels responsible. Social organizations go to great lengths to devise mechanisms for obscuring responsibility for decisions that will affect others adversely. Collective action is still another expedient for weakening moral control. Any harm done by a group can always be attributed largely to the behavior of others. People act more cruelly under group responsibility than when they hold themselves personally accountable for their actions.

Additional ways of weakening moral control operate by disregarding or distorting the effects of one's actions. When people pursue activities that are harmful to others for reasons of personal gain or social pressure, they avoid facing the harm they cause or minimize it. If minimization does not work, the evidence of harm can be discredited. As long as the harmful results of one's conduct are ignored, minimized, distorted or disbelieved, there is little reason for self-censure to be activated. It is easier to harm others when their suffering is not visible and when injurious actions are physically and temporally remote from their effects. When people can see and hear the suffering they cause, vicariously aroused distress and self-censure serve as selfrestrainers. Even a high sense of personal responsibility is a weak restrainer of injurious conduct when aggressors do not see the harm they inflict on their victims. Most organizations involve hierarchical chains of command in which superiors formulate plans and intermediaries transmit them to functionaries who then carry them out. The farther removed individuals are from the destructive end results, the weaker is the restraining power of injurious effects. Disengagement of moral control is easiest for the intermediaries in a hierarchical system-they neither bear responsibility for the decisions nor do they carry them out and face the harm being inflicted.

Dehumanization

The final set of disengagement practices operates on the recipients of detrimental acts. The strength of moral self-censure depends partly on how the perpetrators view the people they mistreat. Correlative interpersonal experiences during formative years, in which people experience joys and suffer pain together, create the foundation for empathic responsiveness to the plight of others. To perceive another in terms of common humanity activates empathetic emotional reactions through perceived similarity and a sense of social obligation. The joys and suffering of those with whom one identifies are more vicariously arousing than are those of strangers or of individuals who have been divested of human qualities. It is, therefore, difficult to mistreat humanized persons without suffering personal distress and self-condemnation. Self-censure for cruel conduct can be disengaged by stripping people of human qualities. Once dehumanized, they are no longer viewed as persons with feelings, hopes and concerns but as subhuman objects. They are portrayed as mindless "savages," "gooks," and the other despicable wretches. If dispossessing one's foes of humanness does not weaken selfcensure, it can be eliminated by attributing demonic or bestial qualities to them. They become "satanic fiends," "degenerates," and other bestial creatures. It is easier to brutalize people when they are viewed as low animal forms, as when Greek torturers referred to their victims as "worms".

During wartime, nations cast their enemies in the most dehumanized, demonic and bestial images to make it easier to kill them. The process of dehumanization is an essential ingredient in the perpetration of inhumanities. The commandant chillingly explained that it was not a matter of purposeless cruelty. Rather, the victims had to be degraded to the level of subhuman objects so that those who operated the gas chambers would be less burdened by distress. In experimental studies of the perniciousness of the combined effect of dehumanization and a diminished sense of personal responsibility, a supervisory team was given the power to punish a group of problem solvers with varying intensities of electric shock for deficient performances. The punishment was administered either personally or collectively to the performing recipients characterized in either humanistic, animalistic or neutral terms. Unbeknown to the supervisors, the administered shocks were never delivered to the recipients. Dehumanized individuals were treated more punitively than those who have been invested with human qualities. In contrast, personalization of responsibility and humanization of others together have a powerful self-restraining effect. The supervisor's self-regulatory evaluative reactions to performing a punitive role differed markedly across the different disengagement conditions. Those who assumed personal responsibility for their actions with humanized individuals rarely expressed self-exonerative justifications and uniformly disavowed punitive sanctions. By contrast, when performers were divested of humaness and punished collectively, the supervisors often voiced exonerative justifications for punitive sanctions and were disinclined to condemn their use. This is especially true when punitive sanctions were dysfunctionally applied in increasing intensities that impaired rather then improved group performance. Self-exonerators behave more harshly than do self-disapprovers of punitive actions.

Many conditions of contemporary life are conducive to impersonalization and dehumanization. Bureaucratization, automation, urbanization and high geographical mobility lead people to relate to each other in anonymous, impersonal ways. In addition, social practices that divide people into ingroup and outgroup members produce human estrangement that fosters dehumanization. Strangers can be more easily depersonalized than can acquaintances. Under certain conditions, wielding institutional power changes the powerholders in ways that are conducive to dehumanization. This happens when persons in positions of authority have coercive power over others with few safeguards for constraining their behavior. Powerholders come to devalue those over whom they wield control. Even college students, who had been randomly assigned to serve as either inmates or guards given unilateral power in a simulated prison, quickly come to treat their charges in degrading, tyrannical ways.

The findings from research on the different mechanisms of moral disengagement are in accord with the historical chronicle of human atrocities: It requires conducive social conditions rather than monstrous people to produce atrocious deeds. Given appropriate social conditions, decent; ordinary people can be led to do extraordinarily cruel things.

Power of Humanization

Psychological theorizing and research tends to emphasize how easy it is to bring out the worst in people through dehumanization and other self-exonerative means. The sensational negative findings receive the greatest attention. For example, Milgram's research on obedient aggression is widely cited as evidence that good people can be talked into performing cruel deeds. What is rarely noted, is the equally striking evidence that most people refuse to behave cruelly, even under unrelenting authoritarian commands, if the situation is personalized by having them inflict pain by direct personal action rather than remotely and they see the suffering they cause. Even when punitive sanctions are the only means available and they are highly functional in producing desired results, those exercising that power cannot get themselves to behave punitively toward humanized individuals. In contrast, when punitive sanctions are dysfunctional because they usually fail to produce results, punitiveness is precipitously escalated toward dehumanized individuals.

The failure of degraded individuals to change in response to punitive treatment is taken as further evidence of their culpability that justifies intensified punitiveness toward them. The emphasis on obedient aggression is understandable considering the prevalence of people's inhumanities to one another. But the power of humanization to counteract cruel conduct also has considerable social import. People's recognition of the social linkage of their lives and their vested interest in each other's welfare help to support actions that instill them with a sense of community. The affirmation of common humanity can bring out the best in others. The moral courage that was honored testifies to the remarkable power of humanization.

Proactive moral action is regulated in large part by resolute engagement of the mechanisms of moral agency. In the exercise of proactive morality people act in the name of humane principles when social circumstances dictate expedient, transgressive and detrimental conduct; they disavow use of valued social ends to justify destructive means; sacrifice their well-being for their convictions; take personal responsibility for the consequences of their actions; remain sensitive to the suffering of others; and see human commonalities rather than distance themselves from others or divest them of human qualities. Social psychology often emphasizes the power of the situation over the individual. In the case of remarkable moral courage, the individual triumphs as a moral agent over compelling situational pressures to behave otherwise. Such moral heroism is most strikingly documented in rescuers who risked their lives, often over prolonged periods fraught with extreme danger, to save from the Holocaust persecuted Jews with whom they had no prior acquaintance and had nothing material or social to gain by doing so.

Humanization can rouse empathic sentiments and a strong sense of social obligation linked to evaluative self-sanctions that motivate humane actions on others' behalf at sacrifice of one's self-interest or even at one's own peril. In the case of the rescuers, a resolute personal obligation for the welfare of persecuted individuals overrode self-concern despite the grave risks and heavy burdens the extended protective care entailed. Rescuers viewed their behavior as a human duty rather than as extraordinary acts of moral heroism. Once the protective relationship was initiated, the development of social bonds heightened the force of empathic concern and moral obligation.

Blaming one's adversaries or circumstances is still another expedient that can serve selfexonerative purposes. In this process, people view themselves as faultless victims driven to injurious conduct by forcible provocation. Punitive conduct is, thus, seen as a justifiable defensive reaction to belligerent provocations. Conflictful transactions typically involve reciprocally escalative acts. One can select from the chain of events a defensive act by the adversary and portray it as initiating provocation. Victims then get blamed for bringing suffering on themselves. Self-exoneration is also achievable by viewing one's harmful conduct as forced by compelling circumstances rather than as a personal decision. By fixing the blame on others or on circumstances, not only are one's own injurious actions excusable but one can even feel self-righteous in the process. Justified abuse can have more devastating human consequences than acknowledged cruelty. Mistreatment that is not clothed in righteousness makes the perpetrator rather than the victim blameworthy. But when victims are convincingly blamed for their plight, they may eventually come to believe the degrading characterizations of themselves. Exonerated inhumanity is, thus, more likely to instill self-contempt in victims than inhumanity that does not attempt to justify itself. Seeing victims suffer maltreatment for which they are held partially responsible leads observers to derogate them. The devaluation and indignation aroused by ascribed culpability provides further moral justification for even greater maltreatment.

Moral Disengagement

Disengagement practices will not instantly transform considerate persons into cruel ones. Rather, the change is achieved by gradual disengagement of self-censure. People may not even recognize the changes they are undergoing. Initially, they perform milder aggressive acts they can tolerate with some discomfort. After their self-reproof has been diminished through repeated enactments, the level of ruthlessness increases, until eventually acts originally regarded as abhorrent can be performed with little personal anguish or self-censure. Inhumane practices become thoughtlessly routinized. The gradual disengagement of morality is illustrated by a prison guard, who assisted in the execution of convicts by gassing. Putting people to death requires subdivision of the task to get someone to do it. The guards role was limited to strapping the legs to the death chair. The process of radicalization involves a gradual disengagement of moral sanctions from violent conduct. It begins with prosocial efforts to change particular social policies and opposition to officials, who are intent on keeping things as they are. Embittering failures to accomplish social change and hostile confrontations with authorities and police lead to growing disillusionment and alienation from the whole system. Escalative battles culminate in terrorists' efforts to destroy the system and its dehumanized rulers.

Disengagement of moral control mechanisms has been examined most extensively in military and political violence. But it is by no means confined to extraordinary circumstances. Quite the contrary. Such mechanisms operate in everyday situations in which decent people routinely perform activities that bring them profits and other benefits at injurious costs to others. Selfexonerations are needed to neutralize self-censure and to preserve self-esteem. Certain industries cause harmful effects on a large scale, either by the nature of their products or the environmental toxification and degradation their operations produce. Disregarding or minimizing injurious consequences, or discrediting the evidence for them is a widely used disengagement practice.

For years the tobacco industry, whose products kill more than 400,000 Americans annually, disputed the view that nicotine is addictive and that smoking is a major contributor to lung cancer. The vast supporting cast contributing to the promotion of this deadly product include talented chemists discovering ammonia as a means to increase the nicotine "kick" by speeding the body's absorption of nicotine; inventive biotech researchers genetically engineering a tobacco seed that doubles the addictive nicotine content of tobacco plants; creative advertisers targeting young age groups with merchandising and advertising schemes depicting smoking as a sign of youthful hipness, modernity, freedom and women's liberation; ingenious officials in a subsidiary of a major tobacco company engaging in an elaborate international cigarette smuggling operation to evade excise taxes; popular movie actors agreeing to smoke in their movies for a hefty fee; legislators with bountiful tobacco campaign contributions exempting nicotine from drug legislation even though it is the most addictive substance and passing preemption laws that block states from regulating tobacco products and their advertising; United States trade representatives threatening sanctions against countries that erect barriers against the importation of U.S. cigarettes, and even a President firing his head of the Department of Health, Education and Welfare for refusing to back off on the regulation of tobacco products. Much work remains to be done in analyzing the particular forms that moral disengagement practices take at industry-wide levels and the justificatory exonerations and social arrangements that facilitate their use.

Advances in the measurement of moral disengagement hold promise of furthering understanding of how this aspect of morality develops and influences the courses lives take. Developmental research shows that moral disengagement is already operating even in the early years of life. It contributes to social discordance in ways that are likely to lead down dissocial paths. High moral disengagers are less troubled by anticipatory feelings of guilt over injurious conduct, are less prosocial, and prone to ruminate about perceived grievances and vengeful retaliation, all of which are conducive to aggression and antisocial conduct. The higher the moral disengagement and the weaker the perceived self-efficacy to resist peer pressure for transgressive activities, the heavier the involvement in antisocial conduct. Gender differences in moral disengagement do not exist in the earlier years. But before long, boys become more facile moral disengagers than do girls. Moral development is typically studied in terms of abstract principles of morality.

Adolescents who differ in delinquent conduct, do not necessarily differ in abstract moral values. Most everyone is virtuous at the abstract level. Amorphous abstractions obscure the dynamic processes governing the selective disengagement of moral self-sanctions. It is in the ease of moral disengagement under the conditionals of life that the differences lie. Among adolescents, facile moral disengagers display higher levels of violence, theft, and other forms of antisocial conduct, than those who bring moral self-sanctions to bear on their conduct. Proneness to moral disengagement predicts both felony and misdemeanor assaults and thefts regardless of age, sex, race, religious affiliation and social class. This predictive generality attests to the pervading role of self-regulatory mechanisms in detrimental conduct. Moral engagement against destructive means can be enhanced in children by peer modeling and espousal of peaceable solutions to human conflicts.

The self-regulation of morality is not entirely an intrapsychic matter as rationalists might lead one to believe. People do not operate as autonomous moral agents impervious to the social realities in which they are immersed. Moral agency is socially situated and exercised in particularized ways depending on the life conditions under which people transact their affairs. Social cognitive theory, therefore, adopts an interactionist perspective to morality. Moral actions are the products of the reciprocal interplay of personal and social influences. Conflicts arise between self sanctions and social sanctions when individuals are socially punished for courses of action they regard as right and just.

Principled dissenters and nonconformists often find themselves in this predicament. Some sacrifice their welfare for their convictions. People also commonly experience conflicts in which they are socially pressured to engage in conduct that violates their moral standards. Responses to such moral dilemmas are determined by the relative strength of self sanctions and social sanctions and the conditional application of moral standards.

Sociostructural theories and psychological theories are often regarded as rival conceptions of human behavior or as representing different levels of causation.

Human behavior cannot be fully understood solely in terms of social structural factors or psychological factors. A full understanding requires an integrated perspective in which social influences operate through psychological mechanisms to produce behavior effects. Some of the moral disengagement practices, such as diffusion and displacement of responsibility, are rooted in the organizational and authority structures of societal systems. The ideological orientations of societies shape the form of moral justifications, sanction detrimental practices and influence which members of society tend to be cast into devalued groups. These sociostructural practices create conditions conducive to moral disengagement. But people are producers as well as products of social systems. Social structures—which are devised to organize, guide, and regulate human affairs—are created by human activity. Moreover, within the rule structures, there is personal variation in their interpretation, adoption, enforcement, circumvention or active opposition. Social cognitive theory avoids a dualism between social structure and personal agency.

Sociostructural influences affect action via self-regulatory mechanisms operating through a set of subfunctions. Neither situational imperatives nor vile dispositions provide a wholly adequate explanation of human malevolence. In social cognitive theory, both sociostructural and personal determinants operate interdependently within a unified causal structure in the perpetration of inhumanities. Unusual forms of malevolence are typically the product of a unique interplay of personal, behavioral and environmental influences.

5

Counselling and Therapeutical Outcome

All the primary psychotherapeutic modalities — individual, group, couple and family therapy—can be used to treat the effects of childhood sexual abuse. For adult male survivors, individual and group treatment are generally considered the most effective treatment formats. Although therapists always need to be flexible and to accommodate to the individual needs of clients, the contributors agree that male survivors are generally best served by first engaging in individual therapy and then moving into group therapy with concurrent individual work on an as-needed basis. Couple or family work may be used as a regular adjunct to the therapeutic process, if this supports a client's recovery. Body work may be a useful addition to a client's heating primarily during the Thriver Phase of therapy. Contributors were quick to point out that the ideal and the possible are not always identical in regards to service provision to male survivors. Circumstances often dictate the realities that both clients and therapists face.

Many clients' choices about therapeutic resources are determined by financial considerations rather than by need. Some geographic areas have limited clinical resources and individual treatment is the only type of therapy available. In other areas, group treatment is available, but there aren't enough individual therapists. Certain aspects of therapy are common to all therapeutic modalities. Developing a therapeutic contract, identifying issues that are contraindicators for therapy, conducting a thorough assessment and evaluating therapeutic outcomes are essential ingredients of therapy, regardless of the treatment modality. These generic components of treatment are discussed below.

Therapeutic Contract

Both sexual abuse and therapy are interpersonal processes. Because of this similarity, for therapy to be healing and not harming, it must occur in a context of ethical and clinical integrity. Both clients and therapists need to have clear guidelines about the relational aspects of therapy. A therapeutic contract clarifies the roles and rules of the therapeutic process. Because therapy is not a static process, the contract has to be renegotiated as therapy progresses. For many survivors, developing a therapeutic contract is an opportunity to practice negotiating their needs. Therapeutic contracts may be written or verbal, depending on the therapist's and client's respective personal styles. Often the formal aspects of the agreement (fee schedules, session times, etc.) will be written down, while the informal, spontaneous aspects of the therapeutic process (planning how to work with particular issues) will be negotiated verbally. For clients who are highly dissociative, writing down therapeutic agreements can be helpful; a written contract provides a tangible record to refer to if they cannot recall what happened during a session.

Some therapists use the contracting process to give their clients information about how they work. For instance, some therapists explicitly inform their clients that they will not become sexually or socially involved with them or create dual roles with them. They tell clients that it is the client's right to pace the therapeutic process and determine its duration. They explicitly give clients permission to debrief or question any interactions that are hurtful, puzzling or unclear, so that the client always has an opportunity to examine the therapeutic process. They may briefly explain their therapeutic style, so that clients can be informed consumers when selecting a therapist. Spending time developing a therapeutic contract is reassuring to new clients. A clear contract circumvents later problems since guidelines for behaviours and actions are outlined prior to needing to use them. Key elements that should be discussed when developing a therapeutic contract are outlined below.

Information boundaries: Clients need to be assured that the therapeutic process is confidential and that their personal history will be respected by the therapist. However, they also need to know that if they abuse themselves or others (including the therapist) or are violent towards their surroundings, it will be considered grounds for breaking therapeutic confidentiality. Therapists should be knowledgeable about the legal aspects of reporting abuse. They must share this information with their clients when applicable. Clients must be informed that if they disclose information about present abuse situations or abusers who have access to young children, police and child welfare agencies must be informed. Safety concerns always precede concerns about confidentiality. Because the abuse occurred in secrecy, some clients are anxious about therapeutic confidentiality. They may need to examine the boundary of confidentiality in some detail in order to feel reassured that therapy will not replicate the abuse process.

Fees: Clients need clear information about how much a therapist charges for his or her services and how he or she expects to be paid. Therapists must be clear about how flexible they are willing to be about fee collection. Clear fee policies assist both clients and therapists.

Structure of sessions: Clients need information about the duration and frequency of sessions. Although these may at times need to be renegotiated to meet unique circumstances, having clear time boundaries is an important way to differentiate therapy from abuse.

Touch boundaries: It is imperative for clients to control when and how they are touched during therapy. Each client must always determine his own touch boundary. During the abuse, the victim was not in charge of how he was touched; therapists must take care not to replicate this experience during therapy sessions. Even routine social rituals, such as shaking hands, should only occur if initiated by the client. Similarly, each therapist must ensure that his or her own comfort zones regarding touch are not infringed; if a client requests a hug, but the therapist is not comfortable with this contact, the therapist needs to own and honour his or her personal boundary. Such behaviour presents the client with a positive role model for respectful touch boundaries.

Prior to engaging in therapy, clients need information about the kind of support they will receive from their therapist outside of scheduled sessions. Clients need to know their therapist's boundaries regarding telephone access and whether the therapist is available for unscheduled emergency sessions. When a therapist goes on holiday, clients need to know whether their therapist has arranged for coverage by another therapist should an emergency arise. Planning for possible crises can reduce a client's level of anxiety. Should a client become sufficiently self-harming that hospitalization is required to monitor his personal safety, he will respond to this plan more easily if he has previously agreed to its merits. Developing emergency contingency plans with clients before engaging in therapy is a useful early step. Some clinicians have a prepared handout for their clients that outlines their policies and procedures. This can reduce the amount of session time that is spent on this information and it leaves the client with a concrete resource for future reference.

In order for abuse-related therapy to be healing rather than retraumatizing, clients need to be ready to address their sexual victimization and therapists need to have sufficient skill to ensure that the therapy is emotionally corrective. Timeliness is an important variable to consider when offering this kind of therapy. These are some of the main reasons that abuse-related therapy would be contraindicated:

Ongoing life crises: If a survivor's life is currently crisis-ridden, working intensively on past trauma will generally only exacerbate his current instability. Clients who have difficulty keeping a job or earning enough money to meet basic needs, or who are in the midst of a relationship breakdown, are not good candidates for abuse-related therapy. They need to focus on these more immediate issues before they engage in abuse-related work. Clients who are actively violent or in an abusive relationship need to address these patterns before they are ready to look beyond these symptoms at the deeper causes of their behaviours. Suicidal or psychotic survivors need to manage these mental health issues before focusing on their victimization. Clients who have active substance or process addictions are not good candidates for abuse-focused therapy until they have developed healthier emotional coping strategies. Although some therapists will work with clients after only six months of sobriety or drug-free time, most therapists working with ex-addicts follow the rule-of-thumb of "one year clean and sober".

Lack of social support: If a survivor is very isolated, therapy must focus on developing social skills and building community before moving into abuse-related processes. Neither a therapist nor a client will be well served if the therapist is the only source of support in the clients life. A lack of social support reinforces clients' dysfunctional beliefs; it supports their self-image of not being deserving of caring and their belief that their victimization experiences are too shameful to be shared with others. Therapy is only a small part of a client's life. Clients need to have companionship and caring within their natural communities as well as in their therapy. Many clients attend 12-step programs as a means of developing new avenues of social support. Interaction with others, in both therapeutic and social ways, is an important part of the recovery process.

Lack of motivation to change: Some clients come to therapy because other people think it would help them. If a client doesn't recognize that he has a problem or that certain aspects of his life are unsatisfactory, he has no motivation to change. Therapy that is focused on childhood sexual abuse requires a commitment on the part of the client; he will have to address painful issues of betrayal and loss in the course of his recovery. If a client does not have an investment in making changes and achieving therapeutic goals during the course of therapy, he is not a good candidate for abuse-related work.

If a therapist is not available to work with a client on an ongoing basis or does not feel competent to work with abuse-focused issues, he or she should refer the client elsewhere. It is very traumatic for a survivor who is beginning to explore the possibility of trusting another person, namely his therapist, only to suddenly have this process threatened because the therapist changes jobs or for some other reason has to terminate the therapy. Of course unanticipated events will occur in both therapists' and clients' lives; however, whenever possible, therapists must respect their clients' needs for stability and safety and try to avoid premature termination.

Client Assessment

When conducting an assessment with an abuse survivor or someone you think may be an abuse survivor, it is very important that clinicians actively solicit information about the abuse and its impact on the client. If you wait for the client to raise these issues, they may never surface. A client may interpret a therapist's lack of active questioning about abuse as support for his own minimization or denial. A client's shame about having been abused maintains his silence about this event; the therapist must gently but actively support and encourage the client to break silence and challenge his feelings of shame. Therapists must be careful not to make assumptions about their clients' abuse experiences; clients must be given time and space to tell their own story in their own words. You can generally assume that most clients will disclose their abuse histories in chunks; clients test their therapists' reactions to partial disclosures before they feel safe enough to make a full and complete disclosure. Usually the parts of the abuse experience that a client feels the greatest shame about will be the last to be told. Therapists have to walk a fine line between opening the door for information about the abuse to surface and being too intrusive.

Therapists' assessment questions need to be specific and worded in a non-judgemental way so as to elicit useful diagnostic material. Instead of asking "Do you have a sleeping disorder?" ask the more open-ended and less threatening question "What is your regular sleeping pattern?" For many clients, dysfunctional coping strategies are ego-syntonic or culturally sanctioned and they do not appear as abnormal. Clinicians must ensure that the questions they ask are precise, straightforward and non-threatening. Some clients' histories are shocking and very upsetting, so clinicians must be prepared to hear the answers to the questions they ask. For example, questions about sexual habits and practices that would be embarrassing in a social context need to be asked as part of a thorough assessment. It is essential that the therapist is comfortable asking questions about masturbation, sexual fantasies, sexual practices, anger, fear and other culturally-sensitive or emotionally-loaded issues. If the therapist is uncomfortable, this will be communicated to the client, who may then disclose only partial information in an attempt to make the therapist feel more at ease.

In general, the more thorough the assessment, the fewer surprises will emerge in therapy. If during the assessment process it becomes apparent that a client is highly dissociative, then the clinician can prepare to work with someone who has possible MPD or other related symptoms. Client confidence and safety are increased by predictability, so time spent in conducting a thorough assessment is generally repaid later in the therapeutic process. Some clients exhibit symptoms associated with abuse, but they do not have a cognitive memory of having been victimized. It is important that clients who have repressed memories do not feel ashamed because they're unable to recollect their experiences and are not forced to remember events before their unconscious is ready to do so. Therapists must let the abuse history come from the client and not contaminate the therapeutic process by placing expectations on the client to disclose memories prematurely. When a client recovers repressed memories in a timely fashion, he trusts his own recollection and doesn't undermine his recovery by questioning the validity of his experience.

If a clinician is uncertain about the dynamics that a client is presenting, he or she should consult with a knowledgeable colleague. The assessment process lays the foundation for the rest of the therapy; it is important that clients are not over or under-pathologized as a result of this process. Certain key areas need to be carefully assessed. These are:

General family/social history: Frequently victims of sexual abuse have traumatic events other than having been sexually abused that have shaped their lives. Clinicians need to conduct a thorough family and social history to understand the important events (and people) in a client's life. Problematic areas, such as violence or a lack of social support, need to be assessed. However, clients also need a clear inventory of their strengths and resources.

Successful patterns and helpful strengths are as important as problem areas and trauma. The survivor's current life patterns must be carefully assessed. The client's status vis-a-vis work, relationships, health, parenting roles and skills and so on, need to be determined. Until a client's day-to-day life is functioning adequately, focusing on abuse-related events can be counter-therapeutic.

Sexual history: During the assessment, a survivor may or may not be able to disclose specific information about his sexual victimization. If the therapist frames his questions carefully, he can increase his client's comfort in sharing whatever conscious memories he does have. Information is then shared with the therapist as the client chooses, leaving the client in charge of his disclosure process. Since many clients are afraid that the therapist will take a voyeuristic interest in their sexual past (as the abuser did), reducing the level of threat and shame in presenting their sexual histories is very important. Dimock suggests providing clients with a means of categorizing their abuse experiences. He gives his clients a list of four categories of sexual behaviour with several examples in each. These are:

a) chargeable offenses
b) growing up in a sexualized atmosphere
c) intrusive behaviours
d) inappropriate relationships where the child is placed in an adult role with sexual implications

To the extent that is possible, the survivor's sexual history should include information about specific behaviours that occurred during the abuse, who was present, how old the client was when the abuse was occurring, how old his abuser(s) was, how he felt at the time and whether he has sensory memories (taste, smell, etc.) from the abuse. If the client has made previous disclosures, he should be asked about these experiences. Whether he was believed or not and whether he was supported or not, can have an impact on his expectation about how you will receive his present disclosure of victimization.

Coping Strategies

Clients need to be asked about the ways, both functional and dysfunctional, that they have coped with the impacts of being sexually abused. Many clients are unable to articulate their coping mechanisms; however, it is often the dysfunctional coping strategies the client has been using that have brought him into therapy. Dissociative behaviours need to be assessed. Frequently, educating clients about dissociative processes and increasing their awareness of when they are engaging in these behaviours is a necessary step before a full assessment. Survivors often exhibit dominant sympathetic nervous system symptoms such as an exaggerated startle response or chronic muscle tension. Many survivors live in a chronic state of emotional fear and anxiety. Hence the normal balance between their sympathetic and parasympathetic nervous systems is disturbed. Anxiety attacks, excessive irritability and hypervigilance are common symptoms experienced by sexual trauma survivors. Eating and sleeping patterns are often disrupted. Difficulty in failing asleep or waking up in the middle of the night, an inability to digest food or rapid weight loss indicate an overworked sympathetic nervous system. Many survivors develop addictions or compulsive behaviours in an effort to mask their abuse-related emotions. The very issues that the addictions were developed to cover will resurface during therapy.

Evaluating Therapy

Both clients and therapists need a means of evaluating the therapeutic process. When questioned about whether they use formal or informal methods to evaluate their work, most of the contributors replied that they used informal methods to determine the success of their work. The small number of contributors who routinely used formal evaluation procedures with their clients tended to use standardized psychological tests in a pre/post test format to measure treatment outcomes. Contributors who use informal methods to evaluate their clients' progress ask their clients for feedback on the therapeutic process. Changes such as a reduction in PTSD symptoms or trauma-based intrusive memories, increased self-awareness, affective improvements and cognitive restructuring are used to measure the success of the therapy. Client satisfaction and life changes, achievement of identified goals, improved work or relationship functioning are other indicators of improvement.

Clinicians who use formal tests need to demystify them with their clients. Tests need to be fully explained to ensure that clients understand their potential usefulness and give informed consent prior to taking them. The limitations of testing (false negatives or false positives) also need to be discussed, so that clients realize that testing is not an infallible process. Contributors who evaluate their clients with standardized tests use both scales which have been specifically designed for use with sexual abuse survivors and other generic psychological tests. The Dissociative Experiences Scale (DES)—a screening tool to identify survivors with high levels of dissociation—is a self-report test that measures three main factors:

1) amnestic dissociation;
2) absorption and imaginative involvement; and
3) experiences of depersonalization and derealization.

The Trauma Symptom Checklist (TSC-33) is a 33-item checklist specifically developed to tap post-traumatic psychological disturbance. The test measures five clinical subscales (dissociation, anxiety, depression, sleep disturbance and hypothesized post sexual abuse trauma) as well as developing an overall measure of trauma. This test was developed by John Briere and his colleagues; the TSC-33 is described in Therapy For Adults Molested As Children. The non-abuse specific psychological tests that some contributors' use to assess and evaluate their clients are the Tenessee Self-Concept Scale, the Beck Depression Inventory, the Hudson Self-Esteem Scale and the Minnesota Multiphasic Personality Inventory (MMPI).

Some clinicians monitor and evaluate therapy on a regular basis; every fourth or sixth session they will review the process of therapy with their clients. Others evaluate less during the course of therapy, but after termination they make follow-up phone calls to monitor the stability of therapeutic changes. Therapists who work with adolescents will sometimes elicit feedback from their clients' parents or teachers to ascertain whether therapy is being helpful. Group clients sometimes use a peer review process to monitor change and progress. Most clinicians define therapeutic success by items such as increased self-esteem in their clients. Relying on a client's self-assessment in addition to the therapist's own observations of a client's change is generally an adequate basis upon which to evaluate therapy. Evaluative tools that are easy to administer are an underdeveloped and underutilized resource in clinical work, especially in regard to therapy with abuse survivors. Impressionistic data is the most common form of therapeutic evaluation.

The success of psychotherapy in general and abuse-related psychotherapy in particular, depends on the nature of the relationship between the therapist and the client. Clients need adequate safety in the relationship to be able to learn and grow. Therapists need sufficient skill and integrity to be able to enhance and support their clients' learning. As clients develop an awareness of their own psychological processes and make their unconscious responses to trauma conscious, they begin to develop options and choices in how they respond to events in their lives. Dysfunctional patterns that were created to cope with trauma in earlier developmental stages can be replaced by more healthful responses that are appropriate to the client's present life circumstances.

The reason that most clinicians suggest male survivors begin with individual work is that an essential feature of abuse-related therapy is safety. Without sufficient safety, a client cannot address his past history of abuse. If he is focused on here-and-now concerns, he cannot free sufficient psychic energy to address his past. Individual sessions provide a client with an opportunity to develop familiarity with both a therapist and the therapeutic process. In individual therapy, the client is encouraged to speak about his victimization and he is believed and supported. Individual therapy permits a therapist to assess his client's skills and deficits and permits a client to develop a safe and supportive relationship with another adult. These two tasks are essential precursors to participation in abuse-focused group therapy.

The focus of early abuse-related therapy is on reclaiming and validating the facts and impacts of the client's victimization. The therapist gives his or her client permission to remember and acknowledge his sexual abuse and listens to his disclosures in a supportive, nonjudgemental manner. The therapist gently questions the client about his past and begins to challenge distorted abuse-generated cognitions that the client has drawn about himself, others and the world at large.

During this stage of therapy the therapist works with the client to ensure that therapy is a safe-enough process; this may require teaching the client containment skills (e.g. techniques for managing flashbacks or anxiety attacks) and expanding his understanding of abuse-related processes by sharing psycho-educational materials. The client's behaviours are normalized and destigmatized. He is encouraged to openly examine his abuse experience and its subsequent impacts on him. He is helped to befriend parts of his experience and parts of himself that he has felt ashamed of or pushed away. You can often facilitate this process by the use of gentle humour.

Inner child work

During the Victim Phase of therapy the inner child metaphor can be introduced. Most clients are helped by the discovery that they have several different ego states. In general, the more dissociated the client, the greater the number of his ego states. Recognizing that different ego states can conflict with one another, or react separately to the same stimulus, can help clients to be more self-accepting, and to better understand their own behaviour. When clients begin to see the "child" part of themselves as having been traumatized and mistreated, they open the door for developing self-loving rather than self-hating ways of being. They begin to develop compassion for themselves, a compassion which is experienced regardless of their affective or cognitive state. Gradually the client is invited to accept responsibility for "reparenting" the parts of himself that were inadequately parented in his childhood; he is reassured that the therapist is available to act as his guide or coach in this process, so that he has sufficient support for the task.

For some men, the inner child metaphor is difficult to accept initially. Being child-like or having childish ways of reacting to situations, is seen in a negative light. This rejection of the immature components of self can sometimes be overcome by using metaphors of captivity. Likening an abused child to a prisoner of war whose captors used him for their own ends can assist some men to have greater understanding of the situation they were in as children. Acknowledging that even battle-trained soldiers decompensate in situations of captivity can help some victims become less self-blaming and more self-respecting regarding their own responses to having been abused. Other men can experience compassion for a girl more easily than they can for a boy. These men believe that males should be more resilient to suffering than females, no matter what their age or situation. With such men, retelling the client's own abuse-related history but changing the gender of the victim can elicit the compassionate feelings that they cannot feel on their own behalf. When they express concern on behalf of the fictional girl-victim, they can be reminded that the very same events happened to them and that they also deserve to be treated with compassion.

Visualization

Visualization can be a useful technique for some clients to acquaint themselves with their "inner child". Before leading a client into this type of visualization, ask him to identify "anchors" for his adult-self and his present resourcefulness. These adult reminders can be concrete objects, such as the client's wedding ring or some other symbol of his adult status. Should the client become anxious during the visualization, he can recathect his adult self by touching this symbolic object. Once the client is grounded in his present reality, lead him into a visualization process by asking him to close his eyes and inducing deep relaxation. If the client is not comfortable closing his eyes, instruct him to focus on one spot in the room while paying attention to his breathing and body sensations. Once the client is deeply relaxed, ask him to get in touch with the child he was just before the abuse began.

When closing the visualization, ask the client's adult-self to ensure that the child is feeling safe and protected before leaving the imagery. There may be some imagined action that will have to occur before the child is ready to say good-bye. At first, many clients have difficulty contacting their inner child. A client may feel self-conscious taking part in a visualization process or may report that his inner child doesn't want any contact because he feels untrusting or afraid. However, if the client is willing to persevere and if you coach him about how to approach an untrusting or fearful child, he will eventually make contact with his child-self. When this occurs, the client is often surprised at how this process can stimulate intense feelings and memories and at how powerfully healing it is to learn to parent the child-self.

Guided imagery is a powerful tool for helping clients develop their abilities to create safe personal boundaries. Contributors use this technique in a variety of ways. Here are two of them.

— *Container visualization:* Clients often experience intrusive memories or find themselves obsessively thinking about their abuse experiences. Helping them develop an imaginary "container" in which they can place these memories or thoughts, knowing that they will be there whenever they want to recall them, provides relief. After ensuring that the client is anchored to his present adult status by some concrete anchors, lead him through a progressive muscle relaxation exercise, until he is deeply physically relaxed. When he shows signs of relaxation, such as rhythmic breathing or closed eyes, instruct him to imagine a container, either a real one or one that he creates in the moment, that is very secure and to which only he has access. Invite him to place experiences, such as intrusive memories and recurring thoughts, in this container and to practice taking them in and out of the container at will. Tell him that whenever he chooses, he can use this container to store his thoughts or feelings. He can always retrieve them when he chooses or he can keep them in the container for as long as he wants.

Some therapists use this exercise to close a session during the early stages of therapy. Just before the client leaves the session, lead him into a trance in which he locates his container and tell him: "Leave any thoughts you don't want to be aware of until your next session in your container." Then gradually bring him back into the here-and-now reality of the therapy room. Training clients to use this technique on a regular basis makes it a familiar way of managing intrusive internal experiences. The more this skill is practised, the more effective it becomes.

—*Place of safety visualization:* As with the container visualization begin this exercise by leading the client through a progressive relaxation exercise until he shows signs of deep relaxation. Tell him to take himself to a place, real or imagined, where he can be by himself in complete comfort and security. Keep your instructions about locating this place deliberately vague, so that the client's unconscious has the freedom to produce a suitable image for his needs at the moment. Ask your client to fully experience this internal place—to hear, see, smell, taste and feel what it's like. Ask him to anchor his safe place with a hand posture or a readily available physical object (e.g. a marble or stone). Then, if he feels anxious, instruct him to make the hand posture or feel the stone and to signal all levels of his consciousness that he's relaxing and entering a safe place. Tell him that he can return to this place whenever he chooses—no one else need know when he's doing this.

Once the client has firmly established a safe inner sanctuary, you can ask him, in a variation on this visualization, to invite someone he trusts and respects to visit his place of safety. If he wants, he can ask his visitor questions or he can receive affirmations from his guest. At all times the client must be in charge of his safe place and if he has any resistance to inviting someone else into it, this must be respected. To close this visualization, ask the client to gradually leave his safe place, return to his body and, when ready, return to the therapy room. Like the container exercise, this technique becomes more effective if it is practised frequently and becomes a regular feature of a client's self-care.

Life book

Invite survivors to revisit the events of childhood with an adult's eye by creating a "life book". Instruct your client to buy a hard-cover lined notebook or scrapbook. The book should be of good quality to reinforce the importance of its contents. Tell your client to assign each page a year, starting with the year of his birth and working up to the present. For each year, ask him to write stories or make notes about himself at that time. The focus is always on the client—if traumatic events happened to others around him, tell him to write about these events as they affected him. The client should leave space at the bottom of the page or in the margin so that he can add later comments to his life story. The life book is an active and concrete task that provides a way to organize flashbacks and memories in a nonthreatening manner. It indicates time periods in which memories are blocked or repressed. It helps clients recognize their own survival strengths and it opens the door for reflection on their life experience. Clients can be as imaginative as they wish in how they create and use their life books. When reviewing the life book with each client, ask "What are you learning about yourself in this process?"

Life story

A similar, but shorter, exercise is having a client tell you his life story. It is helpful to use a structured format so that the survivor has control of the process. Storytelling needs to be a healing experience, not a retraumatizing one. Ask your client to tell you about his family by drawing a genogram on a whiteboard or by bringing in pictures of family members. Symbolic objects, such as rocks or stones, can be used to represent family members. As the client tells his personal history, assist him to identify the ways that he learned to survive his abuse and to look for themes and patterns in his life.

Drawing the abuse

This can be an effective intervention for clients who are more comfortable with creative media than they are with talking. Give your client a large pad of paper—the size of the paper evokes childhood responses—and tell him to take the paper home and "draw the abuse". Make it clear that this is not an art exercise but rather an opportunity for the client to recall and clarify events that happened in his past. Tell him to draw a scene in his life before the abuse occurred and then to draw specific scenes of his abuse, using a comic-strip format. For instance, he can draw a bubble coming out of his head to describe what he was thinking or feeling, or put captions under his drawings to explain what is going on in them. Ask the client to bring his drawings into a therapy session and question him about the information they contain. Don't interpret the drawings—any interpretation that occurs should be the client's. Often concretizing the images of his abuse makes them seem more real to the client and brings his memories and feelings into greater awareness. In touching the client's self-portrait, the therapist symbolically touches the client, which can nurture the client in a nonthreatening manner.

Script recognition

This intervention is relatively common practice for therapists trained in Transactional Analysis (TA) and it is well suited for clients who were intrafamilially sexually abused. Six different ego states are identified and each one is symbolized by a chair or cushion. The first ego state is the "nurturing parent" who is competent in meeting his or her own needs and acknowledges his or her child's needs as separate from his or her own. The second is the "critical parent", who contaminates his or her interactions with the child by his or her own unmet needs. This parent may be critical and punitive, or smothering and overprotective, and does not listen to the child's expression of his own needs. The third is the "adult", who is the rational, logical ego state. The adult is able to analyze situations and seek out new information or skills to support new directions and growth.

The final three ego states are the "natural child", the "compliant child" and the "rebellious child". The natural child is the source of feelings, spontaneity and creativity. It also carries the wound of the abuse. The compliant and rebellious child ego states are reactive adaptations to the influence of the critical parent and distortions of the natural child's energy. Once the ego states have been described and identified, ask the client to sit in the position representing the ego state in which he spent most of his time as a child. The timeframe can be divided into before and after the abuse. Encourage him to talk about his experience of being in this place. Ask him to identify the positions that his father and mother usually occupied and to sit in these respective positions and role-play each parent.

This is generally an intense and useful process for clients. Recognizing family members' scripted roles can be liberating as clients realize their own part in maintaining the script and the options they have to create change. The client's first step in altering these processes is becoming clear about the overt and covert messages he absorbed as a child and the dynamics he continues to enact in loyalty to his family.

During a session in which a client is talking about his history of abuse or his current life, suggest that he sit quietly and focus on the sensations that are occurring in his body. Ask him to notice if one body sensation or one feeling is particularly noticeable. If he says yes, ask him to really develop his awareness of this sensation. After some time spent in exploring the sensation, ask him if he has any images that come to mind that are connected with the bodily experience he was focusing on. Any images or feelings that surface for the client can be explored and worked with. This technique can help clients retrieve repressed memories and honour their kinesthetic awareness. The above interventions are samples of the type of work that occurs in the early stages of therapy. As the client becomes more aware of his victimization and most importantly, the effects it has had on his life, he begins to move out of the victim phase into the survivor phase where the therapeutic journey often becomes more intense. When a client stops blaming himself and starts holding the offender accountable for the abuse, he frees up his psychic energy to address the emotions that he has kept out of awareness.

Individual Therapy

Survivor Phase

During this stage of therapy, the client reclaims dissociated parts of the self (behaviour, cognition and/or affect) and develops new options for handling current life stressors and past traumatic events. The middle phase of therapy, the Survivor Phase, is generally the longest and most difficult. During this phase the client is challenged to identify where, in his current life, he continues to act out the effects of his victimization and to develop more adaptive living strategies. The client's key task at this stage is to develop and internalize new behaviours and beliefs to replace the dysfunctional patterns he has unconsciously developed as a result of his victimization. Generally the client also engages in abreactive and regressive work during this phase of therapy. These processes unlock repressed emotions and, when well orchestrated, allow the client to integrate previously undigested psychic material. By the time a client enters the survivor phase of therapy, his relationship with his therapist will have matured, permitting him to take greater risks in the therapy process. Consequently, difficult tasks such as working with the client's internalized abuser can be addressed in this phase. The intensity of this stage of therapy can be taxing on both client and therapist. Both parties need to have adequate self-care skills to ensure that their stamina and motivation are sustained throughout this often difficult time. There are several key therapeutic themes that emerge in the Survivor Phase of therapy:

— Working with revenge;
— perpetration and sexual fantasies;
— working with addictive and compulsive processes;
— working to increase clients' affective range; and
— working with dissociative processes.

Your clients' fantasies contain important data about their sexual victimization and their reactions to it. The therapeutic relationship must provide opportunities to talk about these fantasies in a non-shaming manner. However, survivors are often reluctant to disclose these fantasies because they feel ashamed of them or are afraid of being judged.

Revenge fantasies

Most sexually abused men have active revenge fantasies in which they imagine getting even with their abuser. Generally, when asked about their revenge fantasies, clients will reveal their most innocuous fantasy first, until they know they are safe to share more information. Clients need to be supported for revealing their fantasies. They need to know that when fantasies are owned and spoken about rather than kept a secret, they are less likely to gain momentum and be enacted. Revenge fantasies expose the client's rage and anger. It can be helpful to suggest that the client draw or symbolically act out his fantasy in therapy, while simultaneously discharging his rageful emotions.

One symbolic enactment that has proven effective is to cover an old cardboard box with reminders of the abuser and the abuse and then to destroy it. This can occur either in the therapy session or under other circumstances. However, the process should be shared with at least one supportive companion so that the client knows that his anger at his abuser is not shameful or secretive. Whenever a client reveals previously hidden fantasies, he needs to debrief both the content of the fantasy and the process of disclosure. Subsequent to disclosing their fantasies, many clients feel very ashamed of having exposed their private fantasy to their therapist. They may become self-punishing or self-harming if they do not have sufficient internal permission to express these feelings and fantasies.

Therapists need to be alert to these dynamics and to ensure that their clients have adequate self-care skills to participate in emotionally intense interventions. Clinicians may frequently need to remind their clients of the difference between fantasy and actual behaviour so that their fantasies can be acknowledged and worked with during the therapeutic process.

If a survivor has perpetrated against another person, he must be held accountable for his behaviour and take responsibility for having offended. He should feel appropriate guilt for this behaviour while simultaneously contextualizing it in relation to his own victimization so that he can own his behaviour in a non-shaming way. If a survivor's offenses are recent or indicate a repetitive pattern, his recovery process will be prolonged while he engages in therapy focused on his offending issues. Although many survivors have never offended against another person, they may have fantasies in which they imagine themselves abusing a child. Some survivors are very fearful that they may become sexual with a child and they are anxious about these deviant thoughts.

To address this issue, a therapist will need to help the client understand where his fears of becoming a perpetrator originate. For some clients, they stem from an over-identification with the perpetrator. For other clients, they are based on having developed "contaminated" sexual arousal patterns during the abuse experience. Having been aroused during his victimization, the client has created masturbatory fantasies which are based on this experience. His subsequent sexual arousal becomes intertwined with abuse-related fantasies. To address the client's fears of perpetration, the therapist may need to teach cognitive techniques such as thought stopping, so that the client can control his fear-related thoughts or deviant fantasies. If a client has used abuse-related fantasies to reinforce his sexual arousal, he will need to develop other, more appropriate fantasies.

The client will also need to reality-test his fears. He needs to examine his current adult life to look for signs that indicate a propensity to abuse children. Generally there are none. The therapist may need to remind him that he has ways of meeting his needs as an adult that were not available to him as a child. If the client's fears persist, with his therapist he can develop a plan to put into place should he begin to exhibit problematic behaviours. Developing a contingency "safety plan" is generally very reassuring to clients who are afraid that they may behave destructively.

Compulsive Behaviours

Alcohol, drug, food and sexual addictions are common among abused men, as are other compulsive behaviours such as overworking or compulsive exercising. Therapists must be careful not to focus on the addictive symptoms at the expense of the underlying issues that the addictive behaviour was developed to mask. Addictions serve many purposes. They can be a means of meeting needs that are otherwise not being met or they can be a way to create a distraction in order to avoid acknowledging certain feelings or awarenesses. People develop addictive behaviours because, at least in the short run, they help them cope with experiences they have inadequate skills to address. In order to change addictive processes, a client has to understand the emotions that drive his behaviour and he must be willing to recognize the cost of his addictions in his life. He must be willing to experiment with different options for addressing the unmet needs that have maintained his compulsive behaviour.

Therapists must be careful not to engage in a power struggle with an addicted client. A client must be invested in changing his compulsive behaviour if he intends to develop alternative coping mechanisms. If the therapist is more invested in this change than his or her client, the therapist will become frustrated. The therapist must always be aware that only the client has the power to change his behaviour. Many therapists recommend that their addicted clients attend appropriate 12-step programs; these groups offer support, information and a predictable structure that can greatly enhance a client's progress in managing his addictive patterns. Towards this end, therapists must keep themselves informed about 12-step self-help recovery and maintain connections with their local 12-step fellowships.

As the client becomes aware of the state of mind, or feelings, that he has been blocking with his compulsive behaviour, he needs support to tackle them directly and develop healthy alternatives for self-care. Often a client will have an abreactive experience as he lets himself feel the affect that he has been blocking with his addictive behaviour. This abreaction may generate information about the seed of the addiction. This may enable the client, either gradually or suddenly, to come to terms with the previously unacceptable state of mind or feeling.

Many male survivors have difficulty contacting their feelings. They equate the expression of emotion with vulnerability and powerlessness. Men often believe that they can rely on their physical strength to protect themselves from feeling fearful or vulnerable. Other survivors fear that if they open the door to the expression of their feelings, they will be flooded by uncontrolled affect. Because repressed emotions are often quite powerful, and, given that the survivor equates feelings with (in some sense) nonsurvival, the former abuse victim may actually believe that emotional release is dangerous. It is important that therapists do not push their clients into affective expression before they are ready. To do so would be counter-productive because it invites resistance and creates a power struggle. Entering intense emotions too quickly may scare some clients away from therapy. Expressing repressed emotions is a natural outcome of the healing process. Therapists and clients must trust that a client will know when he is ready to experience his feelings about the abuse directly.

For some clients, strong emotional release will not be a necessary aspect of their healing. For others, especially those who are unconsciously acting out their emotions in their current relationships, active expressive work will be crucial for them to make the link between their repressed emotions and their current behaviour. Whenever intense affective work or abreactive work, occurs in therapy, it is important that it is structured in ways that increase the client's power and mastery. Recreating the original trauma without making therapeutic gains is countertherapeutic for the client.

Clients need to be taught skills for identifying and handling their emotional processes. Many somatic experiences, such as migraine headaches or chronic back pain, cover unexpressed emotions. As the client develops his full capacity to express his emotions, his physical complaints diminish. Many survivors experience their emotional lives in an all-or-nothing manner. They either block their feelings and push them out of their awareness, or they let their feelings explode and are overwhelmed by them. Until clients learn healthy affective containment skills and develop functional ways of expressing feelings, they are likely to continue all-or-nothing emotional response patterns. Predicting this likelihood can assist clients in managing their emotional inconsistencies while they are developing healthier patterns of managing their emotions.

Many clients need support in developing a vocabulary for identifying their different emotions. Therapists can teach clients that their emotions fall on a continuum and that they can have varying degrees of fear, anger, joy and sadness. Clients can be asked to become keen observers of others to see how different people express their emotions. Personal and cultural injunctions that limit men's expression of feeling can be identified and challenged. Anger is a feeling that most men have cultural permission to express; It often becomes a unidimensional expression of feeling that consumes all other emotions. Other emotions, such as fear or sadness, can become distorted into anger and rage. In order to discover the feelings that underlie their anger, clients must first be helped to fully experience their angry feelings. For this to happen, men need to make a clear distinction between anger and violence. Permission to feel and express anger must never be confused with permission to behave violently.

Usually survivors find that the emotion they most need to express is not the anger they are feeling, but the fear or another underlying feeling (such as profound sadness), that has been hidden by this mask of anger. Separating primary and secondary feeling processes is part of the therapeutic journey in the survivor phase. For example, when a survivor begins to realize that he gets into fights with others when he is trying to avoid feeling fearful, he can begin to address his fear directly. For men who are very afraid of uncovering their emotional responses, creating distance from the intensity of their feelings can, paradoxically, help them to contact their affect. Asking men to talk about their feelings in the third person, as if they were talking about a good friend, can help them reclaim this aspect of their lives.

If survivors have very ambivalent feelings, such as feeling both intense love and intense rage at their abuser, therapists must be careful to support both these emotions. Premature efforts towards integration of ambivalence can slow the course of healing. Although the client may be frustrated by the apparently contrary feelings that he experiences, both his conflicting emotions speak to his emotional truth, and both must be honoured. Many abused clients need to learn that both love and anger can be felt simultaneously and that the two feelings are not mutually exclusive. Since the repressed or disowned feelings that survivors bring into therapy are based on past experience, it is helpful for the therapist to suggest future possibilities to the client to help him change his present emotional patterns. Talking about a future in which the client feels emotionally integrated and his feelings are in harmony with his thoughts and behaviours, can seed the expectation that this is an achievable goal for the client to work towards.

Contributors have used a variety of techniques to assist their clients to increase their affective expression. Some use music to elicit their client's feelings, playing a love song during a session and asking the client to imagine singing it to himself. This exercise may reveal resistance to loving oneself or cynicism about the concept of love.

Whatever specific response emerges, it will be a doorway to further exploration of affective responses. Using the gestalt empty chair technique is a method that some contributors use to assist their clients to discover their feeling responses. Clients who are concrete and practical in their orientation may have difficulty engaging in this type of activity. Clients who are willing to participate in this intervention can have their entry into the exercise "primed" by having them write a letter to the person or the part of themselves, that they want to put in the empty chair. They can then start the dialogue by reading this letter out loud. It is important that clients understand that the letters they write in therapy are not intended to be sent to the actual person to whom they are addressed; rather they are directed to the internalized image of that person which the client carries in his mind.

Clients who are comfortable with nonverbal media can be asked to construct a collage to show what it feels like to be victimized, angry or grieving. During the process of making the collage, or while it is being discussed in therapy, the client will generally contact the affect associated with the events shown in the collage. Some contributors use breathwork as an intervention in emotional release. Increasing the frequency of the breathing pattern, as in holotropic breathwork, can encourage a client to regress. Therapists who use these types of techniques require considerable training in them before they can use them expertly.

Less technical forms of breathwork can occur that assist survivors to develop skills to manage their emotions. Clients can be asked to become aware of their breath while they are focused on a train of associative events that elicit emotional responses. This ensures that they do not start to hold their breath as the intensity of feeling increases. Clients can be coached to send their breath to a particular part of their body or to give a sound to their breath, in order to shift their emotional awareness to a deeper level. The suggestion that a client let his breath carry out the feelings that are flooding him as he remembers a traumatic memory can give a survivor a new option of being able to hold the memory in his awareness without being traumatized by it. Practising breathing techniques which induce physical relaxation gives a client confidence that he can be present with his memories of the abuse without being overwhelmed by them. Various forms of emotionally expressive work are used by contributors to support their client's affective growth. The purpose of this kind of work is to recathect the original feelings that were dissociated during the abuse and to externalize them in concrete form so that the client can increase his comfort with, or reduce his fear of, these emotions. For instance, if a client is feeling loss and sadness about his lack of self-esteem, he can be asked to engage in a tug-of-war (using a towel or some other suitable prop) to take back his self-esteem.

During the tug-of-war, coach the client to verbalize and vocalize his anger at having his self-esteem damaged by his abuser. Similarly, if a client wants to rid himself of his feelings of sexual shame, he can be helped to construct a way of literally pushing these feelings away from himself. The key in such dramatizations is to be alert for clues and cues from the client that suggest a way of concretizing and externalizing feelings and affective processes. Role-plays can be a very effective way to elicit emotions. If a scene from a client's abuse is role-played, it is advisable to subsequently role play scenes which give the client nurturing and protective messages so that the client can develop a supportive and caring inner script.

Clients should not be asked to role-play their perpetrators during the survivor phase of therapy. If this is done at all, it should not occur until the thriver phase. If a client plays his perpetrator before he has thoroughly addressed his own emotional reactions to the abuse, he can become too aware of the offender's vulnerabilities and prematurely forgive his perpetrator without fully exploring his own emotional processes.

Bioenergetic anger releases are used by some contributors to help clients find a powerful, but safe, outlet for their rage. Therapists must ensure that prior to engaging in this type of intervention they make a contract with their clients to stop this work should either the therapist or the client become concerned about the direction it starts to take. Therapists need to be familiar with this type of work so that they are emotionally available to the client during the emotional release and not preoccupied with their own reaction to the client's intense feelings. Clients who engage in anger-focused work need to be coached to keep their eyes open and feet firmly grounded so that they don't move into a blind rage. After this kind of work, the client needs to debrief it thoroughly so that he can integrate any new insights that he gains through the process.

Any props that a therapist needs to support active emotional release work, such as tennis racquets, towels, pillows, etc., need to be readily available in his or her office. Tactile comforters should also be available so that clients can nurture themselves as needed. Many men are reluctant to pick up a teddy bear or other childish symbols of comfort, but they will use a stuffed basketball or a blanket for the same purpose. If emotional releases occur in the presence of other people, such as in a group session, the observers need to be warned that the process can trigger their own reactions. They need permission to take care of themselves during the process. For some men, this will mean covering their eyes and ears. Others may need to change their seating arrangement so that they can sit close to someone they trust. The observers will also need time after the emotional release so that they, too, can debrief the experience.

Dissociative Processes

Children are generally honest and forthright, unless they believe that it is not safe for them to tell the truth. When they are told not to talk about something that has happened in their lives, such as being sexually abused, in order not to lie, they have to "forget" what has happened. In technical jargon, they learn to dissociate from their behaviours, feelings, sensations and/or cognitions. If a child is likened to a house, a child who is dissociative has closed the door on some rooms in his house and acts as if they do not exist. Memories of being abused are kept behind metaphoric locked doors, blocked from his conscious awareness. The abused-self is, in effect, split off and dissociated from the child's self-identity. Although an adult survivor may not have conscious memories of the events that he has stored behind locked doors, he may exhibit behaviours that hint at these ghosts.

Dissociative survivors need to educate themselves about their dissociative processes. They must begin to notice when and where they dissociate. Keeping a journal and making daily entries that help them to track their dissociative episodes is informative. As clients begin to learn what triggers their dissociative states (i.e. certain times of day, parts of a house, kinds of activities, etc.) they have the option of staying dissociated or developing other ways of dealing with the situation that is stress inducing. As clients become conscious of their dissociative patterns, when finding themselves dissociated they can ask themselves "What part of me is needing to leave now?" Learning grounding techniques can be helpful to survivors who dissociate to bring them back into their present reality and present identity. Looking in a mirror reminds a client that he is an adult and not a powerless child. Writing about the situation that is eliciting traumatic memories and writing or telling someone about the memories can validate a survivor's experience and reduce his isolation. Keeping symbols of his adult identity available can also reconnect a survivor to his current self and break his dissociative state. Some survivors are uncomfortable with these interventions because by engaging in them acknowledges their abuse, which can be painful.

The most extreme type of dissociation is MPD. Clients who develop MPD are overdifferentiated and their therapy is focused on assisting them to reintegrate fragmented parts of self. To continue with the analogy of a house, clients who have MPD live in many separate rooms with no corridors to link them together. Therapy needs to help the client reconnect the rooms. MPD is a coping strategy created to deal with abusive situations that are too overwhelming for a child's immature ego to integrate. Although the original intent of the defence was to secure the child's survival, this unconscious coping strategy no longer works well in an adult client's life. Parts of the self are identified with a time that is no longer current and act in ways that are no longer functional. The barriers between the different alters need to be dismantled and the functions that they serve need to be integrated and updated.

In general, if MPD is pathologized, clients tend to act in pathological ways; if MPD is normalized, clients tend to act in normal ways and carry on attending school, going to work and so on. In order for the different parts of the self to fuse, clients need adequate stability in their lives. Therapeutic safety has to be established with all the alter personalities, one at a time, and the specific role of each alter and the information that he or she carries must be brought into awareness. During the survivor stage of therapy, provided that a client feels secure within the therapeutic alliance and is not consumed with current life crises, dissociated experiences are invited back into conscious awareness. This reclamation is often accompanied by the release of intense repressed emotion. The client temporarily enters an altered state of consciousness and, in effect, relives the incidents that he has dissociated. This process is called abreaction.

Traumatic memories may need to be abreacted several times in order to access all the missing pieces. These are:

1. The client has a relatively continuous memory of the traumatic time period(s).
2. He is not currently dissociating in an uncontrolled or dysfunctional way.
3. He is not experiencing flashbacks or reliving the trauma in other ways.
4. He can remember and talk about the trauma without intolerable affect.
5. He has developed a subjective sense of the personal meaning of the trauma.
6. He expresses interest in and hope for the future rather than feeling overwhelmed by the past.

Survivors fall on a continuum of memory repression. On one end of the continuum are those survivors who have total recall of their abuse; on the other end are those who have no memory of their abuse. The majority of survivors fall in between these two poles; they have some conscious memories and some memory gaps. It is not necessary for a survivor to reclaim all or even most, of his repressed memories to heal. Survivors need only have sufficient memory recall to counter their own denial. When clients are doing abreactive work in therapy, it is often necessary to schedule therapy sessions more frequently to give the client adequate support and safety. Healing occurs when old traumatic memories are revisited and new affective and cognitive associations to them are forged. After successful abuse-related therapy, when traumatic memories are stimulated this occurs in the context of powerful new associations. The client has a new context and new skills for processing his past experience. For instance, a new association is made when a therapist witnesses a client's abreaction, so that the abuse memory no longer connotes isolation and shame.

Another new association occurs when a client has permission to fully express the feelings that his abuse memory invokes, without having to temper their expression to meet other people's (i.e. the abuser's) needs.

Therapeutic dissociation

Therapeutic dissociation, which can also be called trance-work or hypnosis, is a powerful tool that can help clients manage their unconscious dissociation. This intervention works paradoxically - unconscious dissociative behaviours developed during the abuse are managed and assimilated in therapy by the use of conscious dissociation. Trance-work in therapy is an extension of a natural process. Daydreaming, highway hypnosis and systematic relaxation techniques are common everyday trance experiences trance that are familiar to most clients. Before engaging in trance-work with clients, it is important to educate the client about this kind of intervention. Therapeutic dissociation is a natural process, but often it needs to be normalized and demythologized for clients. Clients can be told that hypnosis is a method of asking the subconscious mind to help the client in his healing journey. The client need only remember events that will be helpful to his healing process.

Before entering a trance, the client is grounded or anchored in his present adult reality. This grounding is made in as many representational systems as possible, so that the client can call on all of his senses to assist him to leave the trance, should he wish to do so. Clients are advised that spontaneous age regressions can occur in trance states. This is a normal and common occurrence. Using hypnosis, clients can often connect with thoughts and beliefs that they developed as a child that are not available to their normal consciousness. If the client has dissociated core negative beliefs that he developed as a child, this information can often be reclaimed during trance-states and brought into consciousness. Thought errors and mistaken beliefs can then be challenged by the client's adult mind.

Therapeutic dissociation invites less conscious aspects of the client's mind to support his conscious mind in actively creating change. It helps the client gain mastery over processes he has previously used in unconscious and dysfunctional ways. As abuse survivors become skilful at entering trance states at will, they begin to notice the times in their lives when they unconsciously enter a trance state.

This new awareness brings an opportunity to develop more functional methods of addressing stressful situations in their present reality.

Contributors agreed that therapeutic dissociation is a very useful tool to help clients manage their traumatic memories, but less useful as a method of recalling repressed memories. Clients who recall lost memories under hypnotic suggestion often don't feel confident that the memories are valid. The contributors also agreed that therapists who intend to use hypnosis with their clients must obtain adequate training and supervision in this work. Therapeutic dissociation is not a suitable intervention for clients whose motivation to use hypnosis is non-therapeutic (e.g. a client who is not really interested in working through his abuse, but wants more information with which to blame others for making his life miserable). It is also not advisable to use this type of intervention with clients who are psychotic or with clients who are taking legal action against their perpetrator. The reason for this later prohibition is that hypnotically recalled memories are not permissible evidence in court and a client could risk losing his case on this technicality.

The Thriver Phase

With a few exceptions, such as when an abused client either symbolically or actually confronts his abuser(s), many of the issues addressed in this final phase of therapy are the same as those addressed with clients who haven't been sexually abused. The usefulness and appropriateness of body-focused therapy in this stage of treatment for some clients. Finally, address the termination of abuse-focused therapy and make suggestions for making this transition successful. By the time a client enters the thriver phase of therapy, most of the work that occurs in therapy sessions is similar to that conducted with non-abused clients. The hardest part of the client's healing journey is generally completed by this stage.

Often this phase is a satisfying and enjoyable time for both the client and the therapist; dysfunctional abuse-created patterns have been replaced with healthier ones, and the client's self-esteem is dramatically increased. Issues typically brought into therapy by thrivers focus on relational difficulties with their partners, children or extended family, sexual difficulties and dysfunctions, and personal safety and self-care concerns. Typically, therapy to address these issues is no different for clients who have been sexually abused than for other clients.

By this stage of therapy clients should be able to identify and manage their personal boundaries. Some clients choose to engage in body-focused therapies in this stage of their recovery, a task for which they should by now be sufficiently prepared. For some survivors, body-focused therapy techniques reach wounds that would otherwise be overlooked. Body-focused therapies directly raise issues that are central to survivors' sense of safety, such as their degree of comfort with their bodies, and with touching and being touched.

Body Work

Information and memory about abuse is held not only in the survivor's mind but also in his body. Some clients find that as part of their recovery process they need to augment traditional psychotherapy with non verbal body-focused therapies. They intuitively realize that the trauma that occurred to their bodies needs to be addressed by physical as well as symbolic interventions for their full recovery. Bodywork consists of a continuum of interventions ranging from those in which the client is fully dressed and no physical touch occurs, through breathwork and yoga-like stretches, to full massage. The types of healing processes that can occur as a result of bodywork are myriad. They can be both physiological and psychological. A trained bodyworker must be skilful in both physical process therapy and psychological therapy. It is quite common for survivors to reclaim abuse-related memories during bodywork. A trained bodyworker should be prepared to assist his or her clients to work through abreactions should they occur.

A physiological benefit of bodywork is that it helps clients to become aware of any chronic unconscious physical tension that they have developed as a defence structure. The body's defence systems are unconsciously controlled. As a result of chronic nervous tension, muscle fascia can become locked into defensive body armouring. Bodywork helps clients become aware of these areas of chronic tension. This opens opportunities to create change as they learn to relax and discharge repressed affect. The trauma of abuse often causes psychosomatic responses that unbalance the nervous system. Overactive nerve stimulation results in hypertonic reactions such as extreme tension and an inability to relax.

On the other hand, hypotonic reactions result in depression and lethargy. Therapists can train survivors in relaxation techniques and assist them to experience deeper and deeper levels of relaxation, gradually restructuring both their emotional and physical responses. Psychologically, bodywork has many benefits for survivors. Working with a trained bodyworker may be the first time that a survivor negotiates safe, contractual touch with another person. Bodywork is an opportunity to practice receiving nurturing, nonsexual touch in which the client controls the type of contact he receives. This lets the client experience and define his own autonomous physical boundaries.

Many abuse survivors have either avoided physical contact with others or been hypersexualized and had indiscriminate physical contact. In either case, they have experienced little real choice about the degree of touch they receive and the circumstances under which it is obtained. Learning to determine the type of touch they desire by responding to internally defined needs can be very important. Bodywork can be the circumstance under which this learning takes place. Many abuse survivors have distorted images of their bodies or they have developed an avoidant relationship with their physical selves. Some survivors feel very marginally connected to their bodies. Others experience great discomfort with their bodies or their body processes. Bodywork can help clients to reclaim and reconnect with their bodies on their own terms. Many clients begin to feel their feelings for the first time as previously dissociated physical sensations and processes are brought into awareness.

Whether or not to engage in bodywork must always be the client's decision. The therapist should not raise the possibility of bodywork until the client himself indicates an awareness of the physical aspects of his abuse-related experience. If a client feels too threatened by bodywork, he will not follow through on any suggestions to pursue this option. With some exceptions, the bodyworker and psychotherapist should generally be two different people to reduce the possibility of developing negative transference in the psychotherapeutic process. This separation of roles gives the client an opportunity to process his experience in body-focused therapy or any transference reactions he may have to the body worker, with a neutral and supportive third party, namely, his therapist. An exception to this dual role for the therapist occurs when bodywork takes place in a group setting and the psychotherapist is not alone with the client.

Although the two people who provide psychotherapy and bodywork should be distinct individuals, their work needs to be connected. Clients who are working with more than one therapist must be asked to give consent for information to be shared between the various service providers to ensure that the client receives the best possible treatment. Working with more than one professional can lead to their roles being unproductively split or insufficient information being shared among all the parties. Clients who have active addictions or suffer from psychotic breaks are not candidates for bodywork. Neither are clients who have unrealistic or inappropriate expectations about the bodywork process. Some clients who have little memory of their abuse engage in bodywork because they assume that this will unlock their repressed memories. Although this may occur, there is no guarantee that it will. Clients may end up dismissing the usefulness of bodywork, not because it couldn't help them but because it did not conform to their expectations.

If a client decides to engage in bodywork, it is advisable for him to ask other survivors and clinicians for a referral to a bodyworker who has experience working with abuse survivors. He should also rely on his intuitive responses; if he does not feel comfortable with a bodyworker he should not work with him or her. A client's first meeting with a bodyworker should focus on building a working contract focused on the issues the client brings to this type of therapy. The bodyworker needs to assess the client's needs and determine if they are appropriate for his or her practice. Although the bodyworker should not intrusively question the client about his abuse, he or she needs to gather sufficient information to ensure that his or her interventions are appropriate.

The bodyworker should explicitly tell the client that sexual touch or sexual stimulation will not be a part of their relationship. He or she should also inform the client that should the client experience sexual feelings during the session, the client should signal the bodyworker and they will renegotiate the work they are doing together. At all times the client must be in charge of the kind of contact he has with the bodyworker and he must be able to stop the process whenever he chooses. A skilful bodyworker will always ask the client's permission before proceeding with any form of physical contact.

It is important that bodywork occur in a forum in which the highest ethical standards prevail. Both the potential for revictimization and the potential for more complete recovery are present when a survivor decides to pursue nonverbal therapy. A bodyworker must operate with a very high degree of integrity to ensure that the process of bodywork is safe and healing.

Termination

The final step of therapy for a thriver is to plan the termination of his therapy. This final task deserves the same thoughtful consideration that was given to all previous therapeutic tasks. Celebrating a client's successes and acknowledging his ongoing skills and strengths are part of this final process. A thorough review of the client's therapeutic progress and an open acknowledgement of the importance of the therapeutic relationship to both the client and the therapist is essential. The client should leave therapy cleanly without any unresolved loose ends or unfinished business about the therapeutic process itself. Clients indicate their readiness for termination by consistently behaving in self-supporting ways that indicate that they are ready to become the architects of their own recovery. This does not necessarily mean that they no longer exhibit abuse-related symptoms; however, when such symptoms are present, the client feels confident and capable in addressing them.

It is important that the client who is terminating knows that the therapist's door is open should he need to return. Some clients are reassured by infrequent check-ups with the therapist and use irregularly scheduled follow-up sessions to stabilize their therapeutic gains. Other clients need to know that they can reestablish therapeutic support without any loss of face or shame if unexpected events occur, such as recalling previously repressed abuse memories. Leaving the client with an option of renewing his contract with the therapist, should the need arise, creates safety within the termination process.

6

Sensitive Advice to Grow Child

The world is filled with believers in the importance of good care and attention for children during their earliest months and years. That widespread belief is embedded in many cultural traditions. The young child may be seen as a little god still in a state of relative perfection, or be pictured as "the butterflies of Paradise", or a "little sun." Belief in the need for proper care is also grounded in the recognition that children are the next generation; they represent the continuity of tradition as well as the hope for, and fear of, change. There is a need to believe that the children of today can be both a rallying point for social action and the constructors of a better world. Personal experience also creates believers in the value of early childhood care and development.

Parents, professionals, and others who are simply close observers of how the neighbor's children grow up, recognize a healthy effect of good care and attention to infants and young children. They do not need an elaborate rationale or cold scientific evidence to justify their personal feeling that rudimentary health precautions and a good diet, combined with smiles and cuddling, talk and play will enhance a child's development. Such actions are not only seen as right and just, but also as a good investment of time and money.

Unfortunately for children, when it comes to investing in programmes intended to improve early childhood development, there are sceptics as well as believers. Control over purse strings and planning processes often falls to sceptics whose way of viewing the world is conditioned by their job. These sceptics need more to go on than someone else's belief that investing in programmes of child care and development is good. They want to be shown that early childhood is a better investment than roads, dams, primary schools or even bombers. They want visible and hard evidence that the proposed programmes will work. In order to justify action, they demand a rationale, a set of convincing arguments based on something other than unsubstantiated beliefs, combining both scientific and political arguments.

Early childhood programmes, particularly if they are outside the home, are sometimes seen as eroding the traditional role of the mother. Scepticism rooted in this view of the maternal role persists even though mothers, traditionally, have seldom been the only person providing care to their young children. It persists in spite of the fact that many women must work outside the home, and that studies show provision of alternate care in these cases can be good for both mother and child. It persists even though programmes to enhance early care and development can reach into the home and can respect the primary role of mothers and families in the process.

Some sceptics are open to the idea that early development is important and should be fostered, but they lack hard evidence that early interventions produce results, particularly over the longer term. Sometimes, this scepticism simply reflects a lack of information. In other cases, the evidence at hand may show that programme results do not occur, or if they occur, do not last. Sceptics may, for instance, point to findings of studies carried out in the early 1970s, suggesting that the effects of early childhood programmes "wash out" when children reach age seven or eight. They are not aware, however, that over the last ten to fifteen years, these findings have been superseded by new research information. They would like to be able to compare an economic rate of return to programmes of early childhood development with other possible investments in order to choose the one carrying the highest rate. At a minimum, they would like to know that proposed programmes will effectively produce results justifying the cost of the programme. Reasonably, they would like to feel that money is not being wasted. Any rationale for investment in programmes of early childhood care and development should include responses to the different sources of scepticism sketched above. Doing so should, at a minimum, bolster the position of those who would like to support programmes of care and development but are under pressure to support other programmes instead.

The rationale that follows draws upon eight complementary lines of argument for increased support to programmes of early child care and development. These are:

1. *A human rights argument:* children have a right to live and to develop to their full potential.
2. *A moral and social values argument:* through children humanity transmits its values. That transmission

begins with infants. To preserve desirable moral and social values in the future, one must begin with children.

3. *An economic argument:* society can benefit economically from investing in child development, through increased production and cost savings.
4. *A programme efficacy argument:* the efficacy of other programmes can be improved through their combination with programmes of child development.
5. *A social equity argument:* by providing a "fair start," it is possible to modify distressing socio-economic and gender-related inequities.
6. *A political argument:* children provide a rallying point for social and political actions that build consensus and solidarity.
7. *A scientific argument:* the research evidence demonstrates forcefully that the early years are critical in the development of intelligence, personality, and social behaviour, and that there are longterm effects associated with a variety of early intervention programmes.
8. *Changing social and demographic circumstances:* the increasing survival of vulnerable children, changing family structures, country to city migration, women in the labour force, and other changes require increased attention to early care and development.

Some of these lines of argument will be more relevant to one situation than to another. Different individuals will find appeal in different arguments, reflecting their particular concerns about the rights of children, about economic benefits, about social equity, about adjusting to changing circumstances affecting families and work, etc. Let us look briefly at each argument in turn.

1. *Children have a human right to develop to their full potential:* For many people, the obligation to protect a child's human rights is the most fundamental and convincing reason to invest in programmes to enhance early childhood development. The Declaration of the Rights of the Child, adopted unanimously in 1959 by the United Nations General Assembly.

2. *Through children, humanity transmits its values:* We are continually reminded that "children are our future." The transmission of social and moral values that will guide that future begins in the earliest months and years of life. In societies where there is a concern that crucial values are being eroded, there is a strong incentive to find ways in which those values can be strengthened. Early childhood programmes can assist in that effort, both by strengthening the resolve of parents and by providing environments for children to play and learn that include specific attention to desired values. Attending to the development of basic values in children must be a high priority in a world racked by violence but seeking peace, in a world facing environmental degradation but seeking co-operative and sane solutions, and in a world where consumerism, competition, and egotism seem to be winning out over altruism, cooperation and solidarity as core values. If children are future, they are the agents of change as well as the custodians of continuity. For many, that is frightening. But for revolutionary governments early childhood has represented an opportunity. They have consistently

recognized the importance of inculcating values at an early age. The idea that the "New Man" begins with the "New Child" has provided a basic and adequate rationale for massive early childhood programmes following revolutions. Although the centralized, proselytizing nature of many such programmes is not always palatable to outsiders, what the post-revolutionary spread of child care centres and pre-schools shows clearly is that the decision whether or not to invest is early childhood programmes is fundamentally a political decision.

3. *Society benefits through increased productivity and cost savings associated with enhanced early childhood development:* Without recurring to a scientific literature, common sense suggests that a person who is well developed physically, mentally, socially and emotionally will be in a better position to contribute economically to family, community and country than a person who has not. And in most countries of the world, that economic contribution begins at a very early age.

Early childhood programmes have the potential to improve both physical and mental capacity. They also can affect enrolment, progress and performance of children in schooling which is, in turn, associated with important changes in skills and outlooks affecting adult behaviour. Schooling helps build such skills as the ability to organize knowledge into meaningful categories, to transfer knowledge from one situation to another, and to be more selective in the use of information. Schooling also facilitates greater technological adaptiveness. It relates directly to both increased farmer productivity and productivity in the informal market sector.

Productivity increases may also occur through changes in employment. Child care and development programmes not only affect positively the future productivity of children, they also offer the possibility of increased labour force participation by women and can free older siblings to learn and earn as well. Furthermore, they can provide employment for local individuals, both as caregivers and as suppliers of materials and services needed to make the programme function.

One way in which investments in health, nutrition, and psychosocial development during the early years can bring an economic return is through cost savings—by reducing work losses, by cutting the later need for social welfare programmes, by improving the efficiency of educational systems through reductions in dropout, repetition, and remedial programmes, and by reducing health costs.

4. *The efficacy of other programmes can be improved through joint investment in early childhood development:* Because investments in early childhood care and development can help to make other programmes more efficient and effective, it is not appropriate to look at them as a direct "trade-off" against, for instance, primary schooling or primary health care. They should be considered as part of the same package, with increased benefits at marginal, or even no additional cost. Combining programmes takes advantage of the interactive effect among health, nutrition and early stimulation. In addition, child care and development programmes are potentially useful as vehicles for extending primary health care. For instance, parental education programmes will not only help parents to help their children at home; such programmes can

also improve the ways in which health care services are drawn upon. If children arrive at primary school better prepared, they can make better use of the school. Not only will dropout and repetition decrease, affecting costs, but the quality of education will rise because one of the most important "inputs" into the school system is the child. When children are better prepared, teachers are stimulated more, facilities and materials are used better, and children learn more from each other.

5. *Programmes can help to modify distressing inequalities:* Investments in early childhood development can help to modify inequalities rooted in poverty and discrimination (social, religious, gender), by giving children from so-called "disadvantaged" backgrounds a "fair start." Poverty and/or discrimination produce stressful conditions and unequal treatment that can inhibit healthy and comprehensive development in the early years. For instance, children from poor families often fall quickly and progressively behind their more advantaged peers in their readiness for school, and that gap is never closed.

Boys, traditionally, have been better prepared for schooling than girls and have had more opportunities to enter and continue in school. The differences begin with gender-linked disparities in the patterns and practices of early development that need to be changed if the discrimination is to be overcome. These are often deeply rooted in culture, but there is evidence that integrated attention to early development can produce changes in ways families perceive the abilities and future of a girl child. By not intervening to foster early childhood development where it is needed, governments have tacitly endorsed and strengthened inequalities. Ironically, one argument used against early education programmes is that they are discriminatory—favouring the upper class. That is certainly true if no special effort is made to assist the poor and if programmes of early education are left to those who can pay for them. But evidence shows that early childhood programmes can moderate rather than reinforce these social differences. As an example, one evaluation of the huge Integrated Child Development Service of India shows clearly that benefits are greatest for lower castes and for girls. Several Latin American studies have also shown results favouring children from lower socio-economic backgrounds and/or children from rural areas.

6. *Children provide a rallying point for social and political actions that build consensus and solidarity:* Mozambique, Peru, Sri Lanka, El Salvador, Ethiopia, Iran and a significant number of other countries are victims of violent actions that place the problem of living together in peace high on the list of social goals. In many locations, lesser political and social tensions make it extremely difficult to mobilise people for actions that will be to their own benefit. In such circumstance, it has been shown that placing "Children First" can be an effective political strategy. Perhaps the most dramatic, but short-lived examples of mobilization around programmes to benefit young children are those in which ceasefires have been obtained between warring groups in order to carry out national immunization campaigns. Children have constituted a "zone of peace." Less spectacular are the many community-based programmes that take children as a point of common interest, as an "entry point" for common action. The welfare of children is

less politically charged than most issues. Moreover, community improvements in health, sanitation and nutrition that benefit children are likely also to benefit the community at large.

7. *Scientific evidence demonstrates lasting effects of early attention to child development:* Evidence from the fields of physiology, nutrition and psychology continues to accumulate to indicate that the early years are critical in the formation of intelligence, personality and social behaviour. This evidence begins with the not-so-new discovery that brain cells are formed during the first two years of life. But recent research has strengthened the argument for early attention by showing that sensory stimulation from the environment affects the structure and organization of the neural pathways in the brain during the formative period. Thus, opportunities for complex perceptual and motor experiences at an early age favourably affect various learning abilities in later life and are able to compensate, at least partly, for the deficit associated with early malnutrition. And, research also demonstrates that children whose mothers interact with them in consistent, caring ways will be better nourished and less apt to be sick than children not so attended. In the 1970s, evaluations of some early intervention programmes in the United States indicated that the effect of these programmes on the Intelligence Quotient of children seemed to "wash out" by the time they were in the second or third grade of primary school. More recently, longitudinal data clearly demonstrates major long-term effects associated with a variety of early intervention programmes. These effects include: improved school attendance and performance,

increased employment and reduced delinquency during the teenage years, and reduced teenage pregnancy .

8. *Changing social and economic conditions require new responses:* Over the last decade, the effects of a world recession have been felt increasingly both by individual families and by governments seeking to adjust their behaviours and programmes to the new realities. But even prior to the recession, and in some settings, independently of it, major social changes have been occurring that call for new approaches to early childhood care and development.

   a) *Increasing labour force participation by women:* The increased pressure for women to work for wages and the need to take over men's farming chores as they have migrated to cities or sought work in mines has brought additional burdens affecting child care and creating a need for alternative forms of care. The trend toward increasing labour force participation pre-dates, but has been strengthened by the world recession of the 1980s. These trends are likely to continue, and even to increase in the coming years. The mother in these or other settings who works so that she and her family can survive may love her child and believe that she should devote time and energy to her baby, but she may not be able to do so; she needs help.

   b) *Modification of traditional family patterns:* Extended families are no longer as common as they once were. As migration and progressive urbanization occurs, members of an extended family are not as available for child care as in the past. Grandmothers are no longer as easily available, either because they remain in rural areas or because they too are working outside the home in wage-earning jobs. The number of women-headed households has increased. In some developing countries the percentage is high. In these households, women must work, creating a major need for complementary child care. If care is available, the earnings of these women are more likely than would be the earnings of men to go toward improving the welfare of the children in the household. Associated with these changes in families are increases in the numbers of abused children and of street children. These growing problems are often dealt with after the fact rather than seeking solutions in the earliest years by helping distressed families with very young children.

c) *Increased primary school attendance has decreased the availability of older siblings to act as supplementary caretakers:* Or, siblings have been forced to drop out of school to provide such care, in which case there is a strong argument for child care initiatives that will help siblings continue their education, at least to the point of literacy.

d) *Changes in mortality and survival rates:* Over the last 30 years, the infant mortality rate has been more than cut in half. More children are surviving who in the past would have died an early death. As survival to age one has increased from 5 of 6 in 1960 to 14 of 15 in 1992, the pressure increases to establish programmes for those who survive.

Child Survival and Growth

Somewhat ironically, survival is usually defined negatively: to survive is not to die. Infant survival is not dying before age one; child survival is not dying before age five. Consistent with this view of survival, programmes of child survival place emphasis on avoiding death, usually measured by reduction of the infant mortality rate (IMR) or the mortality rate of children under five years of age (U5MR). That emphasis is made easier by the fact that death is a dramatic and final event and can be counted with relative ease and accuracy, even allowing for failures to report infant and child deaths. However, death seldom occurs instantly. Most deaths follow a period of illness and deterioration that can be painfully prolonged or relatively short. Dying is a process, the end of which is death. Likewise, living is a process, the end of which is not only survival, but physical, mental and social well-being.

Thus, child survival can be defined more positively, being thought of as something more than simply avoiding death. Surviving children fall along a continuum running from near death through sickness to a healthy state. The further a child is along that continuum toward a healthy state, the better the chances are of continued survival. The process of surviving, then, can be thought of as actively seeking a healthy state, of moving toward the healthy end of the death-sickness-health spectrum rather than simply preventing or arresting the process of dying. Accepting this positive reconceptualization of child survival—as a process of seeking a healthy state at birth and in the early months and years of life—requires looking beyond the analysis of causes of mortality and beyond programmes that reduce mortality. It means examining where children are along a health-growth-development continuum. It means searching for programmes that will improve their health. This requires clarity about what, in a positive sense, constitutes moving toward a healthy state which necessarily include seeking mental and social health as well as physical well-being for young children. The success of programmes should be measured by increases in a survival ratio rather than by decreases in a mortality ratio. An Infant Survival Ratio (ISR) simply turns the IMR upside down. For instance, in 1988, the IMR was approximately 77 deaths for every 1000 children born, i.e. 1 of every 13 children born was expected to die before the age of one year. The ISR would be 923 per 1000, emphasizing that 12 of 13 children live to age one. Using the ISR, we can say that the rate of survival has increased from 5 of 6 children born in 1960 to 12 of 13 children born in 1988. Suggesting an ISR in contrast to an IMR is more than just an alphabet or numbers game. To emphasize living, as represented by an ISR, provokes a different way of thinking than emphasizing the avoidance of death, as represented in the IMR. It dramatizes the fact that many children somehow manage to live in spite of being "at risk." It provokes questions about the condition of those who live and about what is being done for the welfare of the increasing number of poor and "at risk" children who are surviving.

Growth occurs as cells are added to the body or as cells increase in size. The measures of growth most commonly used are weight or height or both. These measures are relatively easy to obtain (compared with measures of social or psychological development), and norms have been developed against which the measures can be compared. This ease of measurement and the availability of standards has given rise to the use of growth charts, based on height and/or weight for age, as a convenient means of monitoring a child's growth. Growth, for children, can be thought of as having attained a certain "growth norm" or it can be seen as a process of steadily increasing in size. There has been a slow shift in recent years from the normative emphasis toward viewing growth as a process. Steady growth indicates progress. Failure to grow (as indicated by failure to gain weight, for instance), points to a need for remedial action. Thus, the particular point where a child falls on a growth chart is less important than the pattern of change, i.e., whether there has been an increase or decrease since the previous measurement. The shift toward viewing growth as a process parallels the shifting conceptualization of survival sketched above, and, as we will see, is consistent also with changing ideas about child development. Obviously, growth depends on the amount and kind of food a child eats.

The relationship between food intake and growth has been a main concern of nutritionists. However, there is a strong tendency among nutritionists to overlook the fact that intake is not only a matter of whether or not food is available; it is also affected by the fact that feeding, particularly in the early years, is a social process. Feeding involves an interaction between the mother, or another caregiver, and the young child. Growth depends not only on the quantity and quality of the food a child takes in, but also on how well that food is assimilated and used by the body. How well food is used is influenced greatly by the health of a child. A child with diarrhea certainly will not use its food well. Although it was not always the case, the combined effect of food intake and health status on growth is now widely recognized. However, physical growth (and survival) can be influenced also by how well a child is developing socially and psychologically, and by the freedom from stress of a child and the child's caregiver. In most discussions of growth and nutrition, the social and psychological health of caregiver and child is not included. The importance of the effect on nutrition and health of developmentally sensitive interactions is not properly understood and is not given its due.

A child who learns to co-ordinate eye and hand movements in order to grasp an object shows a sign of developing a more complex way of thinking, independent of the size of the child. The ability to grasp signifies greater control over one's environment. These changes are very different from an increase in height from 70 to 75 centimetres or in weight from 10 to 12 kilograms. As with survival and growth, development can be conceptualized as attaining a certain state, as measured, for instance, by a developmental or intellectual quotient or by whether a child has achieved the co-ordination that allows walking by a certain age. However, as suggested in our definition above, child development can be viewed as a process with several characteristics:

1. *Child development is multi-dimensional:* within its field of action are included the physical motor dimension (the ability to move, coordinate); the cognitive dimension (the ability to think and reason); the emotional dimension (the ability to feel) and the social dimension (the ability to relate to others). To describe adequately a child's development, therefore, requires more than measuring how well a child is developing its ability to think or to walk; it requires looking at all of the developmental dimensions. Throughout this essay, emphasis will be placed on the mental, social, and emotional dimensions of development. Accordingly, reference will be made

periodically to psychosocial development, a term that encompasses these three dimensions.

2. *Child development is integral, that is, the several dimensions of child development are inter-related and must be considered together:* Changes along one dimension both influence and are influenced by development along the others. Emotional development, for instance, affects physical and cognitive development. If a child is under emotional stress and has not developed an ability to cope with that stress, the ability to develop physically and to learn will both be affected. This interaction among conceptually distinct but organically interrelated dimensions requires attention to "the whole child" and emphasis on a "total" or "integrated " approach to programming for child development. Our emphasis on "psychosocial development" cannot therefore be exclusive and must be seen within the broader view of development that includes physical development.

3. *Development occurs continually:* The process of development begins prenatally and continues throughout life. In its time dimension as well as its content, then, child development must be seen as part of human development occuring over the entire life span. We are concerned here with the child from conception to age 5 or 6 when a child moves beyond the home. But that concern also requires attention to the effects of early development on later development and on behaviours and attainments in all of later life. Viewing development as a continuing process means that a child is always developing; whatever happens at a given moment helps to prepare the way for what happens in the future.

However, the idea of continuity, as used here, does not imply that attainments at one point will continue indefinitely or that the path of development is always positive. Changing conditions can undercut or support what has been attained. Nor does the notion of continuity imply that a child suffering delays and problems in early life will necessarily remain forever behind others. On the contrary, children are very resilient, particularly in their earliest years. Changed circumstances can open the way to improvement. If the environment does not change, however, deficits can accumulate, leading to developmental delays. Conversely, appropriate interventions can have a recuperative effect, as will be shown later on.

4. *Child development occurs in interaction:* Development happens as a child responds to, learns from, and seeks to affect his or her biophysical and social environments. It occurs in interaction with people and things. For this reason, fostering development requires more than providing a child with "stimulation." It also requires responses to initiatives taken by the child. Achild helps to construct its own environment. Achild takes initiatives and influences its surroundings. This fact is central to an understanding of how health and nutrition are affected by a child's psychological and social development, and vice versa.

5. *Development is patterned but unique:* All children develop and there is a general sequence or outline to that development. But the rate and character and quality of development will vary from child to child. Individual variation is the product of a child's special biological makeup and the particular environment in which it struggles to survive and develop. The rate of

development will vary from culture to culture as well as from child to child.

The developmental goal of adaptation to, mastery and transformation of one's surroundings differs radically from the goals of survival, of being healthy, of attaining a certain level of co-ordination or of achieving a higher intelligence quotient. It requires a disaggregated and decentralized view of early childhood development and takes into account the different cultural and ecological surroundings that place different demands on the child.

Protection from Ritualistic Abuses

Ritual or ritualistic abuse refers to abuse at the extreme end of the spectrum of child sexual abuse. Individuals who have experienced ritual abuse often identify both as survivors of childhood sexual abuse and ritual abuse. Ritual abuse usually involves a combination of physical, sexual and emotional abuse, and frequently refers to abuse suffered by individuals as part of a group, and in the context of a powerful belief system. Some describe there are three subtypes:

1) true cult-based in which sexual abuse is only one element of the child's involvement in cult rituals and beliefs,
2) pseudo-ritualistic, in which sexual abuse is the principal activity and cult rituals are secondly, and
3) psychopathological ritualism where mentally disturbed individuals abuse children while using idiosyncratic rituals.

Ritual abuse is sometimes used synonymously with the term "satanic abuse," but this would be correct only when child abuse is combined with rites and practices by people who worship Satan. Reports by children and adults of horrific abuse, torture and brainwashing have been repeatedly received from many parts of the world, and many of the reports are virtually identical in detail, even though the informants are unknown to each other. While police have been able to find physical evidence for some allegations, for many they have been unsuccessful. Consequently, there is controversy regarding the prevalence of this form of abuse. Since ritual abuse often involves sadistic acts and degradation of the victim, it can have very serious longterm effects.

The 1984 Royal Commission on Sexual Offences Against Children and Youth reported that 22% of women and 10% of men had experienced childhood sexual abuse before the age of 18 years in Canada. While there is some variation in prevalence rates reported by different studies in the literature, most reviewers have concluded that at least 20% of women and from 5% to 10% of men in North America have experienced sexual abuse during childhood. The percentage of adults reporting histories of childhood sexual abuse may vary in part because of the use of different ages to define the end of childhood, and whether experiences such as abuse by peers, witnessing exhibitionism, exposure to pornography, or receiving unwanted invitations to engage in sexual activities are included within the definition.

Difficulties which survivors may experience when seeing health professionals can result from past abuse. While the clinician cannot change a survivor's history, an appreciation of the dynamics and long-term effects can provide a better understanding of the client's reactions during treatment.

The following summary has been derived from mental health research, clinical literature and interviews with survivors.

1. *Sexual abuse is traumatic:* Many of the reactions of childhood sexual abuse survivors are similar to those experienced by survivors of other kinds of overwhelming life events such as military combat, sexual assault in adulthood, and natural disasters, and are included in the criteria for Post Traumatic Stress Disorder. While some adults who were sexually abused as children do not report long-term negative effects, most mental health professionals and researchers agree that a history of childhood sexual abuse is associated with a range of significant difficulties in adulthood.

Our society tends to place violent acts on a continuum: certain acts are judged to be "not as violent" as others. We then proceed to place trauma that results from violence and the victim's reactions to the violent acts on a similar continuum. Such judgements are harmful to those who have experienced violence. It is not the role of health professionals to make judgements about the relative severity of the violence, the resulting trauma or an individual's reactions to the experiences.

The violations of body, boundaries and trust can affect the survivor's relationships with herself, her body and others. When a child is abused, she feels out of control and powerless. She is invalidated: her sense of reality is challenged and what she wants does not count. As a result, the child learns that her body does not belong to her and that she has no right to have any say over what happens to her body. She learns to disown and not care about her body. To live through the abusive episodes, she may have learned to disregard or ignore signals of pain, injury, alarm, danger or other sensations that her body generates, or to disconnect from her body. Thus, the survivor's relationship or connection with her body can be damaged.

Childhood sexual abuse is a violation of boundaries. Most children learn about boundaries early in life through day-to-day interactions. They internalize ideas about what is personal or private, and about what physical and emotional closeness and distance mean. When a child sees and experiences that others respect her boundaries and her wishes for privacy and separateness, it reinforces the idea that she is a valuable person. She learns that she is separate from others, that she is a self, and that she has an identity of her own. But the child who is sexually abused learns that her body belongs to someone else. Her body is used to meet someone else's needs, and her feelings, wishes and needs are not important. Thus, her relationship or connection to her sense of self, and her sense of who she is, are damaged.

Most sexual abuse is perpetrated by people known to the child—family members, baby sitters, friends of the family, teachers, coaches, clergy, etc.—people given responsibility for protecting and nurturing the child. The consequences of this experience can be profoundly devastating. When such people take advantage of her, the child is betrayed. The world becomes an unsafe place as she learns that people who say that they care, or are in care taking roles, cannot be trusted. Thus, her relationship with others (including health professionals) can be damaged.

Numerous studies have documented that childhood sexual abuse is associated with mental, interpersonal and physical health problems in adulthood. Long-term sequelae can affect many aspects of function, including cognitive, emotional, behavioural, interpersonal and physical. The following describes some types of difficulties that have been documented by researchers and health professionals.

Cognitive: Child abuse is often associated with distorted beliefs and perceptions about one's self, one's behaviour, and the intentions of others. These distortions can lead to guilt, self-blame and low self-esteem. Perceptions of helplessness, chronic danger and consequent hypervigilence (extreme sensitivity and watchfulness for possible danger) are common. Belief that one is powerless may present as passivity or, conversely, as behaviour that others experience as controlling.

Emotional: Long-term correlates include depression, anxiety, anger, fear, dissociation and numbing of feelings.

Behavioural: Studies reveal a number of actions used by survivors to cope with or avoid distress or emotional pain. These include substance abuse and addiction, self-harm, suicide attempts, eating disorders and health risk behaviours such as earlier onset of smoking, earlier sexual intercourse and multiple sexual partners.

Interpersonal: Difficulties include reluctance to trust others, avoidance of intimacy and close relationships, sexual problems and fear of being alone. Because survivors have had basic boundaries violated and have experienced a lack of sensitivity to their feelings and needs, some may have difficulty learning usual social behaviours that require sensitivity to the feelings and boundaries of others.

Physical: Traumatic childhood experiences, including childhood sexual abuse, are associated with higher rates of lower back pain, chronic pelvic pain, gastrointestinal disorders, chronic headache and general medical problems.

Some painful conditions may be a direct result of past abuse which has left permanent structural damage and becomes more problematic as the individual ages. The stress of traumatic incidences can have long-term adverse effects on normal physiological functioning. "The growing fields of psychosomatic medicine, psychoendocrinology, and psychoimmunology are increasingly providing information about the relationship between external events, brain biochemistry, the body, and the way the mind interprets all these events."

Research of traumatic memory supports the concept of "somatic" or "body memory." Traumatic memories may be encoded as part of the non-verbal "non-declarative" memory, independent of normal language-based memory. Such traumatic memories can be triggered by stress in the present that reminds the person of past trauma, and can be experienced as "somatic" or "body memory."

A feeling or perception of safety is a crucial need for the survivor because of the violations she has experienced in the past. This need to feel safe is compelling in all aspects of the survivor's life, including her interactions with health professionals.

A number of psychological theories propose that we all experience transference in our lives. While transference can be positive or neutral, it can also be negative and may interfere with healthy and adaptive functioning. For example, as a child, the survivor may have been frequently criticized by a parent or the person who abused her. She may then expect that the clinician will also criticize her, and perceive a critical attitude where none is intended. Understanding the concept of transference may help the clinician to avoid taking these responses personally.

Counter-transference occurs when a health professional transfers feelings and perceptions from past situations to the relationship with the client, or allows the client's transference response to evoke a non-therapeutic response. Countertransference may manifest as: needing to be liked or admired by one's clients; expecting to have one's opinions on any and all topics endorsed." Both transference and countertransference responses are normal, but must be resolved ethically, so the client does not develop resistance to healing, and the care that the clinician provides is not compromised through emotional over-involvement or exploitation of the therapeutic relationship.

Feelings and experiences commonly associated with childhood sexual abuse can impede the therapeutic process by compromising the survivor's sense of safety. It is not possible to present a complete list because feelings, experiences and behaviours can vary widely among individuals. Some of the common feelings, experiences and behaviours that survivors may bring to their relationships with health professionals. Clinicians who broaden their understanding of childhood sexual abuse will be better prepared to respond well to unusual reactions to treatment that may be related to past abuse. However, that these reactions and feelings are not limited to survivors. One cannot draw conclusions about a client's past solely on the basis of these feelings and behaviours.

The Principles and Guidelines for Sensitive Practice that follow provide ideas for client-centred care that address the difficulties that are briefly outlined in this section.

a. *Fear and distrust:* Many survivors experience tremendous anxiety and fear of being hurt during treatment. The survivor may distrust the health care professional and therefore be hesitant to adhere to treatment.

b. *Physical pain:* For many, the experience of physical pain is cognitively associated with past abuse. This may be seen in various ways: some survivors have learned to numb their pain or dissociate from it; others may feel the full force of both current pain and the pain of the abuse.

c. *The need to feel in control:* The need to feel in control often arises from past violations in which the child had no control over what was done to her. As a result, a perceived lack of control will diminish the survivor's feeling of safety during treatment and may affect treatment adherence.

d. *Discomfort with men:* Perpetrators of childhood sexual abuse may be men or women; however, statistics suggest that the majority of perpetrators are men. As a consequence, the female survivor may feel unsafe and uncomfortable in the presence of the male health professional. Some survivors may also feel uncomfortable around male clients.

e. *Ambivalence about the body:* Many survivors feel hate or shame about their bodies, and/or feel disconnected from their bodies. The conflict between a survivor's need to seek treatment for a physical problem and her difficulty in caring for her body may affect treatment. She may, ignore symptoms that could offer valuable insight into diagnosis or response to treatment.

f. *Conditioning to be passive:* Abuse often teaches children to avoid speaking up or questioning authority figures. As adults, survivors may have difficulty expressing their needs to the health care practitioner who is now the authority figure.

g. *Triggers:* A flashback is an experience of reliving something experienced in the past. Some survivors have a susceptibility to flashbacks and being overwhelmed by feelings related to the past. Examination and/or treatment may trigger or precipitate flashbacks or overwhelming emotions such as fear, anxiety, terror, grief or anger. This may occur momentarily or for a longer period. Such experiences are thought to involve a dissociative process.

h. *Dissociation:* Dissociation has been described as a disruption in the usually integrated functions of consciousness, memory, identity, or perception of the environment. It may be sudden or gradual, transient or chronic. Dissociation should not be considered inherently pathological and often does not lead to significant distress, impairment or help-seeking behavior. One common experience of dissociation is highway hypnosis where an individual who has been driving a car suddenly realizes that he or she does not remember what happened during all or part of the trip.

Dissociation can be viewed as a skill which the survivor used to alter her attention for adaptive purposes—as a child, she used this skill to cope with the abuse. When the survivor continues to use this coping strategy in adulthood, it can interfere with adaptive functioning. Many survivors report that they are not able to have consistent control over this ability to escape from the current (usually stressful) situation and some report having been unaware of their tendency to dissociate for many years.

Some survivors describe experiencing themselves as being outside their bodies, watching the present situation from a distance, an experience which is thought to be the result of a dissociative process. Some find it painful and difficult to come back to the present. Researchers continue to study dissociation, a phenomenon which has been said to be "devilishly complicated." Considerable empirical research supports the hypothesis that dissociation is a common response to a traumatic situation and a response which is not exclusive to survivors of childhood abuse.

i. *Self-harm:* Self-harm (such as scratching, cutting or burning the skin) is a method of coping for some survivors. Health professionals may see evidence of self-harm in the form of injuries or scars on the arms, legs or abdomen. There are many reasons why survivors harm themselves. It may serve to distract or numb the survivor from her emotional pain; it may shift her feeling of pain to one concrete area; it may serve to end episodes of feeling numb. Others may seek to punish themselves because of a sense of self-blame for past abuse. One of the primary goals of treatment must be the development of feelings of safety for the client. Safety can be seen as a protective umbrella: when it is open, the survivor can participate in the treatment at hand. The spokes that keep the umbrella of safety open are the principles of sensitive practice.

   1. *Respect:* Respect can be defined as realizing the individuality of the other person. The survivor may be very sensitive to any hint of disrespect as a result of past abuse during which she was not respected in a fundamental way.

2. *Rapport:* While establishment of rapport is important in every therapeutic relationship, it is an all-important component of facilitating feelings of safety for the survivor. Development of rapport must begin at the first moment of clinicianclient interaction and must be given ongoing attention. The balance of professionalism and friendliness that contributes to positive rapport is partly a function of individual style. But the clinician who is distant and cold in his or her professionalism is not likely to facilitate a positive connection with the client. Conversely, an overly familiar style can feel invasive and disrespectful. Developing a balance is crucial, keeping in mind that effective professionals convey genuine caring while maintaining appropriate boundaries.

3. *Sharing control:* As a child, the survivor was not allowed control over her own body. Consequently, in adulthood, the sense of having control is of paramount importance in the establishment and maintenance of safety. By sharing control, the client can become a respected, active participant rather than a bystander during treatment. The clinician can act as a coach or facilitator, working with, rather than on the client.

4. *Sharing information:* Sharing information with the client about the initial examination and about every component of treatment also helps the client to develop a sense of safety. Information sharing must be extended to the ways in which the client can best retain information about her body and her treatment when she leaves her appointment. Information must flow both from clinician to client and from client to clinician. The onus for this two-

way flow of information rests with the clinician; she or he should explain the examination and treatment and seek ongoing feedback about reactions to treatment as well as about the client's perceived progress.

5. *Respecting boundaries:* Respect of boundaries is a crucial safety issue. The word "boundaries" refers to the outer limit of the space we consider personal, in both physical and psychological terms. Boundaries define or delineate the areas of the body and the limits of information that we feel are appropriately under our control. Touching a person without consent breaches a physical boundary; asking very personal questions breaches a psychological or privacy boundary. When a breach occurs, the individual feels violated. The concepts of power and responsibility in the therapeutic relationship factor prominently in any discussion of boundaries.

In the position of power, health professionals are responsible for ensuring that, first and foremost, the therapeutic relationship serves the client's needs. In failing to set or respect boundaries, the clinician allows his or her needs to come before the needs and best interests of the client. A boundary is violated if a practitioner, rushed for time, decides that she or he does not have time to ask for consent before beginning a procedure. In doing so, the clinician is addressing his or her need rather than the client's needs. Boundaries can be confusing at times for both the client and clinician. Boundary violations are often inadvertent. It is up to the clinician to remain focused on maintaining appropriate boundaries for both the client and herself or himself. While less common, the clinician may also experience boundary violations. The survivor may sexualize authority figures because as a child she learned to relate to the abuser primarily in a sexual way. It is the clinician's responsibility to be alert to boundary violations and potential violations and to address both, should they arise. The onus is always on the clinician to clarify the situation and guard against violation of boundaries.

Some survivors who, experienced boundary violations as children, may have only just begun to appreciate the importance of boundaries. By demonstrating respect for and sensitivity to boundaries, the clinician may serve as a model for the survivor who is learning to establish healthy boundaries in her life.

6. *Fostering a mutual learning process:* The principles outlined above underpin ways of interacting that the survivor may not have experienced as a child and is only now learning as an adult. She may need encouragement in her journey to become a full, active participant in her health care. Concurrently, the clinician must discuss shared responsibility for the survivor's health with the client in a way that invites participation without creating unrealistic expectations of treatment outcomes. At the same time, the clinician is learning about working with survivors. The survivors who participated in this research reminded us that mistakes and uncomfortable situations are inevitable, but that two remedies are invaluable.

— The clinician needs to recognize his or her mistake and offer an apology.

— The clinician should discuss the situation with the client to resolve the problem that has arisen.

7. *Consideration of ebbs and flows:* Neither coping with the effects nor healing from childhood sexual abuse are linear processes. As a result, the survivor may vary in the degree to which she is able to tolerate and participate in treatment at various times. Such variations in the survivor's tolerance may occur rapidly (day-to-day) or may develop over longer periods of time. To address the possibility for such change, the clinician must repeatedly "check-in" with the client and be willing to adjust the treatment approach accordingly.

8. *Demonstrating an awareness of the prevalence and sequelae of violence and childhood sexual abuse:* Many survivors look for indicators of a clinician's awareness of issues of violence and abuse. Demonstrating this awareness can take a variety of forms. External indicators such as displaying posters and pamphlets from the local sexual assault centre offers a cue that health professionals have such an awareness of the prevalence of violence and abuse.

All survivors are not the same. Some survivors experience few negative effects of past abuse. Some have learned to manage the long-term effects in ways that do not interfere with their daily functioning. Other survivors experience these effects in all aspects of their lives. Concurrently, survivors are also at different points on the continuum of healing from past abuse. Some do not remember the abuse; others are aware of the abuse but have avoided thinking about it or seeing it as significant; still others have just begun or are well along in their journeys of healing from childhood sexual abuse. Not all survivors will share the same perspective on the relationship between their physical and psychological health and past abuse. Some survivors feel that their physical health and reactions to treatment are intimately connected with their psychological state. Others have not made such connections. All of the women who participated in this research had begun their journeys of healing. They spoke about the strong links between their physical health and past abuse.

Many described their interactions with health professionals at various times in their lives: before they had begun to remember past abuse, before they had begun to see connections between their health and past abuse, and during or after the development of this awareness. Thus, the clinician may be working with survivors whose responses to their past abuse vary greatly. The Guidelines in all sections other than Dealing with the client who is upset and Disclosure of childhood sexual abuse represent a respectful way to work with survivors and non-survivors alike. The guidelines in these sections refer specifically to survivors of childhood sexual abuse. Readers are also cautioned that the guidelines section of this handbook is not a stand-alone document but, rather, builds on the dynamics and long-term effects of childhood sexual abuse and on the Principles of sensitive practice.

The client has a right to make an informed choice about health professionals with whom she will work. She also has the right to request a referral to another clinician or facility if she is not comfortable with her current situation. Such options may not be easy or even possible in every situation; nonetheless, health professionals are encouraged to seek ways to support this principle.

The following discussion expands upon some of the suggestions for initial evaluation and presents additional ideas and suggestions for clinical practice.

Consent: Consent is a crucial issue for safety. Clinicians are advised to review the guidelines for consent established by their professional licensing bodies. Consent must be an ongoing, interactive process. Do not assume that consent given today applies to all successive days: ask for consent in each successive day of treatment.

— Always ask and receive verbal permission before proceeding with each component of an examination or treatment each time you see the client.

— Seek the client's consent to allow students to observe or participate in treatment. This should be done as far ahead of time as possible and without the student present. Explain the role(s) of the student and whether the student will be present to observe, treat or both.

— Remind the client that she may withdraw her consent to the student's presence at any time.

— When using an electrophysical agent (such as ultrasound and TENS), describe the physiological effects and what it will feel like. Mention any gels, electrodes, etc., that will be used.

— Ensure that you have obtained verbal consent for use of the modality after giving the explanation.

Language can be used to amplify or minimize the power imbalance in the therapeutic relationship. Avoid overuse of medical terminology: seek with the client a common language that facilitates both a sense of safety for her and a sense of professionalism for you. Seek a balance in the amount of information offered at one time—offering too much information to the client may be just as counterproductive as not offering enough. Monitor the client's body language during treatment and address with her any apparent discrepancies between verbal and non-verbal responses.

Clients are very perceptive of your non-verbal cues. Show your client that you are listening to her. Active listening is one effective technique to clarify what the client is trying to say. Through the use of restatement, reflection and clarification, you are "paraphrasing the speaker's words rather than reacting to them in order to clarify if you have caught the intended meaning." Consider offering a brief written summary of the treatment session. While this can be time consuming, the survivor may feel more involved in treatment as a result. Use of photocopiers or carbon paper can reduce the time required.

Having to undress to undergo treatment may leave the client feeling vulnerable. Explain the rationale for your preference in clothing and ask the client about her preference. Agreement on alternative clothing or providing gowns that do not gape open may increase the survivor's feeling of safety and comfort during treatment. Provide a variety of sizes of gowns and shorts for all body sizes and ask if your client is comfortable with the options. Remember, too, that what you wear may also have effects —although a white lab coat generates a sense of professionalism, it may increase the perception of the power imbalance and intimidate some clients.

Touch may be associated with painful memories for survivors. As a result, many survivors may have difficulty tolerating touch by health professionals. For some survivors, this may change as trust develops; for others the discomfort does not decrease. Your approach to touch must emphasize the principles of sharing control and sharing information.

— Describe the touch that is required during treatment.

— It is critical that you ask for consent to touch throughout a treatment session.

— Some clients may want a step-by-step description.

Other clients may be comfortable giving consent after a description of the whole procedure. Check with the client if her body language suggests a negative response to touch.

— Always be aware of the physical distance between the client and yourself during treatment. Avoid being in very close proximity except when treatment requires it.

— Avoid unnecessary physical contact. If treatment involves bracing part of the client's body against your own body, explain this, and seek consent before proceeding.

Addressing privacy needs of the client is another important step in building and maintaining feelings of safety. The balance between safety and privacy is not the same for all survivors. Some clients will be more comfortable in a private room where no one can overhear them. Some may prefer a private room as long as they can have someone of their choice present during examination or treatment. Others will forego privacy because they feel safer in a larger, common space. Not all clinical facilities can accommodate the client's need for a private room, and this issue should be addressed with her at the outset of treatment. If an agreeable solution cannot be found, the survivor's needs may be better served by referral to another clinician or facility. Post a notice in the reception area offering a private room to clients if they prefer one.

Ask the client about her need for privacy. Discuss alternatives to meet her need for privacy. Ask the client to let you know if her need for privacy changes and check her need for privacy as treatment progresses. Although options for privacy are more limited in acute care settings, clinicians are urged to address this issue with the client.

Pain is another complex issue that is often difficult for both the survivor and health\ professionals to sort out. Acute and/or chronic pain may be complicated by past abuse. While "psychological distress can find somatic expression," researchers are also learning more about the long-term impact of trauma on the physiological responses to stress that can also contribute to the survivor's pain. Remember that:

— Some survivors may respond to pain by ignoring it, not taking it seriously or dissociating when they experience pain.

— Some survivors may not feel pain.

— The survivor may experience pain associated with body (somatic) memories as part of, or in addition to, other problems for which she seeks your clinical expertise.

— The survivor may have had negative experiences with health professionals who discredited her pain because it did not seem to match test results or examination findings. Regardless of whether pain matches examination findings, the client's experience of pain is real.

It is the clinician's responsibility to address the client's pain, other symptoms and problems, in a systematic, nonjudgemental and thorough manner. The clinician needs to set realistic goals with the client and work systematically toward these goals. Despite thorough exploration of all the treatment options within a clinician's scope of practice, there will be clients whose pain the clinician is unable to resolve. If pain is not resolved satisfactorily, it is the clinician's responsibility to explain that treatment options have been exhausted and to discuss other options outside the clinician's scope of practice.

— Leave options for further consultation open.

— Consider joining or creating a health care team that will work with the client to address the problem.

Consider referrals to clinicians or clinics that specialize in the management of chronic pain and to other professionals who may specialize in positioning, energy conservation, fitness, massage, etc. Under some circumstances, the clinician may suspect that the client's problem is related in part to psychosocial issues that are outside that clinician's scope of practice. The clinician can discuss this with the client and refer her for counselling. Rehabilitation often follows a functional model rather than a symptomatic model of treatment. In rehab, the client is asked to disregard "reasonable symptoms in the absence of objective signs of harm" in order to develop the functional tolerances required to return to preinjury employment and/or lifestyle. Survivors participating in rehabilitation may require additional education regarding regarding the phases of tissue healing and assistance in interpreting the symptoms associated with "hurt" vs. "harm."

There are many time pressures on health professionals in today's health care system. While it is challenging for the clinician to find the balance between time constraints and good care, it is important to recognize the potentially grave consequences for the survivor when the clinician is rushed. Treatment may feel very depersonalized, robbing the survivor of her sense of safety. Without this sense of safety, treatment is much less likely to be successful. Discuss time pressures with the client in order to plan how best to meet her needs. Because of ambivalence about her body, it may take longer for the survivor to develop the confidence to carry out an ongoing independent program of self-management. A number of follow-up appointments (scheduled, for example, at monthly intervals) may be helpful.

Difficulties with treatment adherence may be linked with past abuse. Some survivors may be out of touch with their bodies and have difficulty identifying signs of over-exertion or other body signals. Others may perform too many exercises, perhaps in an attempt to gain control over their bodies, to please the clinician or as a form of self-harm. Some may have difficulties with certain actions or body positions because of associations with past abuse. The following suggestions may help the client achieve a desired level of adherence.

— Include a daily check-in before each treatment.

— Respond to the feedback before you proceed with treatment: come up with alternatives together to avoid parts of treatment that she finds difficult to tolerate.

— Explain the rationale for treatment.

— Discuss adherence difficulties with the client. Do not use blame and guilt as tools to achieve adherence. Avoid using words such as must and should.

Rephrase objectives using comments such as "do the best you can do."

— Problems with adherence are often very pressing in acute care settings. After surgery, early mobilization can be critical to recovery, but pain may overshadow such goals. The clinician may be tempted to achieve adherence by using the language of "must" and "should." However, encouraging the client to refocus on her initial goals of treatment may be more effective in facilitating adherence.

— In out-patient or home care settings, the clinician may encourage adherence by working with the client to structure the treatment differently so that it fits the client's life and lifestyle better. When incorporating exercise and activity into treatment:

— Offer clear and direct guidelines for exercise programs. Offer written and oral instructions that include what each exercise should feel like. Give upper and lower limits for the number of repetitions and sets to be done.

— Develop and progress through an exercise program slowly to allow the client to build the neuromuscular skill required.

— Describe signs and symptoms of overuse to the client and monitor the exercise prescription for signs of overuse.

— Encourage the client to keep an exercise or treatment log.

— Encourage the client to view the home treatment program as a tool she can use to care for herself.

Some suggests that part of a survivor's healing is reconnecting with her body. Health professionals may have a role in this process.

— Some survivors have difficulty recognizing or interpreting physical sensations and reactions to treatment. She may need to learn to recognize and interpret sensations such as muscle fatigue, stretching within reasonable limits, tension, relaxation, the reaction of a joint to over-exertion, etc.

— Incorporate visualization of the exercise and sensations expected during exercise. This may help the survivor develop the kinesthetic sense needed before she begins to actually perform the exercise.

— Use breathing exercises, yoga and relaxation techniques.

— If you know that you are working with a survivor who is seeing a counsellor, you may want to offer to work jointly with the client and her counsellor.

Taking care of one's self—eating well, getting enough rest, performing regular physical activity, taking time to relax, etc.—can be challenging for many of us. Health professionals can model self-care and encourage the survivor to develop strategies for her own self-care. If the client has difficulty maintaining self-care behaviours, she may appreciate knowing that she is not alone.

When a client has difficulty with a treatment you suggest, explore different strategies to attain the therapeutic goals. Be respectful and non-judgemental when discussing alternatives to address the problem for which she sought your expertise. If you feel that your authority has been challenged, engage in a dialogue instead of becoming defensive. Offer treatment options. These may include treatments that you recommend, and treatments for which you feel the goals will take longer to achieve or which are not as effective but might be more acceptable to the client.

Switching clinicians without prior discussions with the client can result in a feeling of a violation of established trust and/or of the treatment contract.

— If you know that you are going to be away from work, give the client as much notice of your anticipated absence as possible.

— Discuss alternatives with the client; recommend a colleague who is informed about, and sensitive to, survivor issues.

Introducing the client to the clinician who is covering your caseload would also be helpful. If you practise alone, discuss the practical aspects of your absence with the client. Whenever possible, for unexpected absences, the survivor should be notified and given a choice of whether to attend an appointment with an alternate clinician.

Treatment may "trigger" the client to relive past abuse or to experience an overwhelming emotional response. Such reactions may occur regardless of whether or not the survivor has disclosed past abuse to you or even remembers past abuse. Thus, this section applies both to those survivors who have disclosed past abuse and to those who have not disclosed but appear very uncomfortable or upset during treatment.

There is no complete, predictable list of triggers for all survivors. Touch is frequently described as a trigger. Traction and electrophysical agents such as TENS, ultrasound and interferential current may also act as triggers. Some survivors may be able to identify their triggers while others may be unaware of their triggers.

Some survivors describe body language that communicates a high level of discomfort:

— stiffening
— cringing
— pulling away
— shaking
— startling
— muscle tension and inability to relax
— sudden strong emotional reactions

Survivors have described many different physical reactions to being triggered. Some of these may be understood as physiological reactions to stress:

— shallow, rapid breathing, breath holding or a change in breathing pattern
— rapid heart rate
— decreased concentration level.

If your client is in a dissociative state, she may seem:

— distant
— unable to focus
— uninvolved in the present.

Some survivors feel that disclosing past abuse to the clinician is important because of the impact of the abuse on their health or their reactions to treatment. They may look for ways or times to disclose to the clinician. One of the things that may hold the survivor back is uncertainty about the clinician's response to a disclosure of childhood sexual abuse.

It is important to offer appropriate verbal and non-verbal responses to disclosure. The basic elements of appropriate responses are as follows.

— Acceptance of the information (that is, letting the survivor know that you heard her words)

— Offer an expression of understanding and support.

— Acknowledgement of the prevalence of abuse Acknowledging your awareness of the prevalence of abuse has the effect of reducing shame. You might say:

— "We know that at least 1 in 3 to 5 women (or 1 in 7 to 10 men) are survivors of childhood sexual abuse.

It is a terrible thing that so many children have suffered in this way." Validation of your belief in the survivor's words and the consequences of the abuse for her

— Validate the courage that it took to disclose.

— If your client is visibly distressed, acknowledge it.

— Let her know that you do not think she was responsible for the abuse. Allow the survivor control over the timing and extent of her disclosure. If you are under time constraints, find a way to inform the client of this so that she will not feel dismissed or think she has done something wrong by disclosing.

Canadian law in most provinces requires that suspected abuse of children be reported to child welfare officials. There is no legal obligation for you to report disclosure of past abuse by an adult survivor to child welfare officials unless the client also reveals current abuse of a child.

The survivor may feel more vulnerable and exposed after disclosure. Reassure her that:

— disclosing was not wrong,

— you respect her,

— you respect her decision to disclose as well as the information that she revealed, and

— you will respect her confidentiality.

The client may still feel more vulnerable the next time you see her. It may help to repeat these points again briefly at her next appointment. It is also important to talk with the client about how she feels her past abuse may affect her response to treatment. Explore practical issues within treatment. You may have to balance the importance of taking time to discuss disclosure with the client versus either beginning or continuing treatment. Discussing the implications of disclosure on treatment will take additional time but is likely to increase a survivor's feeling of safety in future treatment. After disclosure, it is important to clarify what the survivor's expectations of the clinician are. Some survivors hope for, or expect, a response that is beyond the clinician's ability or scope of practice. It is therefore important to delineate clearly what your scope of practice is, and identify your clinical abilities and limitations. If you feel the survivor requires help beyond your scope of practice, suggest additional resources. Focusing on what treatment involves and can achieve and on how to best work with the survivor's sensitivities provides both the clinician and client a solid basis from which to proceed with treatment after disclosure.

While health professionals consider client charts confidential, it is important to recognize the meaning and limitations of confidentiality in each clinical setting. A client should be made aware of the level of confidentiality that applies to her health care record. She should be told:

— who has access to her chart within the health care setting both in the present and future; that her record(s) can be released to other individuals only with her consent; and

— that her records will be released when

— required by law.

When charting, the clinician should be mindful of the limits of the confidentiality of the health care record.

If the client has an unexpected reaction to treatment or to the clinician, the clinician is advised to chart the events in as much detail and as objectively as possible, as soon after the incident as possible. Include the words and actions of the client, the clinician and any other staff. The same advice is appropriate when the client expresses discomfort with anything professionals do or do not do.

Task-centred disclosures can be documented in a way that allows for the identification of specific sensitivities or discomforts without revealing the abuse history. Charting in this manner allows for communication of relevant information to other clinicians without revealing more than the survivor is comfortable with. In determining what and how much information to include in a client's record, the clinician should be guided by his or her assessment of what notes are needed in order to provide the best service to the client.

Documentation of abuse may have legal implications for the client who is (or may in the future be) involved in a court case. This may occur, for example, if the client chooses to proceed with criminal charges or a civil action against an abuser or in relation to civil litigation after a motor vehicle accident. These are a few of many possible instances when health records may be subpoenaed. In some instances, the records will be sought to support the client's case; in other instances, the records will be sought to try to challenge the client's credibility or the client's account of events. An in-depth discussion of the legal implications of health records is beyond the scope of this handbook. The clinician is advised to seek legal advice in any situation in which a client's health records are requested by a third party in the absence of the client's consent. A clinician should\ not release confidential records at the request of the police or a lawyer without the client's consent. If records are subpoenaed, the clinician should seek the advice of a lawyer. Subpoenaed records should not be released until a court orders their release, usually following a hearing on this issue.

Many survivors have experienced feelings of abandonment, rejection and subsequent shame in childhood that are carried forward into adulthood. Under some circumstances, being discharged from treatment may leave a survivor feeling as though the clinician is rejecting her or minimizing her problem. The clinician can do several things to help the client with closure.

— Discuss discharge during the first appointment, as part of the introduction to treatment. As treatment progresses, raise the issue of discharge again to ensure that the client's needs are addressed. Plan the timing and other details of discharge with the survivor as far in advance as possible.

— Review initial goals with the client and ask about other goals that the client now has as the end of treatment draws nearer.

— Consider a follow-up appointment, telephone call or email exchange 6 to 8 weeks after regular treatment has stopped.

— Leave the door open for the client to return in the future if her condition worsens.

Losing a job or income affects all members of the family. Adults frequently become so preoccupied they forget that tough times have an emotional, as well as a financial, impact on their children. Children depend on their parents for emotional security. When parents are tense, upset and inattentive, much of this security is gone. Reduced income can mean sudden lifestyle changes for the entire family. There's less money to spend, so decisions must be made on how to spend what's there. It may mean other family members must find jobs. There may be less family time.

Unemployment can mean a parent is home more, which might call for adjusting schedules and space. It may involve a move for the family. Whatever changes tough times bring, all family members feel the impact. Discussing these feelings and concerns, as a family, is important.

Role of Family Communication

Communication has two parts—talking and listening. Each must occur for communication to be successful. As families undergo changes in their lives, they need to talk about them. This includes adults and children. According to Gerald Kaplan, Harvard psychologist, people who are not ashamed to express fears, anxieties and sorrows and to seek help from others, deal with crisis the most successfully. Children who learn this at a young age will be more likely to cope with stress as adults. Being able to discuss and vent angry feelings can help keep those feelings from creating more severe problems, such as emotional difficulties, family violence or alcohol abuse.

Listening is as important as talking. Everyone needs someone to listen to them— someone who supports them and allows them to openly express feelings. Sometimes a person can find a solution or discover the sources of stress through talking. The listener should not feel obligated to advise, analyze or have all the answers. Listening and responding with concern and understanding may be all the help that is needed. Open communication within the family is vital to good relationships. During stressful times we frequently need people outside the family willing to listen when we need to vent feelings. In some families, listening without judging is difficult because we want to help, but have strong feelings and opinions. Also, family members are sometimes too busy or preoccupied to be good listeners.

Even though you feel overwhelmed with your own problems, as a parent you can help your children cope with stress. Here is a list of tips for helping children cope:

— You can help your children best by first helping yourself. Try to gain control of your own stress; then you are ready to help your children.

— Provide your children with information about your family's situation in a way that is within the child's understanding. Don't keep the income loss a secret from children and other family members, despite the urge to spare them or "save face."

— Recognize symptoms of stress that may affect your children: sleeplessness, diarrhea, withdrawal, headaches, and/or angry outbursts. Encourage the child to share feelings and fears. If you feel ineffective in helping your children manage stress, talk to their teachers, a school psychologist, clergy member or mental health professional.

— Promote balanced diets, get adequate rest and plenty of exercise to guard against health problems.

— Try to keep other major changes to a minimum. Too many changes at once can be overwhelming. However, some changes, such as a move, may be unavoidable, so try to keep them in perspective.

— Help your children focus on the positive aspects of their lives. Look at family and personal strengths and draw on talents and contributions of all family members. Recognize these contributions, no matter how small.

— Hold a family discussion on how the income loss affects money available for extra activities and allowances. Talk about family spending priorities. Discuss how each person will help control family spending.

— Spend family time together doing low-cost or no-cost activities that family members enjoy. If older children can find jobs to supplement family income, decide as a family how their money will be used.

Bibliography

Albee, G.W., "The Futility of Psychotherapy", *Journal of Mind and Behavior* 11(3/4): 369-84, 1990.

Axline, V.M., "Dibs: In Search of Self", London: Penguin, 1964/1990.

Bass, E. and L. Davis, "The Courage to Heal: A Guide for Women Survivors of Child Sexual Abuse", New York: Harper & Row, 1988.

Briere, J., 'A Self-Trauma Model for Treating Adult Survivors of Severe Child Abuse', in Briere et al.; pp. 140-57 of first edition, 1996/2002

Draucker, C.B.,. "Counselling Survivors of Childhood Sexual Abuse", London: Sage, 2000.

Dryden, W. and C. Feltham, "Counselling and Psychotherapy: A Consumer's Guide", London: Sheldon Press, 1995.

Gatchel, R.J. and E.B. Blanchard, eds., "Psychophysiological Disorders", Washington, DC: American Psychological Association, 1998.

Jehu, D.; C. Klasssen and M. Gazan, 'Cognitive Restructuring of Distorted Beliefs Associated with Childhood Sexual Abuse', *Journal of Social Work and Human Sexuality* 4: 49-69, 1986

Legg, C., "Psychology and the Reflective Counsellor", London: BPS Blackwell (The British Psychological Society), 1998.

Masson, J., "Against Therapy: Emotional Tyranny and the Myth of Psychological Healing", London: Collins, 1988.

Szasz, T.S., "The Myth of Mental Illness", New York: Hoeber-Harper, 1961.

Index